D0847942

KING OF COMEDY

KING OF COMEDY

by Mack Sennett

AS TOLD TO CAMERON SHIPP

Doubleday & COMPANY, INC.

GARDEN CITY, N. Y., 1954

LIBRARY OF CONGRESS CATALOG CARD NUMBER
54-10768

COPYRIGHT, 1954, BY MACK SENNETT
ALL RIGHTS RESERVED
PRINTED IN THE UNITED STATES
AT
THE COUNTRY LIFE PRESS, GARDEN CITY, N.Y.
FIRST EDITION

Towards a land of Mockbelieve and thrills galore,
I set sail in a dream-ship beflagged with ink and flames.
—JAMES ENSOR

Contents

[Illustrations following page 158]

KING OF COMEDY

CHAPTER 1

Unfortunately, I Sang Bass

I AM an old storyteller, long in the tooth and
willing. Once upon a time I was bewitched by an actress who
ate ice cream for breakfast. As I look back on more than half
a century of professional nonsense, my life unwinds like a two-
reel comedy chase sequence—a leaping funnyman flees from the
Keystone Cops, falls off a cliff into a bevy of Bathing Beauties,
suddenly discovers a custard pie in his hand. I spent most of my
life with clowns. Some of them were wistful and wicked little
men, some of them were as gentle and as daft as rabbits in the
moonlight, others were sidesplitting fellows who attacked life
with a bed slat. I believe I have associated intimately with
more fools than any man living, a blessing for which I thank
God. I made my debut on the New York stage in a character
part, playing the end of a horse. I recall more pretty women
than a seed catalogue has dahlias. This often inspires me to
mourn over my many youthful discretions. From time to time
I laid hands on absurd sums of money long enough to fling it
in various directions. I once owned a mountain populated with
pigs.

Today I am a healthy, oversized, long-winded man with a
crew haircut and a face like a rumpled reticule. I enjoy eighteen holes of golf and a scotch-and-soda before dinner. If you
insist, three scotches-and-sodas. I live on Hollywood Boulevard where from time to time I find someone to insist.

I have been thinking things over. I have supplied myself
with a comforting quantity of cut plug, lined a tin wastebasket with yesterday's newspaper—never missed in my life up

to thirteen feet—and my intention is to start yarning. As I have been indicating so you will know what to expect, maybe, this tale is episodic, like the way we used to make pictures. Take a seat on the aisle.

No autobiographer from a sainted country doctor to the town drunk on the mourner's bench ever consented to make a deposition purely for the sake of confessing himself. Most of us want to brag, and we'll do it even if we have to invent a few sins to fancy up the account. The things that I am going to brag about are these:

Many people, some of them astute, allow that I was the originator of motion picture comedy. That may be stretching things a bit, but I like the idea and my denials are weak.

I am honestly proud of the many unknown talents I discovered and of others, better-known, which I brought to the screen. I mean such people as Charlie Chaplin, Gloria Swanson, Buster Keaton, Carole Lombard, Marie Dressler, Polly Moran, W. C. Fields, Bing Crosby, Ford Sterling, Charlie Murray, Hank Mann, Harry Langdon, Phyllis Haver, Marie Prevost, and a good many others. Not to forget, either, the Keystone Cops, the Mack Sennett Bathing Beauties, and the only pastry that became an international star.

Mainly I am proud of being a citizen of the United States. Why are many people timid about coming right out and saying that? It's like speaking of the Deity. Preachers seem to be the only ones who can mention God in public without making excuses.

I was a Canadian farm boy with no education. I moved to the United States and worked as a boilermaker. A man who was to become President helped me, in an odd sort of way, and I wound up as a motion-picture producer, many times a millionaire when I was on top of the heap. Where else but in America could a thing like that happen?

Those are the brags. As the sequences flicker, my happiest and my saddest memory is Mabel Normand, the actress who ate ice cream for breakfast. I suddenly recall that she often read Sigmund Freud at the same time. She was the most gifted comedienne Hollywood ever knew. There was a time when I could spin a romance, a made-up boy-and-girl story, with the best of them. That was when I had Mabel herself to act in

Molly O or *Mickey*. But I did not play leading man in those films, or in any other films. A story about a true love is the most difficult of all to relate. I am hard-pressed here, but we'll see.

Nowadays people often ask me, "Mack, why aren't movies as funny as they used to be?"

The incidence of injury from being doubled-up with snickers, or from strain on the vertebra from whooping and hollering, is low this year, I have to admit.

Any honest insurance company will confirm the fact that not one citizen of the United States has died laughing in a theater since the days of Ben Turpin. Mr. Turpin, as many lucky survivors recall, used to murder entire audiences as a matter of course. But times have changed.

You will probably remember many of the funny people who worked for me not so long ago.

They set about all over the place with slats and pies. They made fun of everybody and everything. They rolled audiences up and down the aisles. They would exhaust the people with nonsense, inducing a state of hysteria and even semiconsciousness. Then they would top their foolishness with something zanier before the money-paying victims could catch their breath.

This was just to get warmed up. My boys and girls would then go to work in dead earnest. The result was always the same: pandemonium and chaos. Restraint, logic, and inhibition took flight and roosted on Cloud Seven with their sides aching.

This kind of motion-picture making relaxed the people and was good for them. Only the furniture industry suffered. There was no demand for secondhand psychiatric couches.

What's happened to laughter? There used to be so much of it.

If a modern movie director accidentally lets a junior-sized snicker slip into one of his pictures he has to run to a head-feeling clinic and apologize to his analyst.

Hollywood ought to be rocking the national boat with whoops and yells. Instead Hollywood is whimpering and bailing out tears.

Come to think of it, this may not be Hollywood's fault, or

Broadway's, or Red Skelton's, either. Only a handful of years ago *everybody* was funnier. I mean ordinary, plain people, uncles and aunts and suchlike, the kind we all know. They opened their mouths wide and laughed out loud without having to look around to see if somebody mightn't accuse 'em of subversion.

In Canada where I was fetched up life was cold and serious. Canadians are not congenitally comic. To this day they have not caught onto getting funny with cops, the naturalest comedians in the world. Ever hear of them cracking wise at the Royal Canadian Mounted Police?

But even in Canada years ago things were a good deal more comical than they are around Hollywood now.

I was born in Richmond, province of Quebec, on St. Anthony's Day, January 17, 1880.

My people were pure Irish. At the time I arrived, weighing twelve pounds and not considered large for my age, the family and its connections had been in Canada about a hundred fifty years. One of our brags was that James Masterson, a great-great-great-uncle and a well-known brickmason, had built the fortifications at Quebec.

My father's name was John Francis Sinnott and my mother, before her marriage, was Catherine Foy. My real name is Michael Sinnott.

The Sinnotts and the Foys, like most of their neighbors, were "mixed" farmers. They raised everything they consumed and were the most independent people in the world on their little holdings, which averaged about a hundred fifty acres. When I was a small boy my family wove its own cloth and made its own clothes and shoes. Later, as the charms of Sears, Roebuck and Montgomery Ward catalogues influenced us, we had store-bought cloth and footgear.

My people—indeed, all the neighbors around us—were large, well fed, full-blooded, tough, and pious. They were realistic. When they left County Waxford they brought over a few legends about Brian Boru, the recollection that Ireland was the center of European culture until the vikings sneaked up on our forefathers about A.D. 700, and the conviction that

an Irishman can lick any ten men in the world, including ten
Irishmen. But we did not bring any pixies or leprechauns with
us. We left the little people in Ireland, where they are now in
politics.

As I say, we were realistic. We were good, practicing
Roman Catholics. When we made a gift to St. Anthony we
stated explicitly what we had in mind and counted on the saint
to keep his end of the bargain. My mother and St. Anthony
were on excellent terms all of her long life and neither one
ever let the other down.

I had two brothers, John and George, and a sister, Mary,
of whom John is the only one now living. He is in Montreal,
almost as far from Hollywood as possible on this continent.
My sister used to write things. She would set down long, detailed essays about Rome, or St. Petersburg, or Budapest.
These were vivid descriptions and won her considerable respect as a literary person.

I asked her once how she managed this.

"Why, Mike," she said, "I copy them from the ency-
clopedia."

Uncle Mike Foy, my mother's brother, was the pride
of the family.

Uncle Mike was a big man, like all Sinnotts and Foys,
standing six foot three and weighing 225 pounds. We admired him particularly because of his prowess at wakes.

In our part of Canada (about midway between Montreal
and Quebec) there was a dearth of entertainment—and although we certainly never looked forward to the demise of
any of our neighbors, it was a fact that once the good man
was blessed and gone we enjoyed giving him a grand send-off.
Uncle Mike was a specialist in wakes and Saturday-night shin-
digs. He performed house-shattering jigs when the fiddle
played and I believe his capacity for 186-proof high wine is
still unchallenged. But he excelled in wakes.

An Irish-Canadian wake would be attended, not only by
the Irish and some undersized people of British, Scot, or
German descent, but by the French—the Canucks. Never
underrate the Canucks. They are among the most powerful
men in the world, stronger than bears, which they sometimes
resemble.

Uncle Mike was one of the few men in our county who could outwrestle Canucks in the kitchen.

When these gentlemen were fortified by puddings, stews, sweet cakes, and brandy—which even they could not swallow without a chaser—they were very powerful and very entertaining.

They usually began with "twist the wrist," straining their ham-sized biceps to see who could force the other man's hand to the table. Uncle Mike always won, even over Canucks. Then the real wrestling began, and it was worth a lifetime pass to the circus to witness one of those matches. Uncle Mike usually prevailed.

But one late evening while we were paying our respects to a beloved friend who had gone on his long journey, a Canuck named Jean Paul twisted Uncle Mike's neck most uncomfortably, tortured him with a hammer lock, and threw him over his head against a cupboard.

Uncle Mike landed *heavy* and was barely able to get back on his feet. As he groped for support, his hand fumbled against a three-foot iron chisel. His fingers closed on it fondly.

When Jean Paul lunged at him Uncle Mike laid the chisel against his head. The Canuck stumbled like an axed bull, then collapsed in a state of delightful unconsciousness.

Uncle Mike stood over him, swaying, and looking at the chisel with affection.

"Now, *that's* a handy tool!" he said.

Our churches were maintained by tithings, which we pronounced "tidings." If you wound up with five hundred bags of grain after a harvest, you were supposed to give a percentage to the priest. Uncle Mike was a prominent churchgoer. He lived in Tinwick Township, which was predominantly French, and so, of course, the father was French and preached in French.

One Sunday morning the priest said to Mike, "My son, that load of hay you sent over was pretty small, don't you think?"

Uncle Mike pulled himself up until he looked about nine feet tall and roared.

"Father!" he yelled. "If you'll tell us Irish in English as

much as you tell them French in French, we'll increase the damn tidings!"

My mother was always fond of Uncle Mike.

"Brother is a humoristic man," she said.

I was educated, so to speak, at Shipton and Tinwick. We left the farm when I was small, and my father—who was almost as large as Uncle Mike—ran a small hotel in Richmond. Later we lived in another small town nearby, named Megantic, in the hunting country. At a time when I suppose our total cash income could not have come to more than $1400 a year, my mother wore a handsome beaver coat, a product of the local forests, which cost her exactly nothing. It would be envied in Beverly Hills today.

One of the schools I went to was at Pointe aux Trembles, nine miles out of Montreal, and there I learned to speak French. I speak French now about as fluently as I despoil English, but my French is of a certain kind—Canuck, laced with Canadian idiom and Irish overtones. A few years ago I went to Cannes as a guest of the French Government to receive an award for making funny pictures. I delivered a speech in my best Sunday patois, but it turned out that the French and I had almost no system of communication.

When I went to school in Richmond and later at Lake Megantic with my sister and brothers we often had to walk six or eight miles in ice and snow at below-zero temperature. Usually it was about forty below. People who could afford it banked their houses with manure to keep warm. We were bundled in furs and bogged down with leggings and heavy shoes. To sustain us, Mother always dosed us with a *soupçon* of the 186-proof.

As a result, and perhaps for other reasons, I was not bright in school. I was sleepy. I never did learn to express myself quickly or precisely in any language that involves grammar. I spoke slowly as a ponderous child and I speak slowly now as a ponderous man. They tell this one on me in Hollywood:

Charles Chaplin, when he was young and shy and working for me at Keystone, said, "Mr. Sennett, do you think it will rain this afternoon?"

Three hours later I sent him a message.

"Looks like rain," I said.

The story is true. I like to think things over.

Another handicap to articulation revealed itself when I was about fifteen years old. I turned into a basso.

Please consider this. Canadians have an accent of their own, almost as distinctive as Southerners. To this I added a little French and a little Irish. Then I became a bass.

Irish tenors are admired by some people—but an Irish basso! Nobody ever listens to an Irish bass.

I am about as bass as anybody outside of the opera house can get, ranging safely from low "F" to high "F." In moments of dolor I can sometimes fetch up a low "C," but this "C" sounds like the melancholy comments of a frog in a crypt.

I mooed on lonely roads in Canada. I was not encouraged to sing in public. Indeed I was not encouraged to sing in privacy. My father and my brothers gave out that my voice reminded them of a moose in a bog. When I sang they impersonated victims of poisoning. My father was a sound and upright man, a practical husband, good at carpentry, contracting, and operating small hotels. He advised me that no good ever came to a man who insisted on singing bass.

It might be argued that he was right. It was bassing that eventually got me into show business, changed my life drastically—from Canadian farm boy to Hollywood—and changed the lives of so many other people.

My mother encouraged me. It did not occur to her that I was ridiculous when I confessed to her one night that what I actually yearned to do was sing *in Italian*, a foreign and sinful tongue. More than likely my mother never thought I was talented, but one of her sayings was "Never step on my dreams." Somehow or other, with no background of aesthetics or formal education, she had worked out the belief that a dream is a worth-while thing and should be respected. She knew no music at all.

That was how it all started.

Perhaps I should credit Uncle Mike Foy, too. He was a humoristic man. Perhaps his "Now, *that's* a handy tool!" motivated more comedy and motion pictures than I can explain. At any rate, it sometimes appears to me that I never left my early Canadian influences far behind. Without them, certainly, I would never have known Mabel Normand.

We moved to East Berlin, Connecticut, when I was seventeen years old. My father was employed by a contractor, Mother took in boarders, and I went to work at the American Iron Works.

Possibly you have never been lucky enough to meet an ironworker. Let me tell you about them. They are the toughest, hardest men in the world, excepting only Canucks. I have known lumbermen, prizefighters, and strong men in circuses, but for muscle and durability the iron men can make small pies from these fellows. Everything you touch, pick up, or use in an iron or steel mill is heavy. In my day it was commonplace for four men to hoist a four-hundred-pound rail, place it on the shoulders of a single man, and expect him to tote it a hundred yards.

I was a big, black-haired boy standing six foot one and weighing 210 pounds, so a job in the ironworks seemed the most natural thing in the world. A cousin of my mother's named Pete Comisky found this employment for me. I soon despised him.

Cousin Pete was a "rusher." He was paid on a piecework basis and it was his assignment to work hard and fast and make us by-the-day workers look slow. I made $1.50 for working ten hours a day. I also loathed a "bucker-upper" named Smith, who caught white-hot rivets in a bucket as fast as he could—he was a pieceworker too—and ordered me to slam them home at high speed with a ten-pound sledge hammer. The faster I slammed, the more money Mr. Smith made.

An ironworks is a hot place. Iron is produced from four ores, hematite, magnetite, limestone, and siderite. This is heated in smelters, some of them one hundred feet tall, and poured in a molten liquid often as hot as 3500 degrees. When you ladle the slag off a pool of iron it sometimes sputters like fat on the stove. My hands are scarred with white marks from doing that when I was seventeen.

In this atmosphere, drinking tepid oatmeal water to control perspiration, struggling, lifting, hammering, and getting burned, men lose their tempers.

There was a boy named Novak, who did not like my looks. He did not like the Irish, the Canadians, or the Sinnotts. One afternoon when I was singing at the top of my lungs while hammering a girder, Mr. Novak declared that my voice was driving him insane.

"Tunes I like," Novak said. "Noise, no. You are a noisy ape."

I was used to that kind of musical criticism. I grinned and suggested that he stop me.

Novak walked twenty feet away, picked up a ten-pound hammer, and turned.

"I *will* stop you," he yelled, letting the hammer fly.

It caught me on the right arm and sliced meat from shoulder to elbow.

I had to run after that man and attend to him. Cousin Pete Comisky was annoyed and did not give me a day off.

My mother's boardinghouse accommodated about ten paying guests at seven dollars a week each. They were iron-workers, big men with appetites, and the quantities of cabbage, meat loaf, fresh hot bread, biscuits, pie, buttermilk, and gallon tins of coffee they consumed were prodigious. Four or six fried eggs for breakfast were routine. In the evening they gathered around the fireplace in the living room to discuss William Jennings Bryan and William Howard Taft, or to play checkers, and cribbage, or to talk shop.

We were soon joined in the evening by a small man who was considerably out of place among these giants. This was Signor Fontana, a gentle, learned little man who wore a greasy frock coat and a frayed collar from which flowed a black and artistic cravat. Signor Fontana got his dinner for nothing —he ate very little—plus a fee of fifty cents. He was my music teacher.

Like my mother, the professor was convinced that a dream should be nourished. He encouraged me as a singer. And it required bravery to encourage me in front of our nightly audience. He taught me my notes over the protests of the boarders, who complained that the ironworks was more peaceful. Gradually he taught me a few songs. "Asleep in the Deep," naturally, prime equipment for any bass, and "Bartlett's Dream."

What my brothers said about my singing is unprintable. My father objected too.

"This is awful, wasteful nonsense," he said. "This kid isn't a singer and he never will be a singer. Catherine, you are pampering the boy and giving him bad ideas. And we have to sit here night after night and listen to a good ironworker being ruined!"

Professor Fontana's deep eyes would water like a sad spaniel's.

"Maybe you like better when he sing like Feodor Ivanovich Chaliapin," he would plead. "Someday you hear this boy in the Metropolitan Opera House singing Moussorgsky's 'Boris Godounoff.' And you will have to fork up two dollar to get in, I bet!"

"Pay no attention," Mother would say. "You sing good, Mike. Maybe a little loud, but good."

"*Sì*," said Signor Fontana. "Beginning next week, we tone him down. We study *bel canto*, and Mike will sing soft and sweet, like a bird at sunset."

My brothers and the boarders would then try to exceed each other in describing what *kind* of a bird I would sing like.

I never did get the hang of *bel canto*. When I sang the neighbors banged their windows shut.

We lived in East Berlin about a year, then moved to Northampton. Professor Fontana continued to come over from Holyoke to teach me. I said to Mother, "I think I should get some stage experience before I sing at the Metropolitan Opera House. There is a show in town starring Marie Dressler in *Lady Slavey*. She's a Canadian, and I wish I could go ask Miss Dressler how to get on the stage."

Mother said that would not be easy to do. "Miss Dressler is famous and busy," she said. "How are you going to get in to see her? You are an ironworker, Mike. And to tell the truth, you look like one."

"I can dance," I said.

"Yes. I have seen you. On the street corners with the other lads, jigging to keep your feet warm. It might help, Mike, but frankly I have me doubts about you as a dancer. Oh, you are a powerful singer, Mike—but let me try to think up something."

A few days later she said she had thought up something.

"The lawyer," she said. "He has influence. He is a Republican."

I didn't know we knew a lawyer.

"Draws up our leases and things like that when we rent a house," Mother explained. "Practical man. Keeps his mouth shut tighter'n a pickle jar. He'll go far, maybe be a municipal judge or something as grand as that, and I'll vote for him. Mr. Coolidge is his name."

At that time Calvin Coolidge was twenty-eight years old, sandy-haired, pinch-mouthed, and regarded as a comer. This was before he was elected mayor of Northampton and almost twenty years before he had trouble with the cops in Boston when he was governor of Massachusetts. By 1919 I was having trouble with cops myself, and I always admired Mr. Coolidge for the firm way in which he handled his.

We went to Mr. Coolidge's little upstairs office.

He greeted us with a limp hand and pointed to some chairs.

"Mike wants to meet Miss Dressler," Mother said.

"Why?" Mr. Coolidge said.

"He wants to go on the stage," Mother said.

Mr. Coolidge church-steepled his fingers and rocked for a long minute.

"Why?" he said.

"He can sing," Mother said. "He has a big bass voice. If you would like to hear——"

Mr. Coolidge winced.

"Unnecessary," he said.

"Well, so he wants to meet Miss Marie Dressler, who is acting here. She might be able to help the boy get a start," Mother said.

Mr. Coolidge considered.

"Be a mistake," he said. "Why give up a good job in the ironworks to become a mountebank?"

My mother and I did not know what a mountebank was, but we gathered from Mr. Coolidge's inflection that it was something awful. We kept quiet.

"All right," he said, seeing how determined we were for me to become a mountebank. "Write a letter."

He wrote it carefully in longhand and handed it to Mother. It was a model of New England prose. It said:

"*Dear Miss Dressler:*

"*This boy wants to go on the stage.*

"*Yours truly,*

"*CALVIN COOLIDGE.*"

Show people always doted on Calvin Coolidge with a special affection. Mr. Coolidge, especially after he became President, was easily the best actor we ever had in the White House, not excepting Franklin Roosevelt. Dead-pan humor is the most difficult humor of all. It requires a true comic gift and a sense of timing that many professionals never get the hang of. Mr. Coolidge was no amateur—he knew when he was giving the people a show, and he knew what he looked like when he let them dress him up in Indian suits and war bonnets. Will Rogers loved him, and Will would never have cottoned to a man who had no sense of humor.

We called on Miss Dressler at the Academy Theater. The doorman looked at us sourly but let us in, backstage. We stood there solemnly, getting in the way, until the first act of the matinee was over. Then we were shown to Miss Dressler's dressing room.

She was the first actress I ever saw. I stared at her, especially at the mascara on her eyes, looked around at all her frilly underthings tossed around the room, blushed, and stared back at her eyes.

Mother did the talking.

"Mike can sing," she explained. "He wants to go on the stage to get ready for the Metropolitan Opera. Can you tell us where to have him start?"

Miss Dressler looked at me and her eyes grew wider. She saw a shock-headed young man whose shoulders strained a cheap, tight suit. My arms hung like a gorilla's. My hair jutted —I never could brush it much and can't to this day. My face was red and wore its customary expression, a scowl.

Miss Dressler turned to my mother.

"Mrs. Sinnott, I have to tell you the truth. The theatrical profession is very uncertain. Only a very few ever reach anything like the top, even when they have great talent. I know —all this looks very fine and rich and easy, but you never have a home, you're out of work a great deal of the time. Even if your son has enormous talent he will need years of study and training and experience and work.

"I can't be too emphatic about this. Anything to do with show business is hard work."

I interrupted.

I said, "Lady, talk about hard work, have you ever driven hot rivets all day long?"

Miss Dressler looked me over and grinned. I grinned back.

"I guess you ought to have a chance, Rivets," she said. "I'll write you a note—and make it a mite longer than this lawyer feller's letter to me. You take this to Mr. David Belasco in New York and God help you."

So far as I know, I am the only person who was ever introduced to show business by Calvin Coolidge. I never saw him again and I doubt very much that he ever saw me or my motion pictures. I saw Miss Dressler again sooner than I expected.

Marie was twenty-nine years old and already a comedy star when I met her at the Academy in Northampton. She is possibly best remembered now for *Min and Bill*, with Wallace Beery, and for her lusty acting in the *Tugboat Annie* series by Norman Reilly Raine.

But her first big picture was *Tillie's Punctured Romance* in 1914 with Charlie Chaplin, Chester Conklin, and Mabel Normand.

She made this film for me only a few years after helping me escape from the ironworks at $1.50 a day. I paid her $2500 a week.

CHAPTER 2

The Horse in the Bowery

DAVID BELASCO was forty-seven years old. He was already a theatrical monument in a clerical collar when I arrived in New York to become a Metropolitan Opera star. Two of his plays, *The Auctioneer*, with David Warfield, and *Madame Du Barry*, with Mrs. Leslie Carter, were in their second year, and *The Darling of the Gods*, starring Blanche Bates, was in rehearsal. His office above his theater was like a cathedral with images of matinee idols instead of saints, and as you approached him in a dim light you couldn't be sure whether you were about to meet an archbishop or an actor. It is remarkable that I got in to see him at all, but Marie Dressler's note worked the magic. I approached on the biggest feet known to chiropodic science and scowled at the great man.

Mr. Belasco fingered Miss Dressler's letter, sniffed it, waved it, let it flutter to his desk, then regarded me soulfully with his big dark eyes.

"Dear me," he said.

I was twenty years old. I had $25.38 to my name in the world, a straw suitcase containing one extra shirt, two pairs of socks, and a clean collar. My hair jutted this way and that way and—being fresh from the ironworks—I could have picked Mr. Belasco and his desk up and juggled them. My coat sleeves were short. I used to put my hands in my pockets to keep my paws from dangling around my knees.

"I want to learn to be an actor, Mr. Belasco," I said.

"You *can* act?" Mr. Belasco asked.

He may have said, "You *can* act?" Or, "You can *act?*"

There would be three ways of reading that line, but I forget. At any rate, Mr. Belasco managed to express both astonishment and dismay in three words.

"Well, sir, mainly I sing. Bass. My teacher says—but if you would like, I'd be glad to sing for you."

"I hardly think that will be necessary," Mr. Belasco said.

"And dance," I said.

Mr. Belasco peered around his desk at my feet. He looked at me sadly.

"Mr. Sennett," he said, "almost anyone else in our profession would know that I have no singing and dancing acts at the moment."

I assured Mr. Belasco that I did know that, and that Miss Dressler knew it too, and that I did not expect to act with Mrs. Leslie Carter or Miss Blanche Bates, not right away.

"But where does a fellow start?" I asked. "Now, suppose I can sing—and I can—I have got to learn something about acting so I will be able to get up on a stage and sing. I thought you might give me a little advice."

"My son, I will do just that, and I mean this in the kindliest way. I say to you in the solemnity of this confessional: go home."

"Why, I can't do that, Mr. Belasco. I have told everybody at home and parts of Canada that I am going on the stage. And Rose Guilfoil——"

"Charming name," Mr. Belasco murmured. "An actress, of course?"

"No, sir. Sort of my girl. Her folks run the City Hotel in Northampton, and Rose believes I'll make good."

"All the charm and guile of the Irish lakes in that name," said Mr. Belasco. "I should send for Rose Guilfoil and make her a star, on the strength of the name alone. But let's be practical about you. If you won't go home, young man, the best way for you to start is this: go down to the Bowery and start in burlesque. There you will learn the rudiments, how to get on and off stage. That is what you should do. And it strikes me forcefully that burlesque is something you might be uncommonly good at."

I don't want to portray myself at any time as more of a

boob than is necessary, but I was not certain then what burlesque was. I assumed it was some kind of vaudeville.

Mr. Belasco stood up, indicating the interview was over. "But how do I get in?" I asked. "I don't know anybody."

Mr. Belasco walked me to the door. "That will be no problem," he said. "With your gall you will get in anywhere."

I went back to my boardinghouse and pondered this advice for several days. Gall or no gall, I was awed by show business and by Broadway. Such great restaurants as Shanley's, Churchill's, Rector's, Bustonaby's and Keen's Chop House were flourishing in splendor. Give or take a year or so, the great stars of the time were John Drew, Billie Burke, Mrs. Fiske, Ethel Barrymore, Ellen Terry, E. H. Sothern, Maude Adams, Maxine Elliott, De Wolf Hopper, Alice Brady, David Warfield, Willie Collier, Laurette Taylor, Jane Cowl, Fay Templeton, and Otis Skinner. These people and their hangouts were as far removed from anything in my experience as Versailles from a general store in Vermont. They moved in a world of white ties and tail coats, ermine wraps, and tasteful supper parties that were stimulating to hear about but in which I naturally had no part. As a matter of fact, of course, this kind of thing never did become my métier. Theatrical society has its high tones and its low tones just like any other. We read about the fashionable stage in the newspapers and magazines. Our own kind of show folks finally appeared in print when Sime Silverman established Variety in 1905.

In the cheap boardinghouses I lived in—along with midgets, fat ladies, tap dancers, carnival entrepreneurs, and unemployed snake charmers—our chief interest was money. We knew that a Gertrude Hoffmann could earn as much as $3000 a week. Annette Kellerman, the first swimmer to wear one-piece bathing suits, made $1500. Eva Tanguay earned $2500 a week for showing her legs and singing "I Don't Care." Harry Lauder was worth $2500 and later got $4000. Lily Langtry demanded that a carpet be laid down from her dressing room to the stage in order to protect her flowing petticoats. The carpet was red and the legend of "Roll out the red carpet" started right there. Eddie Cantor, Fanny Brice, and Al Jolson had not yet come along.

Most of these were names that we marveled at from far

away. Two comedians, however, started at this time with whom I later did business. Charlie Chaplin was a minor player in a vaudeville act called "A Night in a London Music Hall," and Buster Keaton was part of an act called "The Three Keatons," and was constantly in trouble with the Gerry Society, which tried to keep children under sixteen off the stage. Buster worked at Proctor's Twenty-third Street Theater in 1905. Will Rogers was just getting started. Fred and Adele Astaire were child dancers and had not yet come to New York.

When I was young in New York, "Kiss Me Again," "Sweet Adeline," "Chinatown, My Chinatown," "In My Merry Oldsmobile," and "I Love You Truly" were the songs we sang. A young man named James J. Walker wrote a ditty called "Will You Love Me in December as You Do in May?" "Take Me Out to the Ball Game" was new. Some of the songs were not considered nice by nice people, but we liked "I Love My Wife, But, Oh, You Kid" and the "Angle Worm Wiggle," which Sophie Tucker presented, perturbing the police.

Today Jimmy Durante looks out and down from his suite at the Astor Hotel (which was not there when I arrived) and sees a Broadway so glittering with electric signs that I wonder how he can sleep. Perhaps he can't see beyond his nose. Broadway was gaslit when I came to town, and not very well lit by modern standards. There were no cabarets—the night club as such did not actually get going until 1909, started, I believe, by Jesse L. Lasky, who made his first dime in the gold-rush days. There were no movies. The nickelodeons began in 1906 and 1907. But in 1902 when I came to New York to be a singer and actor, there were indeed, as I have been saying, great stars and they made great money. I was name-smitten and stage-smitten, but mostly money-smitten. I like money and I like to talk about it.

There seemed to be no chance for me except to follow Mr. Belasco's advice. I went to the Bowery Burlesque (we commonly called it "burley-cue"), watched a performance, and was taken in, as Mr. H. L. Mencken had it one time, "like a Sunday School superintendent at a Paris peep show." The round, fat girls in nothing much doing their bumps and grinds, the German-dialect comedians, and especially the cops

and tramps with their bed slats and bladders appealed to me
as being funny people. Their approach to life was earthy and
understandable. They whaled the daylights out of pretension.
They made fun of themselves and the human race. They reduced convention, dogma, stuffed shirts, and Authority to
nonsense, and then blossomed into pandemonium. Now, I
don't pretend that I analyzed those things when I was a boy:
I merely report that, as a little guy, as a thoroughly accredited
representative of the Common Man (who had not at that
time become a political celebrity), I thought all this was delightful. I especially enjoyed the reduction of Authority to
absurdity, the notion that Sex could be funny, and the bold
insults that were hurled at Pretension.

You will recall a standard burlesque act. A pair of sidewalk astronomers offered looks at the stars for a dime. A fat
lady becomes a customer. She is a Pretentious Fat Lady, representing Society. As she peers at the stars—which she can't see
—the comedians make certain lusty remarks about her shape.
Indeed they go the limit. The act closes with one of them
whacking Fat Lady across the bottom with a slat.

With that whack all the common people took a lick at all
the upstarts, or intrenched, or pretentious people. They saw
demonstrated beyond question the appealing fact that everybody has a vulnerable backside just like our own. You will
excuse me, I hope, for this bit of light-duty thinking, but the
whacking of Fat Lady's backside is the basis for all true comedy, from the paradoxes of Bernard Shaw (who was one of the
best bed-slat wielders of his time) to the Keystone Cops. I'm
told that the ancient Greeks knew this, and that the comedies
of Aristophanes were pretty lusty too when they set out to put
stuffed togas in their place. At any rate, you will find that the
downfall of pretension runs through most great comic works,
emphatically including Shakespeare. I was lucky. The technique was revealed to me when I was very green and young.

I hung around the Bowery, picked up an acquaintance
here and there through boardinghouse connections, and got a
job. At first I was handed a broom and told to sweep out. My
rise was sudden. One night they needed a gifted fellow to play
the hind legs of a horse, and so I made my debut in this character part.

My vis-à-vis, you might say, was a young and handsome man named Stu Krauss from North Carolina. Mr. Krauss, who came from a fine old family of Southern aristocrats, was a beautiful dancer who later performed fandangos with Mrs. Vernon Castle and Mae Murray. He gave up the theater eventually and became an honest real-estate broker, but when I knew him he was the front legs of a horse.

Stu Krauss moaned when I was made the hind legs of the horse. "I have been the front legs for two months," he complained, "and I had hoped for promotion. Now you come along and grab the star part of the act."

I thought that over.

"I don't get you," I said.

"Anybody can be the *front* legs," Stu said. "The front legs is—or are—[Stu was educated] the *straight* part. The hind legs do all the acting and get all the applause."

I thought that over.

"I guess talent will come out," I said. "I have been recognized."

"Indeed you have," said Stu. "The minute you appeared I said to myself, 'Here is a man who is destined to be the rear end of a horse.'"

I thought that over.

"I shall try to be humble," I said.

The star of the Bowery Theater Burlesque was the renowned Little Egypt of World's Fair fame. She was the equivalent, or better, of the strip-teasers, as in Gypsy Rose Lee, who attracted so much attention in literary circles a few years ago. Little Egypt did bumps and grinds. If you do not know what a bump or a grind is, I cannot define them. They consist of wiggles combined with contortions of the belly muscles and alarming extensions of the behind. Little Egypt was a mistress of the art and beautiful to boot. She hid none of her charms. She wore little more than the often-mentioned postage stamp and on some occasions her messages seemed to be franked—no stamp. The police warned the management.

The cops demanded more clothing and fewer wiggles. But Little Egypt was a healthy girl who did not fear drafts. She continued to wear less than a statue and she continued to wiggle. Her generosity incited business: audiences were packed matinee and evening, crowing, yelling, hooting audiences. By the time my end-of-the-horse characterization came on stage, those audiences were warmed to an appreciative frenzy, so that even my own callipygian (Stu Krauss supplied that word) efforts were loudly appreciated.

All this annoyed the police and they did what police do when annoyed. They appeared one evening with a wagon and carted us off to night court. Little Egypt and the management, I believe, were scolded, fined, and warned to cease and desist. What happened to me is the important thing.

"And what do you do?" the judge asked me.

"I am an actor," I said.

The judge looked me over.

"You can act?"

"Yessir."

"Where do you act?"

"On the stage, Your Honor."

"I could have guessed that, perhaps. Now, young man, tell me exactly what kind of an actor you are, how you come to be mixed up with these vulgar proceedings."

"I am a character actor, sir."

"Character actor at the Bowery! What do you do there?"

"I impersonate part of an animal," I said.

"Interesting," the judge said. "Pray explain. And remember you are talking to a police judge."

"Well, sir," I said, "I came to New York to be a singer. I am trying to learn to act so I can sing in the Metropolitan Opera House. I am a bass. So—I am now appearing at the Bowery as the hind legs of a horse."

"I should imagine you'd be good at it," the judge said. "Tell me, where are you from, boy?"

"Canada," I said. "I was working in an ironworks before I came here."

"Boilermaker," the judge said. "Boilermaker, Metropolitan Opera, hind legs of a horse. Son, I am not going to fine you. But I strongly advise you to go back to boilermaking. Show business is not for you. You're dismissed. Get along with you."

In all the theatrical biographies I read I always come across the story of the actor's or actress's first performance. It

is always a failure. Lionel Barrymore, for instance, was fired
from the company by his own grandmother after his first try
at acting in *The Rivals*. Billie Burke was hooted at in a British
music hall. John Drew was criticized as "that dreadful young
man." And so it goes. The debuts of us artists are hard and
painful, seldom appreciated. But at least I am in the great
tradition: my first effort wound up in disgrace, though with a
certain distinction. So far as I know, I was the only actor ever
arrested during his first show while exercising his talent for
impersonating the rear of a horse. It was a large horse.

From the Bowery Burlesque—where, as a matter of fact,
I was rehired several times because of my size and particular
gifts—I turned to ecclesiastical employment. Now, believe me,
I could sing. I had the power and the low notes. I could read
music. There were few choruses that needed more than one
bass when they had me.

A reliable sword swallower at the boardinghouse—a tenor
who would have been a bass except for having strained his
larynx—liked to hear me mumble "Asleep in the Deep" in the
living room after supper. When he learned I was out of work
he made a suggestion.

"Try a choir," he advised me. "Now, Mack, do not get in
a choir that wears robes, or marches up the aisle, because you
will trip and fall down, and I have never heard of a choir that
wanted anybody to trip and fall down. Get in a *big* choir, on
account of big choirs have to have lots of thunder in the bass
section, and you are just the boy for holding forth with glory
notes."

It was easy. I went up Fifth Avenue, found the choir-
master of the biggest Baptist church in sight, tried out, and
was hired. This was John D. Rockefeller's church, and so
I suppose I sang for him at some time or another, although I
never saw him. My singing was admired except for one thing:

Diction. Diction has always been my *bête noire*. I cannot
pronounce, and although I dote on handsome words and use
them whenever I can, I often trip over them like a water-
melon thief scrambling through a fence. The choir of the Fifth
Avenue Baptist Church, in those days, was almost in the laps

of the congregation and my loud attacks on pious words created emotions other than religious.

During my struggle with the vowels Mother made daily representations to St. Anthony. This good saint, who was born about A.D. 250, and lived to be nearly a hundred, appealed strongly to Mrs. Sinnott. St. Anthony, you will recall, was an Egyptian, a hermit, the patron of swineherds, and a famous battler against Sin, a campaign in which Mother vigorously upheld his symbols—the T-shaped cross, the skull, the devils, the crutch, the bell, and the monk's habit. Gustave Flaubert wrote a novel about him, *La Tentation de Saint Antoine,* which Mother never read, fearing it was a worldly affront to her friend. She celebrated his feast day, January 17, carried his medallion, and made gifts to the Church in his honor. Mother's approach to religion was practical in the sense that St. Teresa once cautioned a novitiate: "My dear, we don't want ecstasies here, we want someone to wash the dishes." Mrs. Sinnott did her duty by her saint and confidently expected him to do his by her, but he did not always deliver custom-made miracles on demand. We had to accept his decision that I was not cut out to be a choirster. I never did get the hang of Baptist hymns and I was fired.

This disaster did not compromise Mother's devotion in the least and it did not affect my ambition to become a singer, but it was a setback. It immediately affected my conviction that three meals a day are a good thing and possibly it affected my future. It was something to think about.

If I wanted to be an opera singer—and I did—it dawned on me that Professor Fontana's schooling had not been quite enough. I wrote to him at Mother's suggestion, and he recommended another tutor, a Professor Waldemar, who was impressive: he had a studio in Carnegie Hall. It struck me that a man who had a studio in Carnegie Hall must know everything there was to know about singing. I enrolled.

Professor Waldemar was encouraging. He said I would need a lot of work but that I had good equipment. No control, no diction, but good, loud equipment. He began to teach me, and I missed many lunches in order to pay him his small fee. I have always found that performers in the arts work best when

underpaid and underfed, but in one craft, at least, this theory
is not correct. A bass singer should be well nourished and full-
blooded in order to perform at his peak.

One afternoon when I came to the studio the professor
had not finished with a tenor just ahead of me. I sat on a divan
in his office and listened to a glorious voice. It was a grand
voice, a soaring, controlled voice—as good as Caruso's any day,
it seemed to me.

"Who was that?" I asked Professor Waldemar when the
tenor had departed. Incidentally the tenor was handsome, in
a Clark Gable way.

"That boy is a dedicated artist," Professor Waldemar said.
"He is great."

"How much money does he make?"

The professor looked annoyed.

"He doesn't care now about *making* money," he told me.
"Up to now it is mostly outgo. That young man has studied for
years in France and Italy. Six years, anyway. His family has already invested more than fifty thousand dollars in his musical
education."

"So where does he sing?" I asked. "At the Metropolitan?
How many concerts has he had here in Carnegie Hall?"

Professor Waldemar looked at me with sad eyes.

"As I said, Mr. Sennett, this student is merely preparing
himself. It takes years of concentrated effort and denial to become a true artiste. But since you approach the matter com-
mercially, and always pay me on time, I will tell you that he
does earn money, and very handsome money for a singer. He
works nightly in a café uptown and he is paid thirty-five dollars
a week."

I sat down to think.

"Now we'll start with your scales, Mr. Sennett," Professor
Waldemar said.

I stood up and made one of my few fast decisions.

"Fifty thousand dollars!" I said. "Six years' work—and he
makes thirty-five bucks a week! Professor, grand opera ain't
for me, it just ain't for me. I have made a mistake and you will
excuse me—right now. Good-by."

I grabbed my hat and that was the end of my career as an
opera singer.

I lived at Bartholomew's Inn, at Mooney's Boarding House on Fifty-third Street, and at Cook's Boarding House on Thirty-ninth, all near the theater district and all inhabited by various types of carnival, vaudeville, and show folks who required the cheapest refreshment possible. The only attraction at Mooney's was the daughter of the house, Miss Annie Mooney, who was beautiful. The food was atrocious, but when Annie joined us, picking daintily at her victuals, we lost interest in eating and stared hopefully at her. No romance developed because Miss Mooney was unavailable except at mealtimes. I left that place when I discovered that she always ate a hearty dinner in the kitchen before sitting down with the boarders.

I wrote home. I said to Mother:

"Dear Mom: I am doing fine and making lots of money. I am not exactly a star yet and my name is not up in lights, but that will come soon. I feel good and have lost a little weight."

I borrowed a stamp and mailed that.

Mother answered at once. She said:

"Dear Son: I am glad you are doing so well, we are all so proud of your great success. Here is twenty dollars."

CHAPTER 3

Free Lunch for the Actor

THERE WAS a saloon called Brady's on Seventh Avenue between Forty-first and Forty-second streets. It was an oasis of warm, fermented odors—hops, malt, barley, and sweet corn. A stein of beer cost five cents. This was a buxom stein, a tall and nourishing can of the best suds.

Along with it went all the free lunch you could reach for. There were cheese in large yellow slices, thick chunks of ham, corned beef, and slabs of buttered bread. For an investment of five cents in a schooner a man was encouraged to consume a lunch that would come to $2.50 at a first-class restaurant today, or fifteen dollars at Prince Michael Romanoff's in Beverly Hills.

I was shy of nickels, but as I beat my way around the streets of New York in my thin suit looking for work, the thought of all that free ham, cheese, and bread was dearer than memories of a first love. I found a way. I would walk into Brady's, pause at the bar as if undecided what to have, then hurry to the rest room. On my way out I took a direct route to the free-lunch counter and loaded up.

When I did buy at the bar, on odd Tuesdays, or on Fridays that fell on the thirteenth, or when it became necessary to buy in order to maintain good terms with the barkeep, I ordered scotch. My consumption of liquor was frugal, but my inroads on the free lunch were princely.

Unable to afford boardinghouses all the time, three of us young fellows wound up one season in a small apartment on Forty-third Street. On sunny days, and even on chill ones, since we often had no place to go, we sat on the front porch and examined other residents as they came and went. One in particular, a blond and pretty girl named Lucille, attracted our attention. I had heard about such girls. Mother would have described her as "no better than she ought to be," and as such she represented to me a new phase of city sophistication. We passed the time of day.

None of us, of course, could afford the attentions of such an attractive young professional woman, and so our interest was necessarily platonic. We were neighborly, though, and used to exchange magazines and newspapers. One evening I tapped on Lucille's door and offered her a new issue of *Munsey's*, and the lady invited me in.

I was sprawled on a divan telling Lucille the story of Uncle Mike at the wake when a small man walked in without knocking. I do not know this man's name because we were never introduced, but we immediately became intimate. He threatened to kill me and he started to do it.

I do recall that he was greasy, overdressed, and agile. His small black eyes darted from Lucille to me, then fixed on me as he slipped a thin hand into his breast pocket and extracted a razor.

I recall what he said, but I cannot print it.

The gist was that he considered himself a businessman, that Lucille was under contract to him, and that he felt abused and cheated out of his commission. I tried to explain that my presence in Lucille's apartment was purely social—but come to think of it, I have never heard of any gentleman who made such an explanation stick.

Lucille moved toward the man, but he restrained her with a swooping slash of the razor. I picked up a straight chair and held it between me and the small man.

He lunged. I parried in *seconde*. His blade nicked a rung. As I went back *en garde* he attacked again. I parried in *carte* and made a *riposte* that missed his head by an inch. He came in more cautiously next time, feinted, thrust, and slashed in almost one continuous movement. I believe I ran the gamut, parrying from *prime* to *octave*. It was a light chair.

This series brought me around with my back to the door. I managed to hold off my opponent with one hand, jabbing

with the chair, while I opened the door. Then I threw my
weapon at his feet and departed. While the greasy man un-
tangled himself I went down stairs six at a time. He came close
behind, shrilling curses.

Now, I could have broken this razor duelist into two
twisted pieces with my hands. I could have picked him up and
sat him on a mantelpiece. But the sheen of that razor, wagged
by that supple wrist, terrified me. I fled out of the house and
up the street, and that angry man came right behind me,
shrieking. He pursued me for eight blocks before Canadian
stamina won out. As I saw him collapse against a building, I
went up an alley and into a bar where I bought a drink and
paid cash for it.

"To the chair," I toasted. "Now, *that's* a handy tool!"

My fencing match inspired considerable conversation in
Forty-third Street front-porch circles, none of it complimen-
tary to me. I moved away from that place and did not bother
to make a formal adieu to Lucille.

There were times when I worked at the Bowery Theater,
sometimes in the horse act, sometimes as a comic cop, and
other times when I went on the road with burlesque companies before I finally appeared on the legitimate stage on
Broadway. I played "the circuit" with Frank Sheridan's Burlesque, Boston, New York, Chicago, and towns in between. I
played anything there was to play, sang in quartets and trios,
clowned, and carried scenery. I was paid eighteen dollars a
week.

Mr. Sheridan and his wife and daughter were decent, considerate people—off stage. On stage, they were as tough as
their audiences required them to be, and burlesque audiences
in those days demanded the ultimate. Our jokes were blue, our
songs not merely risqué but earthy, and our girls were hard-
boiled. Monday-matinee audiences, when the show changed,
were the hardest, meanest audiences any performer ever faced.
In Chicago they were composed mostly of prostitutes, pimps,
touts, beggars, sneak thieves, and pickpockets. They never applauded. They gave the razzberry to every effort—even the big
girls in union suits with coconut shells over their bosoms to

make them look even more motherly. I learned early not to take dramatic criticism seriously.

I kept my mouth shut. I wrote home faithfully, detailing to Mother accounts of my adventurous travels with distinguished actors, and I was thankful that it was never possible for her to see how I was employed. I was never prudish, but it took no brains whatsoever to see that this kind of cheap and nauseous theater was a long, far moose-call from my dreams of tasteful girls, fine music, and people who were talented and funny. As soon as I could I tried my luck on Broadway again.

One of my first attempts was to make a pass at a musical called *King Dodo*, starring Raymond Hitchcock. I was cast in the chorus on the strength (literally) of my singing. Chorus boys with big bass voices were hard to come by then as now. When I cut loose at the tryout along with a handful of slim and effeminate dancing boys I was regarded as a discovery, and it seemed for an instant or so that my theatrical future was assured. Then came the dancing.

When I lined up with those trained chorus boys who could tap with lightning feet I was a lumbering spectacle. My shuffle was a feature of Saturday-afternoon street dancing in Northampton, but on Broadway it was elephantine. I floundered against people, tripped myself, and finally tripped Raymond Hitchcock. Mr. Hitchcock was annoyed and appealed to the director.

"Kindly remove this bumbler," I heard him say.

"I know he can't dance, but we will correct that," the director said. "He can sing, and we need singers."

"No," said Hitchcock, "we do not require singers that badly. The man is murderous and all theatrical life is in peril."

And so, of course, I was fired.

As I left I brushed against Hitchcock again.

"Good for you," I muttered, "but the day will come when you will be working for me."

(The day did come, but it was far off. I was noble about it and did not remind Hitchcock of his cruelty more than six or eight times.)

I was better in *A Chinese Honeymoon*, which starred

Thomas Q. Seabrooke. No dancing was required of me. I sang,
and my diction didn't matter since it was supposed to be delivered with a Chinese accent.

Fred Mace, who later became a comedy star in Hollywood, was in the chorus with me. With steady employment
we gained confidence and began to act up. An elderly chorus
boy named Schuster was the butt of our jokes. One evening
just before he went on to stand guard over the star in a royal
production number, we filched his helmet and inserted a wad
of limburger cheese. It was a hot night in August. Mr. Schuster
had to stand perfectly still for many minutes in mid stage. The
cheese melted.

Wang, starring De Wolf Hopper, was another show I
worked in.

De Wolf Hopper had an amazingly big voice, and being
similarly equipped, I made up to him as soon as possible. He
was a democratic fellow who enjoyed talking to a chorus boy
as well as to important people, from Chauncey Depew to the
Astors, who frequently came to his dressing room.

"I don't see why you don't let your voice *out*, Mr.
Hopper," I said.

I was referring to his style of "talk-singing" a song. He
cooped up his lyrics, never letting a good, long, big note re-
sound through the theater.

"Do it a-purpose, of course," he told me. "I have a large
baritone, but suppose I let it go? Then I become a mere baritone. There are lots of baritones, but mark you this: I am a
comedian. You might keep that in mind, Sennett. Never give
away everything. Keep something in reserve. Try to be more
than a mere bass, Mack."

We jammed the wings when he recited *Casey at the Bat*
as an entr'acte. We gathered in knots backstage to hear Mr.
Hopper give advice on the subject of love, a course in which he
was indeed professional. He had, I believe, five wives in succession during an era when it was not fashionable to have more
than two. "I marry my sweethearts," he said.

I can display my Broadway credits quickly. They included
A Chinese Honeymoon, Wang, Piff! Paff!! Pouf!!! starring
Eddie Foy, *Mlle. Modiste*, by Victor Herbert, starring Fritzi
Scheff beating the little drum and singing that still wonderful

song, "Kiss Me Again," and *The Boys of Company B*, starring John Barrymore.

The Boys of Company B brings us up to 1907, when Jack Barrymore was twenty-five years old and just beginning his theatrical career. He had tried everything else, from selling patented face creams to drawing cartoons for Arthur Brisbane. Lionel was studying painting, and Ethel had already become a great star after her New York debut a few years before in *Captain Jinks of the Horse Marines*. Unfortunately I was merely one of the boys in the chorus and although Jack Barrymore was a raffish, hard-drinking fellow and as easy to approach as a mailbox, I was not financially equipped to take part in his escapades and therefore have no new Barrymore tales to spin. He had a rasping voice and was no singer, but he was a natural comedian and a hit in musical comedy. Most people have forgotten, in view of *Hamlet*, when Mr. Barrymore finally got around to developing his real voice, that he made his first successes in musical comedy.

I called up Lionel Barrymore on the telephone at this point and asked him if he recalled anything particular about his brother Jack at that time.

Lionel interrupted work on a water color of the Chatsworth landscape and gave me a patient answer.

"You are wrong in assuming that Jack was your financial superior," he said. "He was as shy of cash as a reformer is of integrity. Of course he was. So was I. I was between *Alice Sit-by-the-Fire* and a morality play called *The Fires of Fate*, or maybe it was *The Jail Bird*. At any rate, the consuming passion of all Barrymores at that time—aside from Ethel, naturally—was not art but dinner.

"As a matter of fact, why are we talking about how broke we were? Taxes being what they are, who has a farthing?

"By the way, old man, tell me something if you can. You had geniuses working for you, you know, positive angel-blessed geniuses. Now, I recall a Sennett picture in which the following occurred:

"There is a comedian up in an airplane. Naturally, this craft, being a Sennett contrivance, is constantly falling apart, dropping things from the clouds.

"Underneath a poor fellow flees from a leaping cop. You

know, one of those cops. Well, now, as the poor fellow is
about to be cornered and trundled off to the calaboose in the
Black Maria, he pauses, extends his arms, and makes a fervent
prayer to his Maker.

"'Lord, save me!' he prays.

"At that precise moment, a thing falls from the airplane
and smites the wicked cop on the head, knocking him galley-
west sidewinding. Our hero then turns to the audience and
declaims:

"'Now, that's what I call real service!'"

Mr. Barrymore's chuckles rattled over the telephone like
hail on a tin roof.

"But tell me, Sennett," he went on; "which one of your
boys wrote that charming episode? Or did your scenario department write it?"

"I think it was Frank Capra," I said.

"*He* worked for you?"

"You could call it that," I replied.

I had better get back to wherever I was before Mr. Barrymore interrupted me.

I was rehearsing a revival of *Mlle. Modiste* and Victor
Herbert himself was at the piano in the Knickerbocker Theater
when the San Francisco earthquake shook Jack Barrymore out
of bed and back to work on April 18, 1906. Another vagrant
memory strikes me as I search these years for what happened:
in Chauncey Olcott's *Edmund Burke* in 1905 three girls
named Smith were given billing. They were Gladys, Lottie,
and Edith Smith. Gladys and Lottie became Gladys and Lottie
Pickford, and "Edith"—"Edith" was played by their younger
brother, later known as Jack Pickford.

Between illicit free lunches at Brady's saloon, occasional
chores in burlesque, and few-and-far-between engagements as
a bass chorus boy in musical comedies, I sang for my suppers.
I sang in a quartet called "The Cloverdale Boys." We had
frock coats which could be quickly retrieved from an obliging
pawnbroker when work was offered, and we were willing to
sing anything, anywhere, for a small fee. It was a good, close-
harmony quartet, and I recall it fondly and the other young
men in it: Roland, the baritone and "arranger," who couldn't
read music, Thorndyke, the second tenor (he had a rake-hell

FREE LUNCH FOR THE ACTOR

mustache), Daley, the top tenor and lead, and myself in the basement. We wore Homburgs, had our shoes shined for special occasions, and often made a respectable appearance when called on to perform at weddings in Brooklyn, funerals in the Bronx, Irish wakes all over town, and innumerable birthday celebrations. We charged higher for funerals. We would have sung at banquets for nothing.

Nickelodeons were springing up everywhere. Thomas Edison, who put James J. Corbett, the heavyweight fighter, under contract, thereby making him the first motion-picture star, was operating a studio in the Bronx. The Vitagraph Studio was in Flatbush. The Selig and Essanay companies were in Chicago—do you recall the first cowboy pictures with Bronco Billy Anderson?

Mr. Edison, who had made the first actual motion-picture machine in 1889, was never a showman. He thought he had produced a contrivance, the Kinetoscope, which would make money as a kind of side-show attraction: you dropped a nickel in the slot and peered through a hole into a cabinet. The Kinetoscope merely showed scenes: a train approaching, dancing, boxing matches—no story, no acting. His first film, made in 1893, showed Fred Ott sneezing. In 1896, Edison made a sensational film. May Irwin and John C. Rice in *The Kiss.* All they did was kiss, but it was a sensation at the time.

And in Philadelphia, Samuel Lubin produced an epic entitled *Horse Eating Hay.* It was no wonder that famous actors snubbed the screen and used the phrase, "posing for pictures," with great scorn. But then Edison made *The Great Train Robbery* in 1903. Joseph Jefferson did some film scenes from his stage hit, *Rip Van Winkle,* a full-length drama, *Ben Hur* was made in Italy and pirated in the United States, and almost overnight motion pictures were under way.

It is hard to believe that Mary Pickford joined the Biograph Co. at 11 East Fourteenth Street—an old brownstone house converted to a studio—as long ago as June 7, 1909. She appeared in *The Violin Maker of Cremona* with Lionel Barrymore and in *The Lonely Villa,* an original screenplay by a Broadway actor and singer named Mack Sennett.

I had heard that there was money in motion pictures. As

much as five dollars a day for professionals like me. I went down to 11 East Fourteenth Street and applied to Wallace ("Pop") McCutcheon, head of the studio, and he gave me work. The year was 1909 and the date was January 17—St. Anthony's Feast Day, and my birthday.

The Biograph players included Flora Finch, Owen Moore, Eddie Dillon, Harry Salter, Charles Inslee, Lionel Barrymore, David Miles, Florence Auer—and a young actor from Kentucky named Lawrence Griffith. He changed his name soon to D. W. Griffith.

CHAPTER 4

The Girl from Staten Island

You know, I often kid myself.

I look back on a long life and believe that what happened in the center ring was the big thing. The show is there under the lights. The clowns are funny. The slapsticks whack false bottoms with loud wallops. Comic men and women fall, run, leap, and make faces. Paint and tinsel, and all made up and artificial. Noise, yells, and big oom-pah in the brass. Tumblers, smick-smack girls with gleaming legs. Death-defying leaps, fire, and tricks. Top billing, twenty-four sheets, fancy and over-blown claims. The greatest, the funniest, the most expensive. Saturnalia of nonsense and showmanship . . .

I have been describing a circus, kind of. But much of my life after 1909, when I bumbled my way into motion pictures, was like that. If it wasn't, we had hired hands who said it was. Hollywood in the teens and in the early twenties was an arena, and a Roman one, to boot. But if you should take a pencil and make notes, or sit alone late at night and try to think about what you have amounted to, and why, and what became of your true dreams, you will probably agree with me about this: whatever your center ring was like and no matter what kind of show went on there, this is not where the most important things in your life happened.

The most important thing in my life was a girl. So you say, "Is the comedy-maker going to turn sentimental on us at this date?" I hope not—but then, again, maybe I'll go on and be sentimental. What's so wrong with it? Anyway the girl I have to tell about was an amazing girl. I am a showman and therefore I am dead set against spoiling a good story by leaving off the sauce. But when it comes to this lady I do not have to add anything. All I have to do is try to set her down as she was. This is going to be difficult.

As I was saying, when the clowns went home it was this girl who was important. I must tell you about her, and tell you what she was like before we go any farther.

I have to confess that I did not have the sense—maybe I did not have the integrity—to know what I know now until it was too late. I thought the show under the big top, so to speak, was the real thing. I thought the audience stayed forever and kept on applauding.

I met her at Biograph. Probably we were never introduced at all—in the horde of extras, day workers, actors, vaudeville people, artists' models, acrobats, clowns, and preening dramatic actors that hung around D. W. Griffith looking for dinner and fame, we were not notable enough to require formal presentations. Her name was Mabel Normand. Mabel Ethelreid Normand. She was about seventeen years old at the time.

Now that I am trying to think things through, I wish— aside from regrets—that I had had the good-will and the intelligence to know Mabel Normand better. That is what I mean: *know* her better. How many lovers, I wonder, strong and passionate young men, have the simple kindness to try to understand their women?

I should not belabor this point and cast my clown as a Hamlet: we did not play our funny roles with breaking hearts —the classic, behind-the-scenes heartbreak in all tales about comedians. No. But I was not thoughtful.

In recent years I have tried to know more about Mabel than I knew before it was too late.

The Very Reverend Monsignor William F. Murray, Chancellor of the Diocese of Providence, wrote to the Right Reverend Monsignor Thomas Blackwell, of St. Paul's Rectory, Los Angeles, on August 11, 1953, to say that he had been unsuccessful in a quest.

Monsignor Murray, as a favor to Monsignor Blackwell, who asked the service as a favor to me, had requested a transcript of Mabel Normand's baptismal certificate.

I was trying to start at the beginning of her life. A sentimental, maybe even a sententious undertaking, but possibly
not useless now that I am trying to tell her story and mine.

Monsignor Murray wrote Monsignor Blackwell that he
had searched the archives of the cathedral and also of the terri-
torial parishes of St. Mary's, St. Patrick's, and St. Michael's.
Neither these parishes nor the French parish of St. Charles,
which embraces all of Providence, revealed any record of the
baptism of Mabel Ethelreid Normand, who was born in Providence November 10, 1895, in a Catholic family.

It is impossible that she was not baptized. Her mother
was pure Irish and her father was pure French. Five other children were certainly baptized, and all during her devout but
casual life Mabel Normand professed and practiced the Roman
Catholic faith. I can only suggest an explanation.

Her family was temperamental, improvident, and often in
transit. Her father was a professional pianist—not a successful
concert performer, but a player of tunes in theater orchestras.
So far as I know he never worked for a band on Broadway, nor
did he play with important symphony orchestras. He was in
the pit with small orchestras on the road in and around Boston
and New York. He enjoyed an abiding love for the theater and
for music, and he followed his uncertain profession from here
to there until he met Mary Drury.

Mary Drury, the Irish girl, had night-black hair, gray eyes,
and lashes so long that in late years it was difficult for her to
wear spectacles. She studied singing, but aside from
is no hint that she or anyone else in her provident
any theatrical inclinations. It appears that Claud
mand, the dark and slender French piano player, sw
her feet, tucked her under his arm, and eloped with
disappeared into the raffish life of itinerant musicia
ing band leaders and vaudeville shows up and down
England coast. Mary Drury Normand was kept busy.   *54*
the Frenchman six children.

Their troubles and the quick arrival of half a dozen off-
spring in various towns explain, I believe, why even the mon-
signors could not lay hands on Mabel Normand's baptismal
certificate. This is not the only missing clue in her life.

Three of the Normand children died young. The family

wound up in New Brighton, on Staten Island, where Claude
G. Normand had a job with the Sailors' Snug Harbor, a refuge
for old seafarers. Mr. Normand gave up professional piano
playing and settled down to a life of—I believe the phrase goes
—"quiet desperation." The end of the road for him was Staten
Island. His only legacy to Mabel was music. He taught her to
play the piano. The Normands were often—indeed, always—
without funds, but wherever they moved or however meanly
they had to live, the Frenchman clung to an old and battered
piano. He and his small black-haired daughter played on it
every night. The Normands had more concerts than pot roasts.

Both Miss Hedda Hopper (who became my old friend De
Wolf's fifth wife in 1913, long before she began to write about
Hollywood) and Miss Louella Parsons knew Mabel intimately
when she was at the height of her acting career. Both writing
ladies say the same thing. They say Mabel was a genius and
that she was the finest actress in motion pictures they ever
knew. They are unable to explain Mabel's genius, and neither
can I. This girl seemed able to do anything and to do it the
first time she tried it.

She was barely five feet tall and never weighed more than
ninety-nine pounds. Her formal education was as sketchy as
shorthand. But she learned music from her father, obviously
without many hours' practice, and she became an athlete. The
home she lived in was wild and poor, but she found time before she was sixteen to win a number of medals as a swimmer,
and this was without the years of practice and training usually
needed for any kind of championship performance. She read,
Lord knows when, but she did read, and acquired a peculiarly
baffling skill in—of all things—geography. We can guess, I suppose, that her knowledge of far-off places and coast lines was
inspired by imagination and longing for adventure; but I
plainly don't know why geography fascinated her and I set
down the fact merely as an odd thing. She was only thirteen
years old when she became an artists' model.

Mabel's first job was in the pattern department of a
women's magazine and she took it, not because of any ambition to approach acting by this first-step route, but because her
family was almost destitute and it was necessary for her to
work. The head of the pattern department saw a pretty child

doing clerical jobs and decided that she ought to pose for illustrators. He gave her a note to Carl F. Kleinschmidt, who painted magazine covers. Mabel began to work for Kleinschmidt at the going rate for models in those days, fifty cents an hour. Kleinschmidt introduced her to other artists and within a matter of a few weeks she was pretty regularly employed.

Mabel worked for Henry Hutt, Penrhyn Stanlaws, Charles Dana Gibson, and James Montgomery Flagg. She recalled that one of the first advertisements she appeared in was for Coca-Cola, but she modeled everything from shoes to ermine wraps, lingerie, umbrellas, and soap. A C. Coles Phillips drawing called "The Sand Witch" sold to *The Saturday Evening Post*. Mabel trotted from artist to artist, from Phillips on Twenty-seventh Street to West Sixty-seventh Street, where Flagg held forth. Other artists were in Carnegie Hall and Mabel hung around there, hoping for work.

All of these famous illustrators, Mabel said later, were kind to her. They were workingmen, practicing a profession, with no time for hi-jinks. Mabel did not recall that one of them lived up to the usual conception of casual love and immorality we like to associate with artists. Mr. Flagg was especially kind to her. After she had tried to steal rosebuds from a silver evening gown supplied by Flagg as a costume, he gave her *carte blanche* to take small fancy things from his studio.

Alice Joyce, Anna Q. Nilsson, and Justine Johnstone, later to become famous in motion pictures, were contemporaries of Mabel's in the modeling business. Then Mabel met a young man named Frank Lanning. Lanning posed athletically, made up as a cowboy or an Indian, and it struck him that he might pick up extra dollars if he did the same kind of posing for that new thing, motion pictures.

So far as I could ever learn, Mabel Normand at sixteen had developed no blazing ambition to become an actress. If she had, she would have tried the stage. She would have made good there, and possibly I would never have known her. But when Lanning urged her to try her luck at 11 East Fourteenth Street, she sought the counsel of Orson Lowell, the artist. Lowell said a wise thing, considering what motion pictures were like at that time.

"Most funny women are funny-looking," he told Mabel. "You are not funny-looking, you are beautiful. But you are funny. Now I claim you don't have to be ridiculous-looking to be a comedienne. Go try. If they don't like you, what's the difference? You can always come back and work for us."

Mabel went down to the Biograph Studios, unintroduced, and asked for work, citing her experience as an artists' model. She simply applied to the first employee she met, who sent her to D. W. Griffith's assistant.

This gentleman, Wilfred Lucas, was in need at the moment. He never claimed later that he was smart enough to spot Mabel Normand as a great comic actress the moment he clapped eyes on her. He simply needed a girl with good legs who could be dressed as a page. Neither Lucas nor Mabel recalled what the picture was. It was merely some short-subject picture that needed a page in it, and Lucas sent Mabel over to the wardrobe department to get her legs in silk as fast as possible.

She worked until quitting time and was paid five dollars. But the company was in a hurry and Mabel was told that she could earn two dollars and a half more if she stayed until nine, and another two dollars and a half if she worked on until midnight. She was delighted, never having earned all of ten dollars a day in her life.

When she reached Staten Island it was past 3 A.M. and Mary Normand, Mabel's mother, was hysterical. Being out alone in New York until that unconscionable hour was dangerous enough, she proclaimed, but to spend the time with movie people posing in silk stockings compounded the wickedness. There was a long and tearful session and Mabel was forbidden to return to Biograph, even for ten dollars.

I entered Mabel's life with her first motion-picture scene. I watched her as she made her first "take." Mabel used to claim that she saw me, too, but I think she invented that as a sop to my pride. I was a hanger-on, leaning against a wall, hoping to get noticed and put into the picture myself. For five dollars I was willing to leap, fight, swim, portray grand passion, or even act like a gentleman.

But Mabel claimed she saw me. "You looked like a flat-foot store detective," she said.

At any rate, Mabel committed a cardinal motion-picture sin with her first appearance before the camera. As a page, she carried a queen's train *out* of a room. The scene ended there, and the next sequence, to be shot days later, was to show the queen entering another room, attended by this established page.

No page the next day. Mabel didn't show up.

No one knew where to find her. She had departed sleepily for Staten Island, leaving no address.

It was a week later that I met her on Fifth Avenue. I didn't know her name, but I recognized her as the missing extra with the pretty legs.

"Hi," I said.

"Oh?" she said.

I fell in stride.

"I'm an actor with Biograph, the D. W. Griffith Company," I said.

Mabel did not show that she was impressed, but she did not call a cop to chase me, either.

"You have a future in movies," I said.

"Oh?" said Mabel.

"Matter of fact, you have a *guaranteed* future," I said. "You didn't finish your part. There's another day's work waiting for you. Aren't you interested in five dollars?"

We stopped on the sidewalk and discussed the future of motion pictures.

"I am a Broadway actor," I told Mabel, "now posing in pictures, but I am going to be a director. Matter of fact, I will have my own company pretty soon. My friend D. W. Griffith is giving me pointers."

Some of this was true. D. W. Griffith was teaching me how to direct, although he did not know it. He was my day school, my adult education program, my university. This was possible for two reasons: I was not regularly employed in the occasional bit parts that they gave me or as an extra, and this gave me plenty of time to watch Griffith and his remarkable cameraman, the late Billy Bitzer. And I had discovered that Griffith liked to walk.

When Griffith walked, I walked. I fell in, matched strides, and asked questions.

Griffith told me what he was doing and what he hoped to do with the screen, and some of what he said stuck. I thought things over. I began to learn how to make a motion picture. I even offered a few suggestions to D. W. Griffith, but I discovered he was not so fascinated by comedy as I was, and he went into silences when I brought up my favorite people, policemen. I never succeeded in convincing Mr. Griffith that cops were funny.

"When I get my own company," I told Mabel Normand, "I will make funny pictures and put you in them. I wouldn't be surprised if you turned out to be mighty good. That is, with competent direction. And don't forget the five bucks."

Mabel turned around and went back to 11 East Fourteenth Street with me.

CHAPTER 5

C/o D. W. Griffith, Genius

I KEPT right on telling D. W. Griffith that cops were funny. When I first offered this idea as my original contribution to the drama, Griffith was a hawk-beaked, lean, intense young man from Kentucky who had recently been acting on Broadway and in stock companies. He had turned to motion pictures more or less the way I had and we both caught fire. Well, there was a difference in the way we caught fire which I won't have to explain.

D. W. Griffith, when you come right down to it, *invented* motion pictures. As Lionel Barrymore says, there ought to be a statue to him at Hollywood and Vine, and it ought to be fifty feet high, solid gold, and floodlighted every night.

Griffith knew what he wanted and how to get it and do it from the beginning. He was out to create drama, and he had integrity about that. As for my cops, he was as bored with them when he made five dollars a day as when he was a famous director.

I think you know what I mean about cops. I respect the working force and the plain-clothes men and the traffic officers, who perform their difficult and poorly rewarded jobs of protecting the citizen from himself and from the bunco artists, the sneak thieves, and the murderers who beset him. No matter, policemen are natural foils for comedy. They have dignity, and wherever there is dignity, comics can embroil it, embarrass it, flee from it, and thumb their noses at it. Like me, I imagine, the average citizen is a little afraid of policemen. He enjoys reducing the cop to his own level. I wanted to take a giant step and reduce cops to absurdities.

D. W. Griffith never approved of this. We used to stroll about, gaze at the river, wander the streets, and talk about the future of motion pictures.

"I want to put together full-length stories," he would say. "Not merely little scenes such as we photograph now. And I don't see any sense in always showing so much. For instance, we have a scene in Room A. We finish with it and the characters go to Room B, where more action takes place. Why do we have to photograph the people walking from Room A to Room B? Just cut to Room B.

"Writers do it. It's done on the stage. Why not in movies? And in pictures we can do so many things we can't do at all on stage.

"Why not move the camera up close and show an actor's full face? That would reveal his emotions, give him a chance to show what he is thinking."

"Actors will applaud," I said.

"And this flat lighting! Why not 'mood' lighting, shadows for this scene, bright light for that?

"And feet! Why are we always photographing actors' *feet*? Let's move the camera back and forth, showing part of the actor, the part that means something. Let's use the camera for punctuation. And for vast crowds and spectacles, cavalry charges, burning cities . . ."

I did not know at the time that D. W. Griffith was working out, with me as a sounding board, the great theories which made him the absolute pioneer of the screen. He and his cameraman, Billy Bitzer, invented the close-up, "Rembrandt" lighting, and what we now call the "idiom" of the screen. He did that in 1909 and 1910, and what he did was as fundamental to movies as the wheel is to mechanics. We have widened the screen now, but we are still telling stories the way D. W. Griffith taught us to tell them.

I listened and learned and thought things over. I did not see these factors in the same terms as Griffith saw them. I think that being from the South influenced him: his father had been a notable Confederate officer, and Lawrence Griffith (like Margaret Mitchell years later) had been brought up on tales of Chancellorsville, Manassas, Cold Harbor, and charge the ramparts. He saw stories as mass movement suddenly pin-

pointed and dramatized in human tragedy. He was ready, I
suppose, to make *The Birth of a Nation* many years before he
found the money to start it.

What I saw in his great ideas was a new way to show
people being funny.

"A cop is whacked on the seat of the pants," I said. "Then
the camera moves in for a close-up and you see his face, filling
the whole screen, outraged. Then you cut to the comedian
and you see *his* face—he didn't mean to whack a cop! . . ."

D. W. Griffith endured me largely because I was a strong
walking companion. I discovered that he walked from 11 East
Fourteenth Street to his apartment on East Thirty-seventh
Street every evening, even in the days when he had two chauf-
feurs, a "day" chauffeur and a "night" chauffeur who always
stood by to humor any transportation whim Griffith might
think up. I hung around carefully and just happened to be going his way every night when work was over. So far as any
knowledge of motion-picture technique goes, I learned all I
ever learned by standing around, watching people who knew
how, by pumping Griffith, and thinking it over.

I would have pumped anybody. It was sheer good fortune
that made it possible for me to pump a genius.

Meanwhile I acted, if you are willing to call it that. I did
extra work, played bits with Owen Moore, Flora Finch, and
Florence Lawrence. (Miss Lawrence became "The Biograph
Girl," and was the first motion-picture star, although anony-
mously. It was not until Mary Pickford's enormous success
that players on the screen began to be identified.) I did a fair
job of comic acting in *Father Gets in the Game*, portraying
a character the like of which I had never seen, a Parisian dude.
In 1909 I was in *The Curtain Pole*, a 750-foot comedy, and
some people considered me funny. At any rate, this was my
"hit" picture and now they gave me work I could do.

I could wreck things. I could overturn things. I could
get mixed up with a curtain pole and a door and create
havoc.

The Curtain Pole was one of the first of the real slapstick
comedies, and when it made money I was at long last per-
mitted to work in a film that had cops in it. It was called
The Politician's Love Story and I did not play a cop, to my

enormous regret. Instead I was rewarded with the leading part as a gent in a silk hat, wearing wide mustachios. In the supporting cast was Linda Arvidson, who was secretly married to D. W. Griffith.

I wrote to my mother:

"I am a star now. Please see 'The Politician's Love Story' when it comes to Northampton and also tell Judge Coolidge about it. You may not recognize me but I am the star."

Mother congratulated me. She wrote:

"Dear Son: We saw 'The Politician's Love Story.' I sent word to Judge Coolidge but I do not think he went. We are all proud of your wonderful success but can't get used to it. Have you paid your room rent?"

Although I had played the lead in a picture, I was never at any time among the crème de la crème at Biograph. D. W. Griffith was the Grand Master Panjandrum of all actors he surveyed. He liked me, but he did not consider me any more literate than I was. Mary Pickford and her mother, the Gish girls, Dorothy and Lillian, and Henry B. Walthall (the "Little Colonel" in *The Birth of a Nation*) were kind but superior. Mrs. Griffith thought I was a grouch. She said so in her biography, published in 1925.

"Sennett never approved whole-heartedly of anything we did, no matter how we did it, nor who did it. There was something wrong with all of us—even Mary Pickford."

That was not all true, although it is easy to understand how Mrs. Griffith misunderstood my scowls. I scowl when I think, and I think slowly, so my scowls last. Any idea of mine needs a long period of gestation. So, while trying to use my brains, I frowned. As a matter of fact, comic ideas are the most painful ideas in the world, as any comedian will tell you.

A Frenchman once went to a psychiatrist, one of those guys who charges $25 for a nap on his couch.

"I am depressed," he said. "I am despondent. I want to kill myself. What can I do?"

"You ought to have some fun," said the psychiatrist. "Get away from yourself. Go to the circus and see the great clowns, the Fraternelli Brothers."

The patient sighed. "Alas," he said, "I cannot follow your prescription. I am the senior Fraternelli."

Grouch that I seemed to have been, I did not depress Mary Pickford. I met her first in *The Violin Maker of Cremona*, in which she played opposite David Miles, supported by Lionel Barrymore. I was an extra, part of the Italian street scene. Mary was gracious, as she has always been to everybody, but she was all business. Even then as a dimpled darling, all peaches and cream and very young, Miss Pickford had a bright eye for a dollar. I was an out-sized Irishman and a rough comedian, but Mary and I soon discovered that we shared a common and abiding interest in money.

One afternoon between takes on the set I told Mary my ideas about fun with cops on the screen.

"Now that might be very good," she said, "although as you know, D. W. prefers heavier dramatic material. Have you written some of your cop comedies?"

It hadn't occurred to me to do that.

"No," I said, "I been discouraged. Nobody thinks cops are funny but me. Anyway, I can't write."

"It isn't so difficult," Mary said. "I write stories."

"You do?"

"You bet I do. The studio needs lots of material. I sold four last week."

"They pay you for them?"

"Twenty-five dollars apiece," Mary said.

I became a writer on the spot.

I bought a pad and pencil from a drugstore and attacked authorship. I stayed up late at night staring at my pad and pencil. I wrote, "By Mack Sennett," at the top of a page and stared at it. Nothing came. I walked around the block, had a cup of tea, bought the Sunday papers, and wrote my name again on a fresh sheet of paper.

Inspiration finally arrived. I found a fine, funny, dramatic situation in the Sunday supplement of the New York *World*, changed the names of the persons involved in it, put it in as few scenes as possible for a two-reeler, and made a painful copy in pencil.

I sought out Mary Pickford as soon as I could and showed her my screenplay.

"Good?" I asked.

Mary was a fast reader. "I wouldn't have believed it," she said.

"Terrible?" I said.

"Terrific," Mary said. "This is really superb. A wonderful plot with a neat surprise ending. They'll buy it. I think you'd better take it over to the office right away."

"Not me," I said, "you."

"Me?"

"You're pretty," I said, "and an actress, and you've sold stories before. They wouldn't pay me any never-mind. You take this yarn to 'em and say you wrote it and you and I'll split."

Miss Pickford, as I said, was then, as now, a woman who found charm in finance. She took the story over to the head office and I waited impatiently. We had a quick decision.

"You know Irving Place, only a few blocks from here?" Mary said when she returned.

"Sure, sure, but the story——"

"Tell you about that. At Irving Place lives a writer, pretty famous writer. Do you read *Munsey's?* He writes for *Munsey's.*"

"Used to read *Munsey's,*" I said.

"And the New York *World.* He writes for the *World,* too."

"Sure, everybody reads the *World,*" I said. "What's that got to do with my piece?"

"This writer's name is O. Henry," Mary said. "And when you lift a story, you'd better not lift *his.* He's awfully well known."

I thought that over.

"But I changed it," I complained.

"You didn't change it enough," Mary said.

O. Henry died less than a year later and we all read about his funeral at the Little Church Around the Corner, where a wedding party had to wait until his funeral was over—just the kind of trick ending he would have liked.

Let me get it in the record, though, that I did become an author. It is my theory that almost anybody can become a writer, or an actor, or a hero, or a burglar, or just about anything, if he needs the money. There is no greater inspiration than a hungry vacuum under the belt. I bought a dozen pencils and a stack of paper and set about learning how to write for the screen, in exactly the same way I was trying to learn to be a director. I copied people who knew how.

I learned scenarios by heart, sometimes transcribing them verbatim in order to get the hang. I had to abandon my ambition for a while to make comic pictures about the *gendarmerie*. The big cardboard box that served as a wastebasket in my room was heaped with crumpled sheets of paper and I used up so many pencils that I had to cut down expenses by buying the penny kind. Remember them? One cent apiece with a nub of an eraser, and harder than a pawnbroker's stare. Many a schoolboy, I would bet, grew up to despise writing and writers because he had to use those discouraging penny pencils.

Well, I had an iron puddler's fist and a strong back, so I stayed with it. I wrote about as fast as a monument-epitaph cutter, but I wrote, threw away, thought things over, and wrote more. I still found my ideas in newspapers, but I was careful to find them in news stories, not under the names of professionals. The Biograph executives did not hold it against me that my first effort had been a plagiarism—every studio in those days was larcenous, stealing stories wherever they could and changing them just enough to escape legal action. They read my efforts hopefully and told me to keep trying.

I made the grade at last and began to sell stories to Biograph with tolerable regularity. My screenplays were not much. Few screen stories were much in that era. Most of them were little more than quick dramatic scenes. Even the great classics were tossed off fast for a quick buck. Vitagraph about that time released *Romeo and Juliet, Julius Caesar, The Merchant of Venice, Richard III,* and *Antony and Cleopatra*—in one reel each.

Florence Lawrence (the first movie star) had been making fifteen dollars a week at Vitagraph before she came to Biograph for twenty-five. D. W. Griffith had taken charge at Biograph and was already getting recognized as a master. He saw to that. Griffith earned sixty-five a week and it was a sensation in the trade when he demanded a hundred twenty-five dollars a week and actually got it. So you see that a boy like me who was willing to work and who kept at it had a chance. This was the dawn of motion pictures, and there were opportunities for a few years that never came again.

My stories were too trivial to remember and nobody does remember them, including me. One of them was *The Lonely Villa* and it is worth recalling because I was paid twenty-five dollars for it when I needed money and because it was Mary Pickford's second motion picture.

What happened in *The Lonely Villa?* I haven't the slightest idea, but I can promise you that not much happened. Mary has forgotten all about it, but it would not be safe to give odds that she doesn't recall precisely how much money she was paid for acting in it.

If a swami who could beat the races, or even St. Anthony, had vowed by the United States Mint that pretty soon I would offer Mary Pickford a screen story that would make a million dollars—if anybody had suggested such a ridiculosity, I would have broken a leg laughing. But this did happen. And I became a movie director sooner than seemed possible.

Motion pictures began to get all out of hand about 1910. The nickelodeons continued, but genuine movie theaters suddenly appeared everywhere, in vacant stores, in old city halls and "opera houses." Movies swept the country and they swept me right along with them.

The men who saw this big sweep coming were not college men, Broadway theater producers, or Wall Street speculators. Griffith, of course, was the first artist to understand what could be accomplished with a camera and a spectacle, but the other pioneers were tough men who came from the junk business (the Warners), the fur business (Adolph Zukor) and the glove trade (Sam Goldwyn).

They started out as exhibitors in order to make a dime the fastest way possible. Most of them went into production reluctantly, forced into it in order to lay hands on enough pictures to satisfy their customers.

Famous actors began to come along now. Maurice Costello arrived at Vitagraph in 1909. He was one of the first and one of the greatest American matinee idols, known as "The Dimpled Darling." He created a sensation.

All of us, no matter what rank or talent we had, did whatever was needful around Biograph. We toted cameras, moved furniture, hammered nails, sawed boards, and shifted scenery as a matter of course. Not Mr. Costello.

"I am an act-or, sir!" he announced on the first day he reported for work. "I do not construct sets nor do I shift scenery."

And he didn't. I did, of course. I carried the camera willingly, as often as possible, in order to be on hand to watch Griffith or some other good man direct.

Mainly I was thinking up schemes to get to be a director, notions for stories I might peddle for twenty-five dollars, and ways and means to eat dinner. I can look back now and conjure up the feeling of ambition and tension of those hard days when the magic lantern was a new thing just about to capture a nation's imagination and give it millions of nights of fun and wish fulfillment. The lantern was about to create a new kind of human being on the face of the world, the movie star, a demigodlike person who would be worshiped by dime-store girls and farm hands, millionaires and Society. Come to think of it, no emperor, king, president, or prime minister had ever known the world-wide fame or the affection enjoyed by a full-blown movie star.

As I was saying, fabulous days and nights were just around the corner and some men were moving fast, seeing around the corner a little. I may not have seen very far—let's be frank, I didn't see very far—but I was on the right street to get pushed wherever the excitement took place.

Moonlight and Diamond

WHEN YOU come right down to it, there is no such place as Hollywood. There is a United States Post Office at 1615 Wilcox Avenue, not far from the Garden Court apartments on Hollywood Boulevard, where I now live, and it uses the postmark "Hollywood" on all outgoing mail because people like to see it and because movie producers insist on it as a trademark. But even the Hollywood Chamber of Commerce is hard put to define the exact boundaries of what it is shouting about. "Hollywood" is a roughly defined area of the city of Los Angeles just east of Beverly Hills—which *is* a city all to itself, with cops to prove it.

When D. W. Griffith brought me to Hollywood in January of 1910 as part of a little company headed by Henry Walthall, Mary Pickford, Owen Moore, Jack Pickford, and Tony O'Sullivan, we hired a vacant lot at Georgia and Twelfth streets, put up tents around its boundaries for dressing rooms, and called that our studio. Nowadays Twelfth and Georgia is in the heart of the Los Angeles downtown business district—not far from the modern new Statler Hotel, the slick department stores, and the fancy office buildings of the big oil companies. The last I heard, the Los Angeles Chamber of Commerce and the Philadelphia Chamber of Commerce were competing in a transcontinental yelling contest about which city is the third biggest in the United States. You know who yelled the loudest. At any rate, Los Angeles now has a population of 2,113,942. When we pitched our tents, L.A. had only 319,198.

As for "Hollywood," that was a crossroad out in the

country. It had been a town, they tell me. A man named Horace Henderson Wilcox and his wife, Daieda, who were Prohibitionists from Topeka, speculated in real estate there just before the turn of the century, made a little money, and used to be seen riding fashionably around behind a spanking pair of Arabian horses. But the real-estate boom busted and the retired Iowans who came out to settle in the sunshine gave up their town and ceded it to the sprawling city of Los Angeles in 1909.

Gaspar de Portolá staked out Southern California as a subdivision for Charles III of Spain. Since then all Southern Californians have been real-estate dealers. They are sorry for the wretched people back East and are determined to find them a better place to live at a profit.

There are 12,000,000 people in California today. Any of them will make you a deal. Unlike Florida, there are no lots here that are always under water. On the contrary, there are towns in Southern California so thirsty that the boys can't pucker up to whistle at girls. They just whisper, but the birth rate is going up.

I looked Hollywood over in 1910 and didn't want to buy it. I *couldn't* have bought it, or anything else worth more than a dollar and a half, but I didn't share the prejudice some people have against geraniums and poinsettias and I thought that eventually all motion pictures would be made out this way on account of the sunshine. I was dead sure I was going to make some of those motion pictures.

Glendale was my pick. Glendale is part of the wide gateway to the San Fernando Valley, more or less between Pasadena and Los Angeles. It is a very conservative city these days, population 112,732, but in 1910 it had only 2742. Glendale was settled mostly by Middle Westerners and Southerners, and they were not people who thought highly of actors. It was too bad, because if they had liked us better Glendale and not the community called Hollywood would have become the world center of motion pictures. Instead there are now more dead actors in Glendale than live ones. The famous Forest Lawn Cemetery opened up for business there on New Year's day, 1917, and has since become a favorite tribal burying ground for show folks. Forest Lawn today has a population of 163,000.

I worked in whatever Griffith produced, including *Man's Genesis*, which was cave-man stuff and just right for me. The well-remembered Mae Marsh, then a child actress, was in that one. Whenever I could I plodded around, exploring the countryside, and asking real-estate men what they would take for pieces of property. I tramped all over the present site of the big cemetery in Glendale. It is one of the most beautiful places in the world, but if I could have got my hands on it, it would have been livelier.

If I had been able to scrape up even so much as a thousand dollars in cash I could have founded a fortune in California land. As it turned out, I did eventually found a studio almost in Glendale and within a few years after that I became the largest private owner of real estate in the city of Los Angeles. But that involved me in an adventure with pigs and is a story I'll come to a bit later.

I lived at the Alexandria Hotel at 210 West Fifth Street with a fake Frenchman named Pathé Lehrman. Members of the Griffith company were allowed two dollars a day for expenses and I could not really afford the comforts of the Alexandria, still a fine hotel, but it was about this time that I discovered what a joy it was to take a bath.

In Canada we had bathed on Saturday nights after pouring a bucket of hot water into a tin tub in the kitchen. You froze on one side and shivered on the other during this operation, and you never did feel *soaked* around the edges. Now I could lie back in an enormous tub, let the hot water run full tilt, and *think*. Some philosopher ought to do a piece about the influence of modern plumbing on intellectual America. I believe that a bathroom is about the thoughtfulest place there is. I bet good plumbing has affected our national culture and spirit of free enterprise. I don't see how a man who can lounge around in a tiled bathroom could ever become a communist.

I soaked in the Alexandria bathtubs and thought tall thoughts.

I thought about the Pathé Frères, in Paris, having a kind of affinity for the French on account of considering myself a French speaker. But mainly I thought about the funny pictures the brothers Pathé made. Now, I have been posing for many years as the inventor of slapstick motion-picture comedy

and it is about time I confessed the truth. It was those French-
men who invented slapstick and I imitated them. I never went
as far as they did, because give a Frenchman a chance to be
funny and he will go the limit—you know what I mean. But
I stole my first ideas from the Pathés.

This brings me around to Pathé Lehrman, my roommate
at the Alexandria.

Before I came to California for the first time I had become, in my own mind, anyway, a motion-picture star. Whenever one of my pictures opened on Broadway I would hasten
up town to attend the world premiere. That cost ten cents, so
I often went alone.

One evening I went to the Unique Theater to see myself
in something or other and fell into conversation with an usher.
He was a lean, dark, eager fellow with something of a French
accent, so we tried out our kindergarten-type French on each
other for a while, and then I came around to asking him what
he thought of the masterpiece then on view.

"It has an odor," the usher said.

"You don't like it?" I scowled.

"*Mais oui*, the picture is all right, but the leading comedian, *sacré*, he is no good."

"Do you know who he is?"

"*Certainement, absolument*, I know, *monsieur*—it is you."

"You are a fresh kid," I said. "You think I'm bad? How?
Why? How could I do better?"

"Knew you at once. You're Mack Sennett, the great
actor. I merely wished to see if you could—how do you say?
—take it. You were wonderful. You stole the picture, and you
know it."

I saw at once that this man had good taste.

"Who are you?" I asked.

The usher fumbled in his pockets and came up with a
dirty calling card. It said, "Monsieur Henri Lehrman of Paris."

"I am a student of the motion-picture art," he explained.
"I have come from Paris where I learned all there was to learn
from the Pathés. I wish to bring my knowledge to America,
and learn how you do things, but, alas, I am reduced to this
poor employment."

I thought that over.

If this guy had worked with the Pathés, he would know things I could use and I had better grab him.

"Tell you what," I said. "I'll go in and see the picture and meet you after you're through for the night. We'll have a can of suds at Brady's—I have the money—and we'll talk about your future."

The upshot of this was that Monsieur Henri Lehrman of Paris reported the next morning at Biograph and asked to see D. W. Griffith on my recommendation. Griffith was not interested in Lehrman's promise that he knew all about comedy, but he was at that time making a French period picture featuring lots of swordplay and fifteenth-century prancing. Lehrman said he knew all about that sort of thing; indeed he claimed he was a positive scholar in antique swashbuckling. So Griffith put him on as an extra to find out what he knew.

When Lehrman appeared on the set he had smeared so much make-up on himself that we had to scrape him with a paddle. It was plain that he had never been before a camera.

"He's a frog, I suppose," Griffith muttered, "but I'll wager he is not a French frog. Let him stick around. We need extras."

The scene called for French soldiers to capture a three-story building, rescuing some damsel in distress. Lehrman immediately distinguished himself. He not only ran into the building with the other extras, but suddenly appeared on the roof—and leaped into space.

The fall would have splattered an ordinary man like a scrambled egg, but Lehrman lit on his backside, rolled twenty feet, bounced, and came up grinning weakly.

Griffith was indignant.

"You were not on camera!" he hollered.

"I was just rehearsing," Lehrman said. "I'll do it again." And he did.

Griffith knew we had a fraud on our hands, but he had spotted it right at the start and so he was tolerant. We kept Lehrman on, and Griffith named him on the spot. He became "Pathé" Lehrman and before long he became a director. He was bright, all right. He worked many years for me and gave me an enormous amount of trouble.

Who Pathé Lehrman really was and where he came from

are still mysteries. Some people claim he was from Vienna, not Paris, and others insist that he started life in Yorktown as a streetcar motorman. It doesn't matter. Pathé was a funny man with an instinct for comedy—he thought in terms of nonsense as naturally as Marlene Dietrich deals in her special commodity. As the years went on I found increasing use for Pathé, and it is certainly a fact that he used me.

I was courting Mabel Normand in a mild sort of way at that time, but I was a good deal more concerned with courting a career and she knew it. We went to cheap shows, sat in the gallery at the Metropolitan Opera House (the closest I ever came to that stage), and on such evenings as I did not have to do my penny-pencil and paper work, I would take her home to Staten Island. There wasn't much romance. Boys and girls were more innocent in those days than they are now and it was a long time before I even managed to kiss that girl.

For one thing, she never held still and it is difficult to kiss a girl who won't stand still for it. She was always up to something. On the set there were always people around her. She would tell stories, wisecrack, and play practical jokes by the hour. Mabel was frisky, as skittery as a waterbug and oh, my Lord, how pretty! She turned any place she was into an uproar and if she couldn't think up better things to do, she would pull chairs out from under fat men.

In a way, perhaps, D. W. Griffith missed out on Mabel. Great discoverer of talent that he was, he never saw that Mabel was a born actress. She was no intellectual, like Bette Davis, who thinks out her roles and always asks her director, "Why?" Mabel was pure emotion. All you had to do was say act out this or that emotion, feel this way, or look like you feel this way, and Mabel could instantly do it, throwing herself into the part so thoroughly that she believed it. But on account of the pranks that went on all the time, and on account of her being with me so much, Griffith never took her seriously. I am not alone in my opinion that Mabel might have been a great dramatic actress if some thoughtful director had turned her energies in that direction. Instead, of course, she became a comedienne, and the best.

Before I left for California I bought Mabel a ring. As I don't have to tell you, it was a cheap ring. It cost two dollars

and a half but it had a lot of *shine* to it and I had to save up
to buy it. Mabel knew that.

One evening on the ferry on the way home to Staten
Island I gave it to her. You know how a country boy does that
sort of thing, sort of offhanded, as if, oh well, just happened to
have this ole ring around and didn't know what else to do
with it. Mabel stood very still.

This scared me. I said, "Maybe I'd better go buy us some
popcorn. If you have a dime."

Mabel was staring at the water, which had wide splashes
of moonlight on it.

"Popcorn," she said softly.

So I went off and bought the popcorn and when I returned she was still staring at the water.

We leaned over the rail and watched the yellow moonlight on the dark river. As our ferry ploughed and dipped
toward Staten Island, the Manhattan sky line rose and fell as
if we were standing still and the city was going up and down.
Fog shapes moved all around us, looming and going away, and
we heard the low, sad hoots of other boats on the bay and the
river. It was all magical and I began to feel shivers in my spine.

We went on munching popcorn. Then the moonlight
flickered under a cloud and went out.

Mabel turned to me and she was standing very close.

"Too much butter?" she said.

I heard the popcorn bag rattle to the deck. I took Mabel
in my arms and kissed her and there wasn't too much butter
at all.

"You put the ring on my finger," Mabel said when that
was over, and it wasn't over for quite a while. "It's the most
beautifulest ring in all the world."

"Nothing *to* it," I said. "Just a little old ring. But when I
get famous I am going to buy you a peck of diamonds and a
slingshot and we will shoot 'em at people and laugh when they
jump and we will have all the money in the world, and I will
build me the biggest bathtub you ever saw, maybe nine feet
long, and we will ride around in a Pierce-Arrow."

I couldn't tell whether Mabel was laughing or crying, but
she pulled away from me.

"I dunno about you, Mack Sennett," she said. "I don't

know whether you are a man to fall in love with or not—and I haven't said I *have* fallen for you, mind that—bathtubs and slingshots!"

That is sort of how it was with Mabel and me all the way through.

But when I was in California, Mabel staying in New York to do some work for Vitagraph, and thought things over in the Alexandria bathtubs, and got excited about California real estate and about the possibilities of making great motion pictures out there, and me making them, I got all lonely for Mabel and those shivers began to come up and down my back again.

I mooned around in the bathtub so much that Pathé used to get mad at me.

"Come on, Mack, we'll go over to the Athletic Club and shoot a pool," he would say.

"No, I got to think."

"You think with your *skin?*" he'd say. "Get out of that damn tub before you turn permanently pink. Whatsamatta with you, kid? You in love?"

I thought that over.

I was in love. It wouldn't do to tell Pathé Lehrman that, because we were both having a fancy flirtation with the waitress downstairs, and he would ride me to death, and anyway this was something that needed a heap of thinking over.

"Shucks, no. Me? You out of your silly mind? Nawp, I was thinking about a parcel of real estate in Burbank, near the Los Angeles River. Make a good site for a studio. Go away and let a man think about business."

It did make a good site. Warner Bros. is there now.

Pathé went away and I climbed out of the tub and wrote Mabel a letter.

It wasn't any good, so I tore it up. "She'll die laughing and I'll ruin everything," I said to myself. "Why, I just about ruined everything on the ferryboat as it was. The girl is romantic, why, of course, and I am acting like a clown, and talking about money and real estate and all sorts of impossible nonsense a girl doesn't want to hear about until she is *married*. I have got to write something real romantical."

I just couldn't do it.

I sat there a long time, thinking things over, and finally I heard a phonograph record going in the next room. The windows were open and I could hear it clearly. The tune was "Brown Eyes," and it seemed just right for Mabel.

"Dearest Mabel," I wrote. "I have been thinking about you all the time. I guess you know how I feel. Do you still have the little ring? It isn't much, but it kind of means something if you keep it.

"Well, I have written you a poem and I guess it tells you how I feel about you better than anything else I could say."

Then I copied down the chorus of "Brown Eyes" and sent it to Mabel as if I'd just made it up.

She knew I wasn't any poet, but she never let on. Women are very kind people, when you come to think of it. She wrote me very sweetly and said the poem was beautiful and showed I was a much more romantic fellow than she thought I was. She signed the letter, "Your girl, Mabel," and she was exactly that from then on.

CHAPTER 7

Keystone, World Premiere

An OUTSIZED and handsome fellow named Dell Henderson was with us on that first trip to California. Dell had started with Biograph the way I started, by standing around, looking starved, asking for work, running errands, carrying the camera, doing anything that promised lunch money.

One morning Dell was on hand in his Paddock coat and his Stetson hat—being the leading-man type—and Griffith noticed him. He put Dell in that morning's scene and paid him five dollars. Dell made the second shift and earned another five. Then he posed until 10 P.M., had a free steak dinner in the basement of the Fourteenth Street studio, and earned another five dollars.

Fifteen dollars and steak!

When Dell went home his wife said, "Never give a thing like that up! Stay with it the rest of your life."

This is the same man, of course, who became a famous Hollywood director, the first to be paid five hundred dollars a week by Famous Players. Later, as you may recall, he directed many fine pictures for Charles Frohman and Fox when people really made big money in the days before taxes.

Griffith liked Henderson well enough to fetch him to California with us as a leading man at small pay. But D.W. was a remote person, an extremely difficult man to know, and even the charming Dell Henderson didn't figure a way to get close to him until we went on location.

Dell was a student of character, I suppose, and he observed Griffith from every angle, figuring a way to reach him. He found the chink in his armor at last and exploited it. D. W. Griffith was afraid of snakes.

In the desertlike bush country where we were shooting there was every kind of critter you wouldn't want to meet up with—lizards, toads, rodents, and rattlers. Dell Henderson hadn't much money, but he went to a small town nearby and hired himself a man.

Everywhere Griffith went that man went in front of him, beating the bushes and muttering incantations.

"What the hell is going on?" Griffith asked.

Henderson was on hand to give the answer.

"Snakes, Mr. Griffith," he said. "Place is leaping with 'em. Rattlers, cobras, God knows what kind of poisonous reptiles. I didn't want you to get snake-bit so I hired a snake charmer."

"Snake charmer?"

"Sure, Mr. Griffith. This man of mine is a herpetologist who has a jinx on snakes. Descended from a long line of medicine men and witch doctors. As long as he's around, you're safe from snakes."

Griffith was fascinated by Henderson's delicate attention. Dell's career was made then and there.

Henderson had other talents. He could communicate with the dead. When we had returned to New York and were on location near Cuddebackville, New York, Dell and I were up in Jeanie MacPherson's hotel room holding a séance, touching hands around a table, when we received a tremendous sign from the spirit world. It was a vast thump directly under the table that was more psychic manifestation than we could interpret. We crept off to bed, wondering.

Next morning we were all fired.

"That was no poltergeist, that was my shoe on the ceiling," Griffith explained. "Next time you fools want to talk with the spirits, don't do it in a bedroom right over my head."

By lunchtime he had hired us all back.

I ran all sorts of errands for Griffith, and eager to do them because I wanted to become a director. At Cuddebackville I hired a cop to guard a set for three dollars a day and gave a woman two dollars for the use of her house as a background prop. Dell found me working with a pencil and paper on this elaborate expense account.

"Great jumping Jehosephat!" he hollered. "Five dollars! You out of your mind? Double everything. Triple it. Put in for fifteen dollars or the ole man won't think you're doing your job."

I did it. A few years later when Henderson came to work for me at Keystone I had a special man audit his expense accounts.

The first picture I directed myself was called *One Round O'Brien*, with Fred Mace and Clarence Parr. I got the chance to direct because of the illness of Frank Powell, the No. 2 director behind D. W. Griffith, and because I was on hand, very much available, and begging for a chance. Being a motion-picture director in 1910 was not even a reasonable facsimile of a Hollywood director today. In my case there was a difference of $2935 per week in salary. Biograph paid me $65 a week, which put me in what I considered a high income bracket. I was expected to turn out two comedies a week.

Now that I was rich and famous, I thought I ought to try to look the part. The best-dressed man at Biograph was Owen Moore, Mary Pickford's first husband. I particularly admired Owen's fine shoes. I was like a Georgia field hand about footgear. As soon as I had a dollar in my pocket I wanted to dress up my big feet.

"Good boots, Moore," I said to Owen. "Now, I always have trouble with my bootmaker. Where did you get those?"

"Brooks Brothers," Owen said. "Best place in town. Expensive, though. Ten bucks."

"Oh, that's no never mind," I said.

I bought the shoes at once, a ten-dollar pair in rich, tough, English leather. In ten minutes I was in torture. My feet, as I have said before, are large. They are country-boy feet, accustomed to dirt roads and plowed fields. But Dell Henderson's eyes bugged out approvingly when he saw my new purchase.

"Can I wear 'em sometime?" he asked.

"Well, look, kid, as a special favor I'll let you have 'em for a couple of days. You can break 'em in for me."

Dell wore the shoes for five days and broke them in beautifully. I saw him on Hollywood Boulevard the other day. He was limping. "Mack," he said, "remember those shoes you had me wear forty-four years ago? They crippled me for life!"

Dell Henderson was responsible for my first picture as a director. Like Mary Pickford and me, Dell too tried his hand at scenarios, hoping to make a little extra cash from the studio. He came in one evening bustling with excitement.

"Got a pip," he said. "A knockout. Call it One-Round O'Brien because it's about a prize fighter who can only go one round. Easy to shoot—mostly in a ring, so there's no expensive sets. Now, I'm not a professional writer, you know, so what'll I do with this real good one?"

"Go over to the office and tell it to 'em. Tell 'em I want to make it," I said, trying to sound like a director.

Dell did that and the office bought his story for fifteen dollars.

The trouble was, Dell had forgot to tell anybody he had read "One Round O'Brien" in a magazine. The magazine sued and the studio had to pay $2500 for that piece of plagiarism. Having had experience in this line, I had a quiet talk with Dell and he never made that mistake again. From then on, all Mack Sennett comedies were made up in our own heads. I never bought a story from anybody.

We could make two pictures a week in those days because we set most of our scenes out of doors, used crowds wherever we found them, paying the crowd nothing, of course, and because at most our comedies ran no more than 750 feet. Indoor lighting was used, but sparingly. We used the free sunlight. Billy Bitzer, the first real cameraman (he shot The Birth of a Nation for Griffith), was already experimenting with trick lights, had invented the close-up and the lap-dissolve in collaboration with Griffith, and other technicalities requiring artificial light, but mostly we shot our film "raw."

We did what we could with what we had. If one company, say, had exhausted the wardrobe department's small resources, the other company changed its script or didn't shoot that day. Once I made a cop picture for Biograph, and when we went to shoot it, Griffith had gone off with all the police costumes. There was nothing for it, the company was assembled, we had to go ahead with whatever costumes we could grab.

I sent Dell and Pathé Lehrman to scrounge for what they could, and what they returned with was a dozen or so ancient, moth-bitten, faded police uniforms, none of which fitted anybody in the cast.

"Put 'em on anyway," I ordered. "We got to shoot."

Fred Mace and the others climbed into the old uniforms, some too big, others too tight, some as droopy-drawered as flour-sack lingerie, and we went off to Long Island to make our picture. It turned out pretty good, I thought, and it made a profit for Biograph. I knew it was a good picture, though, when the complaints came in. The Chicago police raised their hands in pious horror about that little film and let on they were insulted something awful. Well! Authority had been ridiculed! That was exactly the artistic effect I was after. I decided to make more cop pictures.

My relations with Mary Pickford became strained at that time because of a fish. I played the heavy in a comedy called *The Hero*, which Mary worked in with Fred Mace. The story required us to work on a dock, where Mr. Mace, the comedian, lurked out of sight and attached a big fish to Mary's line. For some reason or other, I was the man in charge of fish for that picture, and I saved the company money by using the same fish for three days. It wasn't a photogenic fish anyway.

Mrs. Smith, Mary's mother, objected on the second day and was extremely critical on the third. She said I was an indelicate, ordinary, and oafish man to force her Mary to work without a fresh fish every day. Mary, however, understood economics and when she thought it over, she forgave me. As I was saying, this girl knows the value of a dollar.

The pictures I made then were not much. They were quick, fast comedies with thin plots, and they were immediately consumed, the reels actually worn out, scratched, and destroyed, in the grind of the small movie houses. I have inquired here and there, but I have never been able to lay hands on one of my early productions. I have not tried too hard to find them. I think it is just as well.

I was doing tolerably well. I was sure of that when Mother stopped sending me twenty-dollar bills. She even stopped bragging on me. It was not long after my father's death that

she came to New York to live with me. Before she arrived, I
had a small apartment with Pathé Lehrman and Dell Henderson. We lived in a kind of competitive socialism, sharing
everything and fighting each other for clothes, money, and
girls.

I was now making seventy-five dollars a week.

It's a fact that I was never accepted as a gentleman and
an artist by Mrs. D. W. Griffith, or by Mary Pickford's mother,
by the Gish girls, or by the Broadway actors who condescended
to work for a genius, D. W. Griffith. Griffith was kind to me,
as I keep on repeating, but Griffith's kindness was something
like the generosity of an emperor who gives away continents.
He made pronouncements as if he were handing the Ten Com-
mandments to Moses. He was exactly my own age.

Griffith was the first person to realize he was a genius.
There was no one else to announce it. He dramatized his talents as a means of getting hold of the materials he needed to
do his work. I learned that trick from him and when my
chance came I used it—not with the Edwin Booth stance that
Griffith could take, but in more bumptious ways, with side
shows of hullabaloo. One of the educated writers said years
ago that Griffith performed with a rapier while I worked with
a bed slat. That was about it. Both are handy tools.

At the old brownstone studio on Fourteenth Street,
Griffith toiled and grimaced to make his actors and actresses
act. Madison Lacy, a young photographer who came along a
few years later, says today that Griffith made puppets of his
players. The Gish girls, Lillian and Dorothy, who couldn't
have been as much as twenty years old when they joined
Biograph, were instructed and rehearsed in every gesture, stage
cross, smile, and tear. A director could do exactly that in the
days before sound: while the camera ground, Griffith would
fire rapid commands to his players, instructing them exactly
what to think, how to look, and how to stand. But then, as
Lacy goes on to say, anybody who had talent or any creative
ability of his own as an actor came out of the Griffith experience with the finest training possible.

D. W. Griffith's pride in his abilities and in his pictures
made people believe in him to such an extent that even the
accounting department was taken in. My mother was not.

"I'd bet," she told me when she came to New York, "I'd bet that your comedies make as much money abroad as Mr. Griffith's." The foreign market, then as now, was the key to a producer's success on the black side of the ledger.

I thought that over. One day I got into the accounting department and demanded a showdown. It was incredible, but there were the figures. Griffith films were getting the acclaim, but the Mack Sennett films were making more profit for the studio.

"Now go and ask for a raise," Mother said. I did, loudly, and that is how I got up to seventy-five dollars a week.

This inspired me to be a Great Man. I took Mabel to expensive restaurants and tried to wear better clothes. I never did get the hang of wearing a suit or a hat as if I had no regard for it, like Adolphe Menjou or Douglas Fairbanks, Jr. When I was dressed up I looked dressed up. Most country boys do. Also, in order to prove around Fourteenth Street what big brass I was, I took to betting on horse races. I placed my bets with Charlie Bauman and Adam Kessel.

Charles O. Bauman, a small man who looked like a lazy tailor, and Adam Kessel, a big man who was the sea-captain type, were small-time bookmakers around downtown New York. They would even take twenty-five-cent bets. I began to put money on horses running at Belmont Park, Churchill Downs, Pimlico, and so on. But when Donau, with Herbert up, won the Kentucky Derby in 1910, and when Colonel Holloway, with Turner up, took the Preakness in 1912, I had laid my cash on goats that presumably haven't reached the mucilage factory yet. In short, I went in debt to Kessel and Bauman for a hundred dollars, and I stayed in debt.

Dell Henderson recalls that Kessel and Bauman had had some experience with motion-picture people before they had to cope with me. There was a cheap-Jack photographer on Ninth Street who owed them money. When Kessel sent Billy Shearer, a jockey, to collect, this photographer offered a couple of cans of film instead of money.

The bookmaking partners screamed, but the jock was wise. "You just let out these pictures to little houses, they pay you rent, and you get your money back, see?"

Kessel and Bauman did that and collected $90 on a bad

debt. The photographer, by the way, eventually became so famous as a producer in Hollywood that I don't dare mention his name. After he had paid up his horse-betting debt he turned out a quantity of stag reels. This gave him a stake.

Here I was with an impossible-to-pay debt to Kessel and Bauman. I went home by side streets and sent word I was out when they called. I had them barred from the Biograph studio so they couldn't get in there and break my legs. But one day I ran smack into them on Fourteenth Street. There was no escape.

"Hi, boys," I said. "Been looking for you. Why don't you come around any more?"

"Pay up," said Kessel. "You know we been around."

"Sennett, we've had enough," Bauman said. "Now, listen, pay us that dough or wind up in a gutter with your head cracked."

"Boys, that little bit of money I owe you is small potatoes," I said. "Let's you and me get out of the small time and into the big time where the heavy money is."

"And where is that?"

"In the movies, of course. Look. I'm a well-known director now. I know how to make pictures. My pictures make more money than D. W. Griffith's. You know how pictures make money—you make one picture and you rent it all over the country for money, the same picture. Now suppose we had lots of pictures out working for us?"

The boys thought that over. They had already found out that you could make money renting film—indeed, they had invested in a small film exchange—and, I discovered long after that interview, they had actually made a picture themselves with that Ninth Street photographer. They called it *The Big Elopement*, Bauman playing the father and Kessel the sheriff. It wasn't much, just a matter of putting a ladder against a wall, then showing a couple trying to elope and getting chased by the girl's father and the law. But it had been enough. I have never known anybody who got even a whiff of show business who didn't yearn for more.

My argument with Kessel and Bauman was not completed on Fourteenth Street. We talked for days. They gagged like calves with burs in their throats when I said:

"Forget the $100 I owe you and put up $2500 to start a new company. I'll make you rich."

That was a heap of money. But I was sincere. I was scared, but I was sincere. I saw an opportunity to make the kind of pictures I thought would be great.

First they bellowed about the money. Of course. Then they were tempted more and more by the idea of being in show business and owning actresses. They began to argue about what to call the company.

I knew I was saved when they reached that stage.

"Sennett Comedies," I suggested.

"Kessel Kut Ups," Kessel said.

"Bauman and Kessel Comedies," Bauman said.

We were walking in the neighborhood of the Pennsylvania Station during one of those arguments. I looked up and saw the name.

"Keystone!" I said. "That's it. Keystone!"

We decided then and there to incorporate as Keystone. Bauman and Kessel put up $2500 cash, forgave me my indebtedness, and I became head man, on account of I said I knew so much about making pictures. I had a one-third interest in the new motion-picture company and there were papers to prove it.

As Homer Croy, who coined the phrase, would say, "Oh boy!"

To the end of her days, which were many and bright in the faith of the good saint, my mother tended to treat me like a fourteen-year-old boy. She always encouraged me, but at the same time she took it for granted that I required adult direction. As I grew older and could not be considered totally adolescent Mother's main ambition was to get me married.

She could be downright embarrassing about this.

She and Mabel Normand became great friends as soon as they met, and before you could pull the petals off a daisy Mrs. Sinnott was in full cry for a wedding. She was Irishly forthright.

"Now, Mabel, why don't you marry my son?" she would say. "He's a good boy. I raised him right. Go on, have him."

Mabel had a reply for that. "He hasn't asked me," she would say.

Then Mother would work on me.

"I dunno," I'd answer. "It's one of those things. We are just good friends. And I'm too busy. Anyway, I'm scared to ask her. I don't think she'd do it."

I wasn't too busy to realize that Mabel Normand could become a major motion-picture star and I wasn't too frightened to ask her to leave D. W. Griffith and Biograph—where she would most certainly have become a celebrity—and join the new bookmaker-backed Keystone Company. I wish I had asked her the important question. If I had, this story would be different.

Mabel joined Keystone without argument. She was probably the most naïve person that ever lived. Let me put in an aside about naïveté. I was talking to Jim Cagney the other day and he said several astonishing things:

It's the naïve people who become the true artists. First, they have to be naïve enough to believe in themselves. Then, a performer—especially an actor or actress—must be naïve enough to keep on trying, using his talent, in spite of any kind of discouragement or double cross. He doesn't pay attention to setbacks. In his ingenuousness he doesn't know a setback when it smites him. Money doesn't concern him. But most importantly, when he reaches the top and becomes famous, he doesn't change. "That person wouldn't hurt me," is your unconscious reaction when one of these actors comes on the screen or walks across the stage. Even when he plays a villain (like Lionel Barrymore) he does it with such enormous, hard-working good will that you see the truth underneath and continue to like him. But the minute a cynical person walks in front of a camera—it picks up. It photographs. You know it. You feel it. You dislike him.

Mabel was so naïve that she left D. W. Griffith to join a motion-picture company that had no money to speak of, no studio, no list of players under contract, no stories, and no camera.

As a matter of fact, no studio actually owned a camera. The camera was a product of the Thomas A. Edison Co. Mr. Edison, having invented it but not having seen its possibilities for producing entertainment, nevertheless held the mechanical patents in his tight fist. Companies that wanted to make pictures were forced to rent cameras from him. The Patents Company wars of the early movie days were bitter, complicated, and technical. So far as Kessel and Bauman and Mack Sennett were concerned, this merely meant that we had to become bootleggers, like many another small outfit until the patents trust was busted in 1917.

Any time we were shooting, the Patents Company might break us up and take our camera away. We posted guards.

As for a studio, we had almost no need for one. We filmed our comedies at Coney Island, using Fourth of July crowds for backgrounds, on the streets, at Fort Lee, or in private homes. Once I paid a good woman a dollar and a half for the use of her dining room and table for a big scene. About twelve actors worked in that sequence.

"Wouldn't it be better," the housewife asked, "if those actors were eating real food instead of just pretending?"

"It sure would be better," I said.

"I'll put lunch on the table, then," she said. And she did, no extra charge.

When I left Biograph I took Mabel, Fred Mace, Pathé Lehrman, and Ford Sterling with me. Sterling had been a clown in Robinson's Circus and had later played all over the country with small-time stock companies. Mark his name. Ford Sterling was the first American motion-picture comedy star.

We found a camera which Thomas A. Edison did not know about, made up a story, and planned to make a motion picture at Fort Lee as fast as we could. What we needed now was a cameraman.

I'd had troubles with cameramen before. As you probably know, film went through the motion-picture camera in those days at the rate of sixteen frames, or images, per second. If the cameraman cranked slowly, he got fewer pictures per second and therefore when the film was projected at the regular speed, the action on the screen was faster than normal. One day I sent a cameraman to photograph a Shriners' parade from an upstairs window of a hotel. We would steal crowd scenes like that any time we could. But our boy had rhythm. He became enchanted with the beat of the band and cranked in time to the music. The tramp of Shriners' feet is not the correct time for making movies.

How a man named Ishnuff attached himself to us I never knew exactly. He had charm. He had pretty manners. He talked modestly about having been photographer to the Court of Czar Nicholas and he spoke knowingly about tempo and lighting. He bowed from the waist and his beard bristled with enthusiasm. But more than that, Ishnuff was cheap. He was eager to start and willing to work on speculation, getting paid from the profits when the picture was released. That was precisely the kind of man I wanted working for me—an artist of distinction who didn't care about money.

We started. Mabel, Mace, and Sterling began to go through their paces, me directing. My actors were inspired, zanier, funnier, full of more inventive bits of odd business than ever before. I turned to see how Ishnuff was doing. "Getting it all?" I asked.

"Naturally," Ishnuff said. "I am cameraman for the Czar of all the Russias. Child's play you are asking me."

Ishnuff gave me a superior chin lift.

"I have to be certain," I said. "Are you sure you are cranking fast enough? It seems to me that Billy Bitzer went faster."

"Bitzer! Biograph! Phooey! Phooey on Meester Griffith also. I am saving you the money, Mike. This film is expensive, no? Four cents a foot, it costs you? I cheat him a leetle. I go a leetle slower, not use her up so much. Is all right. You see."

I thanked Ishnuff and apologized. We went ahead and shot the works in two weeks, the whole Kessel and Bauman bank roll on five short subjects which would make us rich and famous.

Nowadays a Hollywood studio runs off its day's work every evening, looking at the "rushes" in a screening room. We had no studio and had to wait the pleasure of the laboratories before our film was developed and we could see what we had photographed. I called every evening to argue them into faster service, but D. W. Griffith's film was coming through ahead of mine, and asking for my film ahead of that distinguished product was like demanding a table at the Colony ahead of the Duchess of Windsor. We waited with bitten fingernails.

"Is all right, is wonderful," Ishnuff promised. "Is mood stuff, may I have my soles sliced off and may I drop dead and freeze to death! I have made great tapestry of comedy, of human race, in beauty and laughter. D. W. Griffith will boil himself in oil."

I did not tell Griffith that I had produced five master-works which would inspire him to boil himself in oil. Instead I told him I had some little pictures I'd like to run off in a screening room and begged the use of a Biograph projectionist.

"Why, of course, old fellow," Griffith said. "As a matter of fact, I have had an eye on you and your works and I should be delighted to let you run your film. I'd like to be there, too, to see your pictures."

This was like Rembrandt's saying he would look at the doodlings of a barefooted boy. I set up the screening at Griffith's convenience and made a party of it, asking everybody I knew. My guests included Mary Pickford and her mother, Lottie and Jack Pickford, Blanche Sweet, Lillian and Dorothy Gish, and the great Griffith. Kessel and Bauman took seats in the front row. I sat in the rear. Ishnuff said that he suffered from claustrophobia, which made it necessary for him to stand in the door.

At my signal the projection of my first masterpieces began. The title was fuzzy, but we could read it. This was followed by a blur. The blur shimmered. Fog shapes loomed across it, lurching and fading. Nothing resembling a motion picture or a human being appeared.

I yelled at the projectionist.

"I am running the film at normal speed, Mr. Sennett," he said coldly. "And I examined this film before I ran it. There is nothing on it."

I knew, of course, what had happened. Ishnuff and his slow cranking had produced, not a motion picture, but a blob. I reached for a handy tool and started for the door where Ishnuff had taken his stance.

He had disappeared into the Fourteenth Street night and was never heard of again by anyone being connected with the motion-picture industry. I would try my best to maim that Russian if I came across him today.

Kessel and Bauman screamed themselves hoarse. I bought champagne and we all shed a tear in it, although beer is the proper beverage for crying in.

This was ruination at the start.

But my mother, who knew nothing about motion-picture production or about my troubles, came to my rescue without knowing it, as she did so many times. When I left Northampton, she led me aside and gave me a small chamois pouch. She took my hand and closed it over the pouch and I knew she was giving me the most valuable thing she had in the world.

"Son, this has been in the family for a hundred fifty years. It is the only really good thing we possess. Keep it. It's yours. But promise me never to use it unless you absolutely have to."

The little pouch contained a 1.52-carat blue diamond.

I had seen it only once or twice before in my life. I protested. But mothers do things like that. "Take it," she said, "and remember—only if you need it."

In my trouble with Kessel and Bauman and Ishnuff I reckoned that real need had arrived. I took Mother's diamond to a pawnbroker named Simpson and put it on his counter. He screwed his little magnifying glass in his eye and peered at it for a long minute. Then he stared at me and I thought his eyes looked harder than the diamond.

"How much?" I asked.

"My best offer is $850," Simpson said.

"Give me the cash," I said.

I hurried to Bauman and Kessel's office. I dumped the crisp greenbacks on the desk and they counted them.

"Boys, let's start again. Here's my stake. All I've got. How about it?"

We started a new picture the next day, called *Cohen at Coney Island*. We filmed it all on one of the hottest July Fourths on record, starring our whole studio—Mabel Normand, Ford Sterling, and Fred Mace. The little picture sold well with the small exchanges and put us back in business. But this time no Russian cameraman. I found an expert, Irving Willard, and he made no mistakes.

I was soon able to retrieve my mother's diamond.

By now Charles O. Bauman and Adam Kessel considered themselves professional showmen. They abandoned their bookmaking business, created an exchange and producing company named Bison, and sent Thomas H. Ince to California to make pictures. As a matter of fact, they stole Ince from Uncle Carl Laemmle's IMP Company by offering him $150 a week and 10 per cent of our shaky Keystone Company.

I argued immediately that I, too, should be sent to California.

"Look," I said, "we have no studio here and the light and the weather are always bad in New York. Let me take our people to California. It will be cheaper."

It took my partners only a few minutes to make a decision.

"Go on," they said. "Go anywhere. Get out of our hair."

I packed my company on a train and left town as fast as possible before they could change their minds.

Tom Ince was already there and under the influence of Western scenery. He became the first to make Western shoot-'em-ups and horse operas. Pretty soon he discovered Tom Mix, an authentic Texas marshal, and William S. Hart, the Shakespearean actor who looked like a cowpoke, and went into the epic business.

Ince's pictures made money at once and were the forerunners of "super-production" and "colossal" in Hollywood. Uncle Carl Laemmle then moved in, made a deal with Kessel and Bauman, and created the Universal Film Company with Ince. This left a small studio in Edendale, just east of Los Angeles and almost in Glendale, unoccupied.

This makeshift studio was exactly what I needed and where I had pined to make pictures when I first saw Southern California along with D. W. Griffith.

Mabel, Fred, Ford, and I arrived in Los Angeles in January 1912. We started making a picture within thirty minutes after we alighted at the Santa Fe station.

Cloud-Cuckoo Country

WE HEARD our first picture before we saw it, although sound didn't arrive in motion pictures until fifteen years later. A Shriners' parade, stepping to oom-pah and brass, was marching up Main Street.

"A gorgeous welcome to you it is indeed, O Maestro Mack Napoleon Sennett!" said Mabel.

"Now, hold your gorgeous, yapping mouth shut for just a minute," I said. "Maybe it is exactly that. Let's have a look and make a dollar."

The parade was a whopper and it would take a long time to pass a given point. A given point in my mind was a free lunch or wherever I could set up the camera and shoot unpaid actors.

"We got us a spectacle, kids," I said. "Bauman and Kessel are always hollering about costs. Look at that crowd scene—all free!"

Ford Sterling was hungry, Mabel wanted to go to the hotel. Fred Mace had seen a parade before. They held back. Pathé Lehrman got what I meant.

"What's the story, boss?" Pathé asked.

"Got no story. We'll make it up as we go along," I said. "Pathé, run over there to the department store and buy a baby doll. Here's a dollar and a half. Jim, you get the camera set up on the corner. Ford, you put on a tall overcoat and make like an actor."

Mabel Normand could throw herself into any part instantly, even into a part that didn't exist.

"Who am I?" was all she asked when she saw we were under way.

"A mother," I said.

"I would be the last to know," Mabel commented.

"Now take this doll," I ordered. "It's your baby. Get going. Run up and down the line of march and embarrass those Shriners. Make out that——"

"—I'm a poor lorn working girl, betrayed in the big city, searching for the father of my chee-iuld." Mabel finished the sentence. "This characterization requires a shawl. Who ever heard of a poor, forlorn little mother without a shawl over her poor little head?"

"Right," I said. "Get her a shawl, Pathé."

Mabel put on the comicalest act you ever clapped eyes on, pleading, stumbling, holding out her baby—and the reactions she got from those good and pious gentlemen in the parade were something you couldn't have caught on film after six days of D. W. Griffith rehearsals. Men were horrified, abashed, dismayed. One kind soul dropped out and tried to help Mabel.

"Move in, Ford," I told Sterling. Ford leaped in and started a screaming argument with the innocent Shriner, who didn't know he was being photographed to make a buck for Keystone.

The police moved in on Ford and Mabel. Ford fled, leaping, insulting the police, and they—God bless the police! —they chased him. I helped the cameraman and we got it all.

The Shriners were good, but the best scenes we nabbed were the running cops. I never got their names, but if there are any retired gentlemen of the Los Angeles Police Department who remember taking part in that incident, let them bask in fame: they were the original Keystone Cops.

We didn't even pause at the Alexandria Hotel. We went straight out to Edendale to our little studio, shot a few more scenes and close-ups to tie the picture together, and we had our first comedy. I wired Kessel and Bauman: "Got a spectacle first day and it's a whopper."

Kessel insisted for years later that the wire said, "Got pickled first day and it was a whopper."

Anything on film made money.

The only requirement was that it be reasonably new. Theaters, states-rights franchise holders, distributors were starved for pictures. That is why some of the unlikeliest people in the world became parents of the new art. Some were sweat-shop operators, bicycle repairmen, junk heap scavengers, cloak-and-suit manufacturers, ex-bookmakers, and there was a prominent ex-boilermaker named Mack Sennett.

Well, pioneers are seldom from the nobility. There were no dukes on the *Mayflower*.

We hopped aboard the new thing and went to town. The town you think of in association with movies is Hollywood, but in the era when Woodrow Wilson was proving that a great scholar could be a great president, and tap-dancing with his daughters after supper in the White House, we were mainly concerned with the carryings-on in Edendale. Time does gallop on: the site of the first custard pie, Keystone Cops, and Bath-ing Beauty studio is now halfway between two newer land-marks, Aimee Semple McPherson's temple and Forest Lawn Cemetery.

Overnight our place was busting its seams with idiotics. Anything went, and every fool thing you might think of under the influence of hashish or a hangover went big.

We were awash with pretty women, clowns, and story-tellers who couldn't write. We made a million dollars so fast my fingers ached from trying to count.

Let me catch my breath before leaping into that Cloud-Cuckoo land of *laissez faire* and turvy-topsy. Hear this:

Nowadays it seems to be fashionable among educated writers to claim that we created a new art form in those morn-ing-glory times. They proclaim that our chase sequences and rhythms derived from classic ballet. Critics have come up with grand new phrases like "cineplastic art" and "unfailing pre-cision of technique." A famous Frenchman wrote a book about us in which he claimed we were "poetic creators of myths and symbols who conceived the universe in its totality and trans-lated it in terms of motion pictures."

My!

Charlie Chaplin joined Keystone soon after we got under

way, and of course I shall have a lot to say about him. Not long
ago he let go with these words: "I have aimed all my comedies
at satirizing the human race. The human race I prefer to think
of as an underworld of the gods. When the gods go slumming
they visit the earth. You see, my respect for the human race
is not one hundred per cent."

Charlie's main experience with the human race was during the almost forty-five years he lived in the United States, so
I suppose he meant his respect for America was not one hundred per cent. That's an assumption. I wouldn't know anything about Charlie Chaplin's politics or his philosophies.

When he came to work for me he wasn't famous. As a
matter of fact, he was obscure. But it's been my experience
that giving an actor—any actor—world-wide fame is like hanging a neon-lit Ph.D. on him. As soon as renown falls on his
shoulders, the actor starts explaining everything, even himself.

Why, I know a Hollywood producer of the top-drawer set
who got himself put on the Republican National Committee
and immediately became a widely quoted expert on political
economy. He had never been to college and was too busy making pictures to read anything. He was smart, though. He sent
one of his secretaries to the University of Southern California,
where she took down all the long words and reported them to
her boss. He went out frequently in café society and could pronounce those fancy syllables like a Harvard sophomore. He got
a lot of respect.

Now, I won't contradict anybody, not right out in public,
anyway, who wants to announce me as a wonderful fellow and
the creator of a new kind of art. When you consider it and
when you tell your false modesty to quit squirming, we *did*
create a new kind of art. But while we were doing it we had
no more notion of contributing to aesthetics than a doodlebug
contributes to the *Atlantic Monthly*.

We did the best we could with what we had.

We made funny pictures as fast as we could for money.
We knew we were experimenting with something new—but
has there ever been a performer, or a creative person of any
kind, from a talented potato peeler to Picasso, who didn't
think he was original? But we didn't rear back and publish
manifestoes like the modern poets and painters nobody can

understand. All the philosophizing and the explaining and the phrases with lace on them, like "cineplastic art," came much later.

Of course comedy is a satire on the human race. It always has been. That is what clowns have been up to ever since kings kept fools. Our specialty was exasperated dignity and the discombombulation of Authority. We whaled the daylights out of everything in sight with our bed slats, and we had fun doing it. We cut our pictures sharply, having learned how from D. W. Griffith, and we did get "pace" into them. But if someone had pointed out that our sequences of leaping cops and fleeing comedians were an art form derived from the classic ballet, we'd have hooted like crazy and thrown a pie at him.

I never saw a ballet.

This brings me around to a contradiction. My people were artists, all right, and great ones. Chaplin—well, you can use all the learned words you want to about him and you'll probably be right. A genius. Mabel, and the Conklins, Mace, Buster Keaton, Ben Turpin, W. C. Fields, all those wonderful clowns were persons of enormous talent.

But not self-conscious. We merely went to work and tried to be funny, and there really was a wonder and a miracle then that no amount of expensive grammar can explain: I, Mack Sennett, the Canadian farm boy, the boilermaker, was the head man. And what went on in that Keystone studio was a caution.

CHAPTER 9

Here Come the Clowns!

WE MADE one hundred forty pictures the first year. From the uproar that went on in the studio and all around the town you'd have thought the pictures were made in spite of the comedians, only incidentally with them. As the money rolled in I expanded the lot to twenty-eight acres and my hair turned white.

All kinds of people came out to Edendale and asked to hire out—vaudevillians, wrestlers, cops, old women, children in arms, acrobats, prize fighters, elephant trainers, flea-circus entrepreneurs, famous actors, and pretty women. If they were funny I put them on. I also employed dogs, lions, geese, and chimpanzees, some of which had no talent. An ex-sign painter named Hank Mann became a star, and so did a fat man—Roscoe Arbuckle. All of these people and fauna were roaring extroverts devoted to turmoil. I seemed to have talent for avoiding intellectuals, although I did give Frank Capra a job. Capra had a degree in engineering from the California Institute of Technology, but he had so much sheer ability that he was able to conceal it.

My people competed with each other in murderous antics before the camera and got themselves so wound up that they seldom knew when to stop gyrating. To tell the truth, I was much the same way, but all they had to worry about was eating and I had to worry about feeding them.

As business picked up it began to seem as if every female who could make faces or who had pretty legs pined to work for me. I'll come to the Mack Sennett Bathing Beauties soon, but even at the beginning we set store by women—although, dramatically speaking, a correctly flung pie can motivate a plot just as expressively. One morning Pathé Lehrman showed in a schoolmarm from Vermont, pretty and about twenty years old, and when I said, "Let's see your knees, honey," like a banker might ask a client for a look at the collateral—you know, strictly business—she heisted her dress all the way and spun around buff-naked.

I ran like an embarrassed ape and from that day on I never interviewed girls alone. As I was saying, my hair began to turn white.

I thought that was mighty doleful. I considered myself a young fellow and even when the real talent arrived and I was demoted to playing rubes in my own pictures, I liked to think of myself as an actor. I sat in my tub and moaned about my fading wool.

"Dang it, this is show business I'm in, after all," I said. "I'll dye that fool hair. They call me the 'Old Man' already and I'm not old at all."

I was ashamed to apply for help to what passed for our make-up department (most actors did their own faces), so I sneaked to the corner drugstore during the lunch hour and bought a bottle of heavy black dye. I dosed my head liberally and went out that evening, feeling jaunty, to a party at one of the big downtown hotels.

I was dancing with Mabel under the impression that I was a reasonable facsimile of a leading man when Adolph Zukor came by. Mr. Zukor had left the fur business in Chicago years ago and had already become a grand lama and saint of the motion-picture industry. But fur was something he still knew about.

"Evening, Mr. Zukor."

"Oh, why, hello—it's you, Mack! I almost didn't know you. What fantastic part are you playing tomorrow in green hair?"

I blundered to the men's room and stared at myself and it was true. Those pharmacy pigments had turned my hair the color of stale seaweed. I gave up and I have not tried to be handsome since that night.

All the energies I had went into my two main ambitions—

a big bathtub and making comedies. Indeed yes, I got the tub
of my dreams. It cost several thousand dollars and was hewn
out of marble with silver trimmings. It measured eight feet
long by five feet wide. I had this two-ton *objet d'art* installed
in my office, and charged it to the studio with a clean conscience. I did my best thinking in that tub. Along with it I
acquired a masseur, an ex-wrestler named Abdullah. But since
I was convinced that the entire studio would go Indian-wild if
I did not keep personal and hard-boiled watch on them, I ran
smack into a dilemma. Where can you put a bathroom, essen-
tially a private and intimate place, so that you can also keep an
eye on Mabel Normand and a whole motion-picture studio?

At Keystone we solved problems directly and by obvious
means.

I had a tower erected in the middle of the lot. It soared
thirty feet over all the stages and had windows on all sides. I
had my office, my tub, and my masseur installed there. Thus I
could bathe and soap and splash and shout any time of the
day, and simultaneously keep an eye on my outrageous em-
ployees. Most of my story and business conferences were held
there with the water running. Vernon Smith, one of my early
story editors, has written me a long letter from New Orleans
recalling those days and pranks. Vernon insists that I used to
invite gag men to climb in the tub with me. Maybe, but no
one ever took me up. The tub act was a solo performance.

The Keystone studio needed watching like a reform school
for Iroquois scalp lifters. I used to ride horseback every morning and come in through a back gate at about eight o'clock.
The carpenters would be loafing and I would catch them. "Going to work, fellows?" I'd say unpleasantly. Then they'd start
hammering and sawing on anything within reach. Pretty soon
the carpenters had spies and sentinels all over the lot. No matter from what direction I approached at any time of day, I
would be greeted by a thunderation of hammers and saws.

People could follow my progress by ear. Silence would
fall as I left and uproar would precede me. It was a powerful
orchestration and I got so I would walk all over the place just
to hear it. Then I would hurry up to my tower in time to see
Del Lord, my ace comedy director, helping Fred Mace and
Ford Sterling sneak in over the back fence, late as usual.

Del Lord came to see me recently. "Mack," he said, "you were a sneaky boss. You spied on us."

"I had to," I said.

"Yes, you did. And that chauffeur you had, that Willie James, the Negro boy, I always thought he was a secret agent too."

"He was," I told Del. "Why do you think I had him? He wasn't worth a damn as a chauffeur."

The boys on the Keystone lot played rough. Hank Mann, the stunt man and actor, Chester Conklin, Del Lord, and Dick Jones and Ray Enright (the last three became famous directors) delighted in the uses of a Ford generator. They hooked this up to an appliance in the men's room on the lot and enjoyed themselves hugely. Their first victim was Hampton Del Ruth, a writer and a man of considerable dignity. When the current was applied to Mr. Del Ruth, he emerged with all the sound effects of a herd of Texas steers, charged into a crowd of extras who were in line to punch the clock, and collapsed flat on his face. Restoratives had to be called for, of which Del Ruth claimed he tasted none.

This delicate whimsey amused the fun-loving Rover boys. Now they laid in wait for Charlie Chaplin. Mr. Chaplin, too, had dignity. He was a shy little Britisher who was abashed and confused by everything that had anything to do with motion pictures. He entered the small room, the boys timed him and turned on the juice—and nothing happened.

"Maybe we kilt that limey," Ray Enright said.

"Don't hear a thing," Del Lord said, getting worried.

"Let's go in," said Jones.

They entered hurriedly and froze in shock as if they were getting their own galvanized treatment. On the floor lay Chaplin, pale as a spook and limp as a doll.

"Get an ambulance!" Jones yelled.

"We've murdered the little fellow," said Enright. "This could start a war with England."

At this moment Mr. Chaplin rose, brushed his clothes daintily, thumbed his nose at the boys, and waddled out in a duck-walk, emitting an un-English Bronx cheer. I hollered from the tower then and my geniuses went back to work.

Joe Jackson, the trick bicycle rider, was another gagster

who was enchanted by electricity. One evening he wired the chairs in our projection room and almost fried me to a crisp. It was Slim Summerville, Bobby Dunn, and Mabel Normand who balanced a bucket of water on a door and led me under it. My head was dented and I was soaked, but I had to accept a good deal of this kind of thing to prove that I had a right to order comedians up the outside of tall buildings, have them dragged by wild horses, or smack them in their faces with custard pies.

Comedians are funny people. They either reverse character completely when not working, like Groucho Marx, one of the most comical men alive, but in private life a quiet and well-read citizen of Beverly Hills, or, like the whooping people who worked for me, they prance all the time.

Many of my Keystone playmates of those delightful days are still around. They are as lusty as house wreckers and so far as I know, none of them has read, or at any rate taken seriously, the intelligentsia who claim we were cineplastic artists and/or ballet dancers. They haven't poured water on me, or electrified me, or knocked me down—that is, recently—but even to this day I have never been able to awe them into proper respect. I am still the Old Man.

There's Hank Mann, for instance. Hank was a sign painter, one of the toughest and funniest men that ever risked his life for a laugh. He was brought up on the lower East Side, a few hard-boiled years before Jim Cagney and George Raft made that community world-renowned.

Hank was one of the original Keystone Cops. There is a good deal of dispute today about who had a place in that first edition, but as Hank and I recall it, there were only seven. They were Georgie Jesky, Mack Riley, Charlie Avery, Edgar Kennedy, Slim Summerville, Bobby Dunn, and the durable Mr. Mann.

Hank used to paint the kind of signs known in the trade as "high-lofty." This was steeple-jack stuff and led him into show business. He eventually made the Sullivan-Considine time as a tumbling acrobat, the performer you remember in old vaudeville days slam-banging all over the stage with chairs, planks, tables, and brooms. When the three Sullivan-Considine houses in San Francisco, Oakland, and Los Angeles closed down, Mr. Mann was one of the artistes stranded on Spring Street. He was hungry and frayed at the cuff. As he says, "I hung around and things were very nil." But Hank managed to eat by the same tricks of the trade I had learned in New York: the magic of the nickel beer and the free lunch. All the at-liberty actors slouched around cheap theatrical hotels on Hill Street, mooching drinks and telling each other enormous lies. One particularly hungry afternoon a talented but out-of-work tattooed woman said to Hank, "Whyn't you go in pictures?" Hank said, "What! Tintypes!" And the tattooed woman said, "Well, sonny boy, it's eatin' money. Lend you a dime. Pile your rump on the trolley to Edendale and see the Old Man."

"Who's the Old Man?"

"Sennett. Mack Sennett. Does the damndest things out there. Been known to hire bums, apes, grandmothers—hell, he's even got actors."

Hank Mann, as you know, became a comedy star. But when he arrived at the Keystone studio in Edendale he couldn't get in the front gate or even in the back gate. This was no particular handicap to Mr. Mann, the high-lofty operator. He came over a side fence without snagging his britches and walked into the prize fighters.

I'll have to explain the prize fighters. I had the lot jumping with gentlemen who were quick with their dukes as my answer to Thomas A. Edison. The patents companies headed by Edison, and including Vitagraph, Biograph, Tannhauser, Kalem, and Selig, had all the legitimate motion-picture cameras tied up tighter than an alimony settlement dictated by Greg Bautzer. Their snoops, spies, detectives, and deputy sheriffs sought every opportunity to seize my bootlegged cameras, so I protected the company the best I could by putting up some professional fists.

Hank inquired if the prize fighters were actors and of course they said they were. One said his name was Barrymore. They saw the little man was tough, so they sent him on to me.

"What can you do? How in the name of sin did you get in here? What d'ya want?" I asked.

"I'm a high-lofty boy and acrobat, been working Sullivan-Considine and I need a job," said Hank.

"You been playing all around with Sullivan-Considine?"
Hank said he had.

"Then maybe you know a little limey who does a music-hall act. Does a drunk scene in a box. Can't get his name right. Champion, or Chapin—something like that."

"Sure, boss, I know him. He's good. Name's Charlie Chaplin."

"Be a funny man in pictures?" I asked.

"Sure, sure, sure, be great. Me too."

So I put Hank Mann on. That is to say, I told him to go find a uniform and that he'd get three dollars a day when he worked. That was the initiation of Keystone.

Until some time later, when I could draw on Broadway or big-time vaudeville for high-priced names, I started every new man as a Keystone Cop to see how he worked out. And with Kessel and Bauman riding me about expenses all the time, I gave out as few contracts as possible. This meant that when there was an overcast, or rain, or when my rambunctious geniuses in the story departments failed to come up with what they called a script, I could lay off the actors and cut down the overhead. Hank Mann had not paid his dues to the Los Angeles Chamber of Commerce: during his first three weeks with me it didn't rain any little bitty drizzle-drazzle, it came up a freshet and a gully washer. Hank became not only mildewed but hungry. He departed the lot to paint entertaining frescoes for some of the cheaper saloons catering to the down-and-out trade on Main Street. Then he appeared at the pay window, where I was always stationed when anything resembling legal tender was being passed out, asked for his day's wages, and quit.

I'd been thinking about him. As a matter of fact, Mabel had clapped a bright eye on him and had told me she thought he could cut just the kind of monkeyshines we'd need in her next picture.

"Tell you what I'm going to do," I said. "Like to have you around, kid. Make you a guarantee of four days a week. That's twelve bucks, you know."

Hank took me up. In fact he bit like a carp, and that's how one of my better-known comedians began his cineplastic career. But it seemed to me at the time that Hank was in a hot-

breathing hurry to get away from the benefactor who had just
made him rich and famous. A few days later I found out why.

One of the enterprises which kept my extroverted clowns
healthy and happy was the continuous crap game which went
on under our biggest stage. I had to blink at this sport for the
sake of good private relations and my only complaint was that
since I was the boss I wasn't allowed to get in it.

Hank hurried off to the crap game, swore the sportsmen
to secrecy on the names of eighteen saints, and told them
about his contract. This broke up the game as if manna had
descended from heaven on gold plates. Within an hour I received ultimatums, hard-luck stories, and threats of broken
legs, accompanied by buckets of tears, from every tough comedian on the lot. There was no way out. I had to raise everybody's salary to twelve dollars a week.

As I guess you've figured out so far, I'm a tight-fisted free-
wheeler when it comes to economics. And when the economics
come to units larger than twelve, I try to count on my toes.
But a lot of wordly goods could be purchased with twelve dollars then. It made the boys slap-happy. You could buy a glass
of beer and wolf a free lunch for a nickel, and if you were flush
you went to the Alexandria Hotel for ham and turkey sliced
by the colored man—ten cents!

Putting my actors on big salaries didn't solve the problem
of their antics off camera. They continued to get drunk, to
play impractical jokes, and to bedevil me as if they were
juvenile delinquents from a tribe of head-hunters. I fired them
every week, every one of them, no exceptions.

Then they would go to Mabel and complain about the
bad Old Man. They would put on their droopiest pantaloons,
their most beat-up shoes, and their most doleful faces, and cry
on Mabel's lap. My girl was as tenderhearted as a nun, and if
the tears she shed over these fraudulent toughs had been
bottled there'd have been enough water to float a small yacht.

After listening to horrifying tales of naked children creep-
ing about the streets begging for bread and faithful little wives
who took in washing in order to keep a scrap of meat in the
house Mabel would rise in her stirrups and reach for high
"C." There would be a procession. The mendicant clowns,
headed by Miss Normand, would march on me like an army of

African ants. The bellowing and shrieking that went on during these sessions, along with stomping on the floor and banging on the desk, raised about as many decibels as the American Iron Works in East Berlin, Connecticut.

I never won. I always hired them back.

Keeping all these people on the pay roll, which was examined weekly by Adam Kessel and Charlie Bauman as if it were contagious, was a kind of magic act at that. We had to make our short funny pictures fast in order to meet the demand of the theaters, which were increasing by the hundreds every week, and the pictures were sold like gingham for girls' dresses—at so much per yard. This meant that if we hit the doldrums on account of weather or lack of imagination, we had no money coming in to meet the pay roll. *173170*

I solved this problem part way and kept Charlie and Adam off my neck by making the actors shovel sand, paint scenery, and do carpentry work on off days when we couldn't shoot pictures. I suppose everybody understands that we depended mostly on sunlight, working on stages shielded by gauze. We turned on what few mercury vapor lamps we had only when the sun didn't shine. Charlie Chaplin, I believe, was the first Mack Sennett player who wasn't put into overalls. This wasn't because Charlie was distinguished—he was far from that when I nabbed him—but because he would have been about as useless with a handy tool as your eight-year-old niece.

Of all the funny fellows I had on and off the pay roll from time to time I believe Hank Mann was the toughest. He stayed with me for eight years and worked up to $125 a week, for which he would perform any foolish stunt my psychopaths in the writing room could think up. Once when Hank was working with Arbuckle and Al St. John in a sky-line chase sequence (we had a private sky line along a ridge in the Glendale hills which stood in for skyscrapers, airplane scenes, and cliff-hanging frighteners) he was supposed to be yanked out of the driver's seat of a wagon and spread-eagled on the landscape.

Al St. John was to jerk the pin from the singletree and the horses were to pull Hank Mann off the wagon. St. John had trouble with the pin, sweating and bawling. This delayed the action until the horses had picked up too much speed for such a stunt. When Al did get the pin out, the horses cut loose like runaway ghosts and snatched Mr. Mann thirty feet through the air, like a kite, until the law of gravity remembered him.

By this time Mann and the horses were almost out of Los Angeles County, certainly at least three whoops and a loud holler out of camera range. Hank descended into a plowed field, chin first, and furrowed a belly-whopping trench for ten yards before, with considerable common sense, he let go the reins.

He returned to me in need of a face wash but without a limp.

"Boss," he said, "I think we'd better retake that scene."

Hank preferred flights which were not so agricultural. When Wilfred Lucas was directing a chase sequence on top of a three-story building in downtown Los Angeles, he had seven of the Keystone Cops, with Billy Williams' camera trained on them, set to run along the roof about forty-five feet above the pavement. Whenever we could, or if in a sentimental moment we happened to think of it, we arranged safety devices to keep our boys from committing suicide. This would have been bad publicity.

For this roof scene we had a protective railing out of camera range around the roof. Hank asked Wilfred Lucas if he could be the last cop to make the run.

The other boys made their leaping, hopping scampers across the horizon, and it all looked as dangerous as some of Harold Lloyd's later breath-takers. Then came Hank Mann. He didn't put a toe on the ledge. *He ran across the safety railing.*

He trotted back to director Lucas as smug as a kid with a quarter.

"You like, huh? Good, huh? Maybe a bonus—huh?"

Lucas stared at him with the acid expression of an old maid who's bitten a worm in an apple.

"Why, you sky-blue-scarlet obscenity of a misbegotten obscenity of a maggot-eaten ape! You damn fool, you ran out of camera range again."

My friend Hank Mann not only doted on such cineplastic and ballet constructions as I've been talking about, but was a man with a flair for making arrangements. We had little scenery, no prop houses or street background on flats, so familiar in Hollywood today. When we wanted to shoot a picture of a house, we had to shoot a picture of a house. Hank Mann went out with a company one morning to put such a scene on film and argued a Los Angeles housewife into accepting five dollars for permission to show her dwelling. Thereupon Hank and the director knocked their heads together and came up with the notion that it would be dramatically effective if they moved every stick of the good woman's furniture out on the front lawn. They did that and kept the furniture there for two weeks.

All of my actors were larcenous scene lifters. In the terms of their art this was known as "fly-catching." With the exception of the incomparable W. C. Fields, who could steal a scene from a cooing baby—and often did, having kicked the baby—Hank Mann was probably the most gifted bandit of them all. He always argued that the principal reason Keystone Comedies were funny was not because the writers thought up comical things for the actors to do, but because all the performers were absolute hams and cutthroat competitors. Each man wanted to beat the next man. Hank and Al St. John used to challenge each other to take the highest fall in a scene. The abiding wonder is that I didn't get a lot of pictures of comedians being splattered like eggs.

Hank committed a deft piece of fly-catching in a fire scene with Roscoe ("Fatty") Arbuckle which I was directing. I had about fifteen comedians in droopy-drawered cop uniforms running in and out of a burning building. I kept them moving in a circle so that on film it looked as if I had at least two hundred cops coming out of a house that couldn't have accommodated more than two tables of bridge. Hank again asked to be last man out as the scene was cut. With the camera full on him, he came to one of those hopping-on-one-foot comic stops, searched his pants and his underwear for a cigarette, then calmly lit it from the burning building.

This one scene captured the entire picture for Hank Mann, and he was working against "Fatty" Arbuckle.

In another film starring Chester Conklin, who was as professional a thief as Raffles ever was when it came to stealing scenes, Hank Mann again got away with the loot. Conklin, who played the part of a pixilated prisoner in the witness box being tried for his life, actually had a legitimate claim to this scene. Hank Mann was merely one of twelve jurors in the box and had nothing to do but sit.

But as the closing shot of that sequence was taken, Mr. Mann loosened his four-in-hand tie and began to work the knot up and down like a hangman's noose.

This not only stole the show from Conklin, who threatened to chase Mr. Mann through Death Valley with a baseball bat, but came out so funny on film that we had to use it as a twenty-four-sheet in our publicity posters.

Hank worked for me for eight years. He was under contract to me, and when I made contracts with actors, the few I did make, I hired Philadelphia lawyers whose ancestors were Philadelphia lawyers to put those deals in fine print two sizes smaller and eight times as tough as the paragraphs you can't read in insurance policies. I had Mr. Mann engaged to fight, bleed, and die for Keystone up to a few seconds before his last gasp. More than that, Hank and I always got on. We were as close friends as men can be when one of the friends calls the other one the Old Man behind his back.

But one afternoon Hank climbed up the tower and said he was unhappy. Up to that time I had always known he was a funny man, but I now began to learn from him that an unhappy comedian can be the most doleful critter on the footstool. Hank wanted out. He wanted out because of money, and the sum he mentioned was far more than I could possibly square with Bauman and Kessel.

I knew that no matter how sincerely he tried he couldn't be funny any more for us at the going rate. I canceled his contract and wished him luck.

Hank had a contract to work for William Fox at $250 a week in his pocket all the time.

High Kicks, Starring Mabel Normand

I'VE BEEN talking about clowns. And I'll be talking a lot more about clowns, what with Ben Turpin, Chester Conklin, Harry Langdon, Harold Lloyd and W. C. Fields coming up. And Charles Spencer Chaplin.

But the most important person in this book and in my life was, of course, Mabel Normand. Mother said again, "Why don't you marry Mabel?"

She went to Mabel and said, "Why don't you marry my boy?"

This is the most difficult part of my story to tell because I can't explain it, even to myself. When I try to write about Mabel I seem to get both of my oversize feet in my mouth and my heart in my throat. I have never been able to talk well about Mabel Normand or even to make a tolerably good description of her. And this is a regretful and almost ridiculously late day for a funnyman to say the true things and the dear things that dreams are made of. I'm Irish and as sentimental as Glocca Morra in the mist. But I'm also a Canadian.

Mabel and I were engaged and unengaged more than twenty times, I suppose, and once or twice we set a date. But things being like they were around Hollywood, she would hear stories about me and I would hear stories about her, and our affair was a series of fractures and refractures.

Take this sequence, for instance. Baron Long, now general manager of the great Biltmore Hotel in Los Angeles, was the proprietor of Vernon's Country Club, where all the movie people went when they were on salary. Rudolph Valentino used to tango there with Natacha Rambova long before he became famous. Wallace Reid would be on hand. Charlotte Smith, Mary's mother, would be in a small side room playing bridge for interesting stakes. Chaplin came out now and then, and he set a house record. So far as I know there is no evidence that Charlie ever bought a drink.

Someone invited Mabel and me to a big party at Vernon one Saturday evening and we decided to go. Now, when Mabel Normand went anywhere at all, or did anything at all, it was with all flags flying. When she bought hats she bought thirty, wore one, and gave the others away. When she had those French people make her gowns and evening dresses she ordered by the dozen—and wore only one. For this hoe-down at Mr. Long's she bought enough costumery and jewelry to outfit a parade of Mabels, and at the last minute sent a maid out to buy an extra $600 worth of bangles and bracelets.

But at the last moment before the party Kessel and Bauman began pleading at me on the telephone from New York. They threatened my throat and the collapse of civilization unless I put the final quirks on one of Mabel's pictures and shipped it East that night. So, in a hurry and not so tactfully as a man should be when he's breaking a date with a girl who's fancied herself up as much as Mabel had, I telephoned her and said I couldn't make the party.

Mabel said, "Oh, all right, Mack," and hung up.

I gloomed through the film in a projection room at Keystone, decided it was a pretty fair example of Mabel being funny, had the boys put it in the can and ship it off to New York. Then I telephoned Mabel, but her maid said—and she wasn't too warm about it, either—she hadn't the slightest idea where Miss Normand was. I got in my car and headed for Vernon.

I crept through the shrubbery, parted branches of the rhododendron, and spied.

Miss Normand, in all her glitter, was dancing with one of the handsomest fellows that ever posed for collar ads or became a leading man in Hollywood, and Jack Mulhall had done both. They were giving an exhibition because they had just won a prize as best on the floor. When the cup was awarded, Mulhall bowed and handed it to Mabel. She waved to the crowd and hugged Mulhall. Suddenly they disappeared, leaving me floundering among the ferns and bushes.

I heard Jack's big car roar down the driveway, got into mine, and followed. Pity I didn't have a camera on that chase sequence. It was fast and silly. But when they arrived at Mabel's apartment and went in together, I began to worry and mutter like the ex-boilermaker I was. I tiptoed upstairs, and tiptoeing is a good balancing trick for a man of my oversized heft, and put my eye to the keyhole.

I saw nothing and heard nothing.

But I remembered something. That afternoon I had had a stomping and quarreling scene with one of my writers about a sequence he'd written. He wanted to show a burned-up boy friend squinting through a keyhole at his sweetheart and another man.

"At the Mack Sennett studio we'll do the improbable but never the impossible. You can't motivate a grown-up man doing a thing like that," I proclaimed.

But there I was.

"The great Mack Sennett!" I muttered to myself. Then I hit the door with my fist. It wasn't locked. As a matter of fact, it was barely closed.

Mabel trotted toward me, grinning, and Mulhall came from the other side of the room. I shoved Mabel aside, being a good deal rougher about it than an Irish gentleman should be, put my left hand on Jack's shoulder to measure him, and threw a right-handed fist at his head.

This caught Mulhall off guard, knocked him as flat as a carpet, and blacked his eye. Blacked it! I turned it purple-red-blue-green-yellow and three shades of magenta with stripes.

As the blow landed, Mabel grabbed at my arm, lost her balance, and toppled head-over-heels onto a couch, stirring up a storm of petticoats as her pretty legs kicked in the air.

I came to my senses. I stepped back, held up a hand, and said:

"Wait a minute, kids. You both have to work tomorrow—early."

Sometimes I'm not such a slow thinker. To hold up the

picture while my leading man doctored a black eye, which his own producer had given him, would cost $15,000.

"I'll run for a doctor," I offered.

"No good," said Mabel. "Find a restaurant and get a thick piece of raw sirloin."

I did that as fast as I could. Miss Normand did not give me a fond good night.

I was at the studio early the next morning and telephoned Pathé Lehrman at once to see if the Mabel Normand company was working. It was. I sighed in relief and stayed in my office, avoiding the set in order to stay out of certain battle with Mabel.

Then Adolph Zukor telephoned. Mr. Zukor was already one of the biggest wheels in film distribution. He was soon to invent Paramount, of which he is still chairman of the board, and he was as important as oxygen to the Mack Sennett studios. He said he was coming over immediately to look at the pictures we had in work.

When he arrived, I spread red carpets knee-deep and put the Keystone Cops through their paces. I steered long detours around the Mabel Normand set.

But this set was what Mr. Zukor wanted to see, and when he said so it was an order.

As we entered I could tell that trouble was already boiling. Mabel's small nose was as high in the air as the Statue of Liberty's. Mulhall was protecting his black eye behind a flat.

She was rehearsing a scene and she wasn't doing it the way I had carefully planned it several days ago. The director called "cut" and asked me to come over.

"Mr. Sennett," he said, "is this the way you wanted us to do this?"

"Not quite," I said. "I had in mind that we'd have Mabel do thus-and-so. It'll be better the way we planned it originally, Mabel."

The take involved some business about Mabel's picking up a book from a library table. She picked it up and took a stance.

"Get off this set, Mack Sennett, or I'll break your head with this book, you house dick. And take your cheap-Jack spies along with you, or I'll——"

Mr. Zukor and I went quietly.

"Actresses, you know," I said. "Sometimes very temperamental."

On the ferry to Staten Island that miraculous night when we ate the buttered popcorn I'd given Mabel the two-dollar-and-a-half genuine diamond ring. She always wore it, and, as a matter of fact, I'd seen it glimmer on her left hand as she thumbed Mr. Zukor and me from her stage.

I gloomed and soaped in my tub and had Abdullah slap me with his canoe paddle hands until I was pinker than a spanked baby. I thought things over and decided it was up to me to be a good deal more romantical. I thought I ought to set about being tender, but I couldn't figure out how to start. One of my handicaps was that, although Mabel came to work every day and performed her pieces of funny acting on the set or on locations in Griffith Park, so far as I was concerned she had vanished. I wasn't even allowed on my own stages when she was there. She not only didn't answer when I called at the Murray Apartments on Seventh Street, downtown Los Angeles, but she apparently wasn't even living there. Carlyle Blackwell and his wife Ruth and Alice Joyce also lived at the Murray and were close friends of Mabel, but they said they hadn't seen her.

Even Willie James couldn't find her.

Pathé Lehrman, who was a gossipier back-fence than Louella or Hedda at their best, long before either of those taletellers came to town, gave me a number of reports, all disturbing and all inaccurate. I might as well give away what the writing men call a plot-motivation gimmick now. Pathé was in love with Mabel himself.

He told me that she was trotting around town with that Italian dancing boy named Valentino. There was not even a smidgen of truth in this disturbing report. He said she was having late champagne suppers with Jack Mulhall (a gentleman to the core with the rectitude of an old-fashioned banker and who, come to think of it, probably couldn't buy champagne at that time anyway). Pathé said that Mabel was pretty much upset and grieved by my oafishness. He was the one who

started the rumor that I had broken Mabel's arm during that
scuffle in Jack Mulhall's apartment.

This story gained as wide a circulation in Edendale and in
Hollywood as in Variety. And although, you remember, I took
pains a while ago to show that Mabel was a naïve person, she
wasn't so naïve as not to take advantage of an interesting
whopper like that. She was an actress. She would come to work
in the morning with her right arm swaddled in a dramatic
white sling, but when I sent Willie to creep on the set and
see if she really had anything like a broken arm, he reported
that by 10 A.M. and two cups of coffee Miss Normand was
waving that arm as happily as ever.

But I couldn't get near her.

I took $5000 in cash from the Bauman-Kessel-Sennett
sock and went to see one of those striped-pants jewelers on
Wilshire Boulevard. For my five grand I got a ring with a
diamond in it that seemed as shiny as a Santa Fe headlight on
a clear night.

The trouble with the desert country of Southern California is a lack of ferryboats. I thought it would be just fine
if I could lean over the rail again with Mabel, throw the two-
fifty souvenir to the moonlight, and give her the new ring.

Dell Henderson and his wife Florence lived at 1830 Kings-
ley, between Venice and Ocean Park. They gave a dinner
party one night while I was carrying this ring in my vest pocket
and trying to get within speaking distance of Mabel. They invited Ann Luther, Bobbie Wallace, and Mae Busch to eat a
twenty-pound roast sent over by Eddie Cline's father. Simple
and pleasant as that was—you'd have thought even I couldn't
get myself in trouble again—I made a boob of myself. I made a
play for Mae Busch.

I was just funning, so help me, and so was Mae, but I
suppose we put on a pretty good and noisy act. And I guess
I was considerably on the rebound. I didn't pay any attention
when Dell carved a few thin slices of beef and served a small
tray which his butler took upstairs.

Mabel had ears like a leprechaun. She heard everything.

I comforted myself by spending money. I bought a new,
imported chain-drive Fiat. I didn't need it. Who needs a Fiat?

I already had one, a long, powerful, thundering, gray job, which clanked like eighteen washing machines out of order. At that time these things cost six thousand dollars. I took a loss on the gray and bought a red Fiat that was as rakish as Jack Barrymore's headgear.

I had grief with that car from the start. Everybody wanted to borrow it. Pathé took it out one evening and stayed all night. By noon some interesting rumors were yakking around the studio. Pathé had left the red car out all night, with the engine running, in front of a well-known seminary presided over by a Madame Mamie. I had to send my chauffeur to pick it up. Even Willie was embarrassed.

But the red Fiat did me a service after all. Miss Normand, who couldn't drive anything more complicated than a small nail, clapped her big brown eyes on the new Fiat and decided I was the boy next door after all.

"Can I drive it, Mack? Please! You know me, I'm as careful as an old lady, and when I hit people I practically almost never maim them permanently. Mack, I've just got to drive that big automobile."

I couldn't think of anything prettier than Mabel Normand behind the wheel of that car.

Off she went. From where I stood and as far as I could see, she had at least two wheels on the ground most of the time.

Mabel returned four hours later by taxicab and climbed up to my office in the tower. Her big eyes were as innocent as a small girl's and she came over and sat on my desk and swung her legs and rumpled my hair and grinned at me.

"Mack, the darnedest thing. You do have an exceptional talent for picking bum automobiles. That Fiat's insides just weren't any good and I hadn't got even to Santa Monica before there was some terrible egg-beating noises and some weak kind of put-put-puts and the car stopped and I walked to a garage and you know what the man says? He says the gears are stripped."

She was the most gorgeous thing you ever saw and what did I need with a Fiat?

I said, "Mabel, I see you're still wearing the ferryboat ring.

I thought, well, maybe, I thought maybe you wouldn't be wearing it."

"Mack, I'll always wear it."

"Nope," I said. "No, you won't. I'm going to do better than that and right now. Take a look at this."

I took the new five-thousand-dollar diamond ring from the safe and held it out to her.

Well, it's always been my observation that any woman, from a queen to a dairymaid, gets a special kind of refraction in her eyes when she looks at diamonds. I don't know what women think about when they look at diamonds, but it puts things in their eyes that never were there before. And Mabel reacted the way pretty girls ought to react when a man hands her a diamond.

So that was all right. She liked it, and we were made up again. But this is what she said:

"Mack, this is very thoughtful of you and you don't know how much I appreciate it. It will just exactly match my diamond necklace."

She dropped the five-thousand-dollar diamond in her purse as if it were a streetcar token. When she left she was still wearing the ferryboat diamond.

There was no rustle of dark trouble then or even a shadow. At Keystone it seemed to us that the Southern California sunshine was incapable of marking anything except high noon. I doubt if any one of us really knew what time it was. Certainly there was no suggestion then or for some time to come of anything evil.

Mabel was like—she was like so many things. She was like a French-Irish girl, as gay as a wisp, and she was also Spanish-like and brooding. Mostly she was like a child who walks to the corner on a spring morning and meets Tom Sawyer with a scheme in his pocket.

She piled contradictions on top of contradictions, then kicked at them with high heels and knocked them down like playroom blocks. Mabel became studious. I don't want to exaggerate this, because so many Hollywood players in recent years have let on that they are constant readers of heavy-duty thinkers, economics, and foreign languages, and most of this

is a pose or the dream-up of a press agent. Anyway I was not
studious along with Mabel and I can't give much of a report
on what she read. But she did read a great deal and the more
she read the more she became fascinated with morbid psychology. She began to seek out the handful of people in the
motion-picture business who were reasonably literate. This
was a phase of her life that largely omitted me.

At the same time Mabel went right on playing pranks.
None of these was exactly intellectual. There was a middle-
aged comedian named Nick Cogley who worked for us and
whose bones were brittle and who shouldn't have attempted
some of the pratt-falls he did for Keystone. Mr. Cogley had
a wife, a "Craig's Wife" sort of person, who kept house as if
she lived in a clinic, and wouldn't even let her husband take
a drag from a cigarette in their living room.

One slimy day when the pavement was slick, Mr. Cogley
was egged too far by Ben Turpin and did a back flip on the
concrete which gave him a compound fracture in his left leg.
We kept Mr. Cogley on the pay roll, but it was a matter of
professional pride with my comedians not to break themselves.
Even when he hurt the most, Cogley had to put up with jibes.

On a morning when my fastest director, Del Lord, was
taking Mabel and Walter Wright to Santa Monica on location, Mabel talked the boys into what seemed at the time an
enchanting idea. They stopped all the trucks in front of Nick's
house, unloaded a few lights and all the smudge pots, and
went in.

"Looky here, Nick," Mabel said, "you're sitting there on
your lazy backside, drawing down your fat salary, because you
broke your leg on purpose to get out of work, so we're going
to photograph your living room for a set."

Cogley protested like a bear in a trap, but no one listened
to his howls.

Mabel directed the grips and electricians where to put the
lights and smudge pots, lit the smudge pots, and the company
departed for Santa Monica, leaving Mr. Cogley trapped in
his plaster cast, unable to move six inches. A dozen smudge
pots can belch an incredible amount of smoke in a living room.

They exited laughing and forgot poor Cogley for upwards
of three hours. When they did accidentally remember to re-

turn, the Santa Monica Fire Department had arrived and was red in the face. Cogley was well-nigh asphyxiated and Mrs. Cogley's hospital-clean living room looked like the Black Hole of Calcutta after an Elks' convention.

Mabel was extremely repentant when her pranks back-fired like this, as they so often did. She put up several thousand dollars to clean up the Cogley house and redecorate it.

She still wanted to drive my Fiat.

I said, "Honey pot, if you strip those gears again, I'll flay you with a butter knife and nail your little pink hide on the front gate."

Mabel took the Fiat out again and stripped the gears. But we were going steady again, so I said all I had to say under my breath.

I liked to drive around town fast in those days with Willie sitting importantly beside me. But the Fiat was an open job and when the rainy season began to douse Los Angeles, riding in that thing was like sitting in a bathtub with the shower turned on.

"We got to get us something dry, Mr. Sennett," Willie complained.

I had just made $10,000 on the stock market that morning on a tip from Don Lee, the Cadillac man.

"Joke on Mr. Lee," I said to Willie. "Pull in here."

We went into the Packard agency and looked at a twin-six limousine that made Willie's eyes shine like chinquapins.

"How much for that hearse?" I asked the salesman.

He told me it cost $7800, delivered.

"Will it run? Okay, we'll take it now. Dispose of this bucket we're driving."

The man wanted references for an outlay like that. "Call up Mr. Don Lee at the Cadillac Agency," I told him.

It was a burgundy-red landaulet and it solved the gear-stripping and keeping-dry problem. It was the kind of a car that demanded a chauffeur, so Miss Mabel Normand never got her hands on that one.

With things like this going on almost every day, with Bauman and Kessel whining at me from New York to make more pictures faster and for less money, and with Mabel's pride always standing between us like a wall I never learned to climb, I was not a Fancy Dan in the romance department. I didn't buy red Fiats and Packard twin-sixes every day, or even on odd Tuesdays, and mighty few of the fancy parties at Baron Long's establishment saw me trying to dance. I worked long, hard hours. It always took extra time for me to think up ways to cope with actors, actresses, clowns, bankers, distributors, and partners whose brains went faster than mine. It seems ridiculous, and when I look at it from this late point of view, it *is* ridiculous to say that I was too busy to get married.

But perhaps a weary certified public accountant, or an insurance man, or a man who runs a chain grocery store—perhaps one of these men who come home in the evening with a headache and discover that they are barely acquainted with their own children—will know what I mean when I say that I was too busy to be kind and understanding.

I am not sure that I knew it then, but I think that all along I wanted to marry a wife, not an actress.

There is no way to read a crystal ball in reverse reflection now and say what might have happened had Mabel Normand and I got married. Maybe some of the bad things that came later would not have occurred.

CHAPTER 11

A Variety of Wild Oats

WE WERE under way full tilt at Keystone. We produced a two-reeler every week, and when we could do it we turned out two per week. The mechanical gags to make these comedies laughable cost more money than you might think, because we didn't have the handy tool of dialogue to explain our situations. Talking motion pictures did not arrive until 1928.

It cost between $25,000 and $30,000 to make a two-reeler. Usually we shot about four thousand feet of film and cut this down to two thousand. It took that much editing to get our pictures sharp and precise and to flim-flam the public into believing, momentarily, that something remotely possible was happening on the screen.

Carpenters were paid $8.00 a day during the early teens and a first-rate cameraman got $250 a week, or considerably more than most of the actors.

The $25,000 to $30,000 was for negative cost only. We had to do more than $50,000 worth of business with each picture in order to break even. Sometimes we didn't, but usually we cracked the nut. The theaters and distributors were not demanding particular pictures, or particular stars, or even a particular type of picture. They pleaded for anything new that moved. Most of our two-reelers took in between $75,000 and $85,000. The only thing tidy about Keystone was the profit.

Our financial arrangements, personal and company-wise, were often as dreamy as a college girl's attitude toward a checking account. When my mother came to live with me, some of her fiscal affairs were awesome too.

I increased the size of the Keystone studio to twenty-eight acres in order to give my comedians ample scenery and sky lines to leap around in. Mrs. Sennett (formerly Mrs. Sinnott) thought it was logical to follow suit and increase her acreage in Canada, more than three thousand miles away.

She always clung to her little subsistence farm in Quebec. The only thing it produced that was of any use to us for many years was a few patty-cakes of maple sugar. Mrs. Sennett would come to the studio with her sugar in a shoe box and make herself popular.

As I expanded, Mama expanded too. She found she needed 250 acres. She was in Canada when she bought the extra land and I knew nothing about it for several months. She merely sent a telegram (collect) to the studio business manager and said she needed $1400. He sent it.

Later he climbed to the tower and told me about the outlay as if he thought I might have him decapitated. I said, "What else could you do? When Mother sends for money, better let her have it in a hurry and keep us both out of trouble."

My mother, undoubtedly backed by the good wishes of St. Anthony, tapped my share of the Keystone till on several other occasions. One time the tap was for around $4500 and word of that got to me fast.

I called her on the telephone, made my manners, asked about her health, and finally got around to asking just why in the world she needed $4500.

"Wells," Mother said. "We have got to sink a number of deep artesians and build some windmills so's we'll have enough moisture for the oats. You wouldn't want my oats to parch up and dry like last summer's straw hat, now, would you, Mack?"

So Mrs. Sennett sank deep wells all over her 250 acres. Quebec is noted for its rainfall. The Sennett farm was criss-crossed like a road map with brooks, branches, streams, and creeks. When I was a little boy there, a spring freshet created a new brook which accommodatingly ran through the middle of our barn and watered the stock. Mother needed wells and windmills about as much as she needed a trapeze.

But it's a strange thing how affairs work out. Years later my mother's foolish wells turned out to be important.

Like most country boys, I loathed anything to do with farming and fled to the city and stayed there as soon as I could. But Mother considered her thumb green and she had an uncontrollable passion for growing things. One autumn when I let her talk me into visiting the farm for a brief vacation, she pointed with pride to her magnificent stand of oats. On every acre or cranny not occupied by wood lots, maple-sugar trees, or houses Mother had planted oats. And she had something to brag about this time. She was selling her cereal for $1.35 a bushel while my brother and Uncle Mike Foy and the rest of the neighbors were getting only seventy-five cents for theirs.

I bloomed and bounced with pride in Mother's achievement. That is, until Uncle Mike took me aside and explained.

"Tell you about that, Mike. She put eight railroad carloads of fancy fertilizer on every inch of those oat fields and spread it deeper than a stack of Bibles. You know this soil. It's porous. The fertilizer's good for one growing season only. Now just figure out how much your mother is paying for her oats."

I figured it out. Mother's flyer in oats was costing me in the neighborhood of ten cents an oat.

Since she was preoccupied with farming, I seldom mentioned my own business affairs to her. My affairs were always troublesome all along the line, even when I became the head of my own company in 1915. *The Good-bye Kiss* was one of my most expensive early pictures and the studios stood to rise or fall depending on what kind of deal I made for it in New York.

I wasn't primed with confidence in this investment and so I went to New York to make as much noise about it as possible in distributors' offices. I took Mother with me.

The exhibitors greeted me as if I were the Marines arriving to save the fort, and even the bankers had kind words.

I hurried back to the hotel one afternoon with everything wrapped up and told Mother I'd made the best deal of my life.

"Why, of course, Mike. I know you did."

"You knew I did? How'd you know?"

"How could I help knowing? Didn't I give St. Anthony a five-dollar bill just before we left Los Angeles?"

But mainly Mother let me be the head of the studio and never stepped out of line. She merely said, "If you don't behave yourself, Mike, I'll give you a clout on the jaw."

At no time in her long and enterprising life did my mother ever associate with elderly people. She gave them the back of her hand. She said they were always complaining about their aches and ailments. She was afraid if she had anything to do with them she might have the first illness in her life. She came to the studio almost daily during the twenty-one years she spent with me in California and called on the girls—Mabel, of course, Marie Prevost, Mae Busch, Gloria Swanson, and Phyllis Haver, for instance. When she grew discouraged in her campaign to marry me to Mabel Normand, she tried to palm me off on all the above-mentioned ladies.

One year when Canadian oats and maple sugar were selling for less than usual she rescued my brother Jack from his small farm and gave me instructions to install him at the studio. A Canadian oat grower wasn't by any means the oddest man on a lot populated with clowns and my growing menagerie.

"But when you work here, Jack, you'll get the same treatment as anybody else, even if your brother is head of the studio."

Jack was a heavyweight boxer and at one time had held some kind of local championship in Quebec. If you held a back-yard championship in that part of Canada, you had to knock out a giant.

"And I'll blast yer swelled and potato-shaped head off your shoulders with a flick of me left wrist, brother dear," Jack said.

So I put Jack on the pay roll at $250 a week and took special pains to see that he had nothing to do with the production of motion pictures.

Nothing untoward or rude ever took place within earshot of Mrs. Sennett. What she may have thought about what she didn't hear or see I don't know, but she lent an aura of respectability to our proceedings, meanwhile having a good time

herself. Her limit on alcohol was a half ounce of bourbon before bedtime.

When we went places and did things, Mother usually went
too. We celebrated New Year's at Pebble Beach by hiring an
observation car to take us all there, and we appropriated an
entire hotel when we arrived. These parties were mixed affairs.
Wives and/or sweethearts accompanied their menfolks. When
I went, I was accompanied by Mabel and Mother.

It soon became the custom for any Hollywood people
accosted by a hotel manager to give the password. "We're
with Mrs. Sennett."

Our holidays and feasts were not so Roman Empire style
as some people think. At least it seems to me now that our
affairs were simple in comparison with what goes on in the
big bistros of café society today—in Romanoff's, Ciro's, the
Stork Club or Twenty-one.

Our routine, when we were not pressed to get film off to
New York, was for a few of us to meet at the Alexandria Hotel
for scotches-and-soda between five and six o'clock. Sometimes
it was the Hoffman Cafe round table, or Levi's Cafe at Fourth
and Main streets, or McKee's across the street from the Alexandria. After dinner, if we didn't have to work, we liked to
go to Baron Long's Vernon Country Club on Santa Fe Avenue.
Drinks were two for a quarter. Mike Lyman, who became
famous as a Hollywood restaurateur, beat the drums in the
Vernon band and Buddy DeSylva played the uke. For five
dollars you could stir up a binge as fancy as any evening at the
Mocambo.

Meanwhile toil and nonsense went hand in hand at the
Keystone University of Art and Culture. Miss Normand was
usually near the firing line of whatever was happening.

An obnoxious amateur applied for work. He said, as everybody always said, that he wanted to see Mr. Sennett. Mabel
got to him first and took him to Slim Summerville, who
claimed he was Mr. Sennett. Summerville had this unfortunate
character falling downstairs, taking pies in the face, and re-
citing Shakespeare when I came along and asked what was
going on.

"I'm showing Mr. Sennett how I can act," said the
wretched man.

Now and then Mabel was the victim of my too merry Andrews. It was a wet day in Southern California and the pavement in front of Keystone was half an inch deep in mud and water. Chester Conklin spied Mabel across the street, wondering how to get across, and made a fancy gesture. He bowed like a headwaiter expecting a fifty-dollar tip, snatched off his coat, and spread it in the mud for Mabel to step on. She stepped, and disappeared into a manhole.

I once knew a country parson who was completely against sin—he was an upstanding man of the cloth, fine as they come —and he had made a lifetime study of the matter. He delivered the most educational preachments I ever heard about sin in Paris, or New York, or Hollywood—places his congregation had never been and didn't plan to go. He was a power in the community, all right, and everybody admired him. I expect, though, that some of his people were disappointed when they did get to travel. None of the places he mentioned was as fancy as they'd been led to believe.

Somehow or another the parson never got around to ordinary sins, like lying, cheating, and gossiping on the neighbors. Naturally his folks appreciated his tact and held him in esteem.

Both my secretary, a conservative lady who makes the best cup of tea in Hollywood and parts of Canada, and my collaborator in this candidate for the Pulitzer Prize have been egging me from the beginning to get more wickedness into this account.

There is one question everybody always asks me: "Tell me, Mr. Sennett, do you think there is more sin in Hollywood than there used to be?"

All I can answer is: "Do you think there is more in Cedar Rapids than there used to be?"

Miss Billie Burke, who left Charles F. Frohman and made her movie debut for Ince at Santa Monica, once noted that sin in the theater is like education at the University of Southern California. There is plenty of it, but not so many people take advantage of it as are exposed to it.

But there is no getting around the fact, which everybody knows, that show folks, being by nature excitable and temperamental, and also being the kind of people who want to give themselves to other people, else they couldn't be actors at all, are noticeably casual about some of our better-known conventions.

I had my problems at Keystone and later on at my other studios. Against every reasonable instinct I had I found myself setting up for a duenna. This was especially true after I had invented the Mack Sennett Bathing Beauties (for an odd reason I'll explain later). They were dollipers, all of them, and the man who wouldn't reach for one of them, or a handful of them—well, there is no possible way to describe a man who never existed.

I won't say that I was any better than I ought to have been, but I wasn't as bad as you may enjoy thinking I was. One of my main chores as the pretty girls came and my boys tried to trip them up was to keep the Sennett name and the Sennett studio from being involved in a scandal. I headed studios in Hollywood from 1912 to 1935 and managed to stay out of court.

One of the reasons for this was a six-foot-tall policewoman named Blanche Payson, who had charge of the actresses' dressing rooms with all the authority of the headmistress of a girls' boarding school. Many attempts were made to get around her. In fact I wanted to see Phyllis Haver in a hurry one afternoon and tried to get by her myself.

"Not in here, sonnyboy," Blanche said.

"But I'm Mr. Sennett!"

"That's what they all say," Blanche glowered. "Move on."

It was often difficult to find out if any money had been made, and who had made it, and who had it.

Film distribution in the early days, when new theaters were opening as fast as investors could lease vacant stores and rent chairs from the undertaker, was an adventure for pirates. It was about as well organized as a national chain of lemonade stands operated by small, dishonest boys.

My friends and patrons, Charlie Bauman and Adam Kessel, were now heels over head in motion-picture production and were involved in many companies and deals aside from our original Keystone gamble. The disorganized state of film distribution affairs continued.

This kind of thing frequently got me into misunderstandings with my partners. When we had fallings-out about money matters, we offered to dismember each other's lawyers. In one of my most threatening hassles with my ex-bookie associates, they got me across a barrel and rolled the barrel out on a limb. I was about to be demoted to eighteenth assistant office boy.

I thought things over and called up Tom Ince. Ince, you'll remember, owned 10 per cent of Keystone. Once before he had engineered a dramatic bluff which took Bauman and Kessel in, so I sought his advice.

Tom said, "Okay, feller, I'm mixed up in this too, and I think we can beat 'em. How many negatives you got stashed in your studios?"

I said I had a backlog of eight or nine completed two-reel comedies representing costs of about $25,000 each.

Tom whooped. "We got those New York boys by the short hair. Tell you what we're going to do. I'm going to take my automobile, drive it myself, and pick up all the film I have on hand, both the negatives and the positives. Then I'll come over to your place and pick up all your film and we'll go downtown and rent us some safety-deposit vaults.

"Here's the gimmick: we'll take a whole chain of vaults in different banks under different names. If Charlie and Adam come out here and try to grab this film, they won't be able to trace a single foot of it."

"Holy smoke," I said. "Tom, they'll sling us in the calaboose."

"They could do that," Tom said. "They sure could do that. And knowing Kessel and Bauman, they would do it, too. But so what? They still won't have the negatives."

Mr. Bauman and Mr. Kessel hastened out from New York. They were armed to their back teeth with contracts and commitments and legal documents. They had me.

They said, "Okay, Sennett, we'll take over. Hand us the film."

"What film?" I said.

"*The* film, dammit."

"Got no film," I said. "Excuse me, gentlemen, these big-figured financial arrangements always give me a slight headache. Mind if I take a nap?"

They did threaten to clap Tom Ince and me in jail. They threatened loudly for two weeks. But we didn't surrender a foot of film until we had made business arrangements that suited us.

I was with Tom Ince on Wednesday night, February 1, 1922, when there was a murder. It was a good thing for me that my whereabouts were firmly established. Thomas H. Ince was a loyal, fast-thinking friend who came to my aid in many ways.

He was born in a theatrical family in New York, toted dishes as a busboy at a White Mountain resort for a starter, and eventually became an actor. He worked in only one picture at the old Biograph Studios when I was there, *His New Lid*, released in 1910. On Broadway he had met a lean Shakespearean actor named William S. Hart, who influenced him considerably later on, but, as a young man, he was like me, yearning to become a director. I was too big and bumptious for leading-man parts and Tom was too short.

Tom found his chance with the IMP Company, which had a curious origin. In 1910 a man named Watterson R. Rothacker, who worked for the theatrical trade publication *Billboard*, thought up an idea for producing short pieces of film for industry and advertisers. He was backed by Carl Laemmle and Robert Cochrane, who were the heads of the Independent Motion Picture Company.

Neither Uncle Carl Laemmle nor Robert Cochrane had the remotest interest in industrial films, but they were having a desperate time with Jeremiah Kennedy, head of the Patents Company, which had all the Edison inventions and cameras tied up.

They invented a fancy legal jape. They put up the money for Rothacker's idea with the proviso that he name his outfit "Industrial Moving Picture Company."

That way these smart operators had two movie companies each with the initials IMP. They could transfer assets, players, completed films, or bootleg cameras back and forth when battling Jeremiah breathed too hotly down their necks and threatened to sick the law on them.

Tom Ince wangled himself a job as a director with IMP

and did all right. His first picture *Little Nell's Tobacco* was a drab spectacle, but when he screened it on Fourteenth Street for Mr. Laemmle, Tom's tongue went faster than the sixteen images per second on the screen and Uncle Carl wound up the evening under the impression that he had seen a masterwork. Tom then made the first Mary Pickford picture for IMP, *Their First Misunderstanding*, and this was a good film. So good, as a matter of fact, that Biograph and the Patents Company screamed themselves pink in the face and lit out after Tom's scalp, legally or anyway they could get it.

Tom had brought a company to California, including Mary Pickford and her mother, Mrs. Charlotte Pickford, and Owen Moore. He took Mary and the cameras and fled all the way to Cuba to escape Jeremiah Kennedy's agents and Thomas A. Edison's thunder.

When that escapade blew over, Mr. Ince called on my old friends, Kessel and Bauman, wearing a diamond. The diamond had been borrowed from a friend but it had a hypnotic effect on Charlie and Adam. What Tom wanted was a job as a director at somewhere around $100 a week. Kessel was embarrassed to offer such a small sum to such a smart man with such a big diamond.

Tom started at $150 a week.

He made one short picture on the way to California, then settled in a Santa Monica gully, or makeshift canyon, to think up epics.

While Ince was thinking them up, a Wild West circus called Miller Brothers' 101 Ranch moved into the vicinity for the winter. Tom clapped an aggressive eye on the 101 outfit the minute he heard the cow pokes holler. Here was the harbinger of his epic.

One telegram from Tom Ince to Kessel and Bauman made Hollywood history and, I do believe, considerably influenced the folklore of the nation. Tom wired that he could lease the Wild West show for $2100 a week, produce a sockdolager of a picture with cowboys and Indians—and make a fortune for the company.

It's on record that Mr. Kessel and Mr. Bauman, who after all were a couple of East Side boys and who had never been closer to a live horse than the pay-off window at Belmont Park, thought this over with whatever their equivalent of prayer was.

But the boys were gamblers and Ince had magicked them. They told him, not without threats, to go ahead, and Ince did produce an epic. This was the first of the great made-in-Hollywood spectacles and the first big Western picture—the forerunner of Hopalong, Autry, Rogers—and Trigger.

William S. Hart, the Shakespearean actor with whom Tom had worked on Broadway, and Tom Mix, a genuine Texas marshal, soon joined up. Both made fortunes. Hart earned so much money that he had to retire after twenty-two pictures to escape income taxes.

As Ince thrived and cow pokes went that-a-way, he was able to afford enormous numbers of extras in crowd scenes which were far beyond the Keystone budget. On slack days when he was not chasing them through the hills and the prairies or holding a well-rehearsed stampede, Tom would call me up and say, "Mack, I got a lot of people sitting around here today. Want to use them?"

Naturally this always caught my talented story department without so much as an anecdote between them. But we'd load Chester Conklin, Vernon Dent, and Slim Summerville into a camera truck, descend on Ince's Santa Monica lair, and shoot a picture off the cuff.

Once when he had more than 850 extras, more or less, made up as the rabble of a Mexican army, we decided they were gallant Boys in Gray, and shot a Civil War saga. This was several years ahead of *The Birth of a Nation*.

Tom gave me a good deal of advice about how to get along with temperamental actors. He said that at his studio he found it inspiring and relaxing to stop work daily at four o'clock and serve tea. We tried this only once at Keystone. The breakage was awful and several strangers got scalded.

As he became a famous man and made large sums of money, Tom found a playful streak in himself which up to this time had been overshadowed by business and hard work. He discovered that it was occasionally refreshing and good for his weary mind to take interesting week-end trips to interesting places.

And since Hollywood had then, just as it has now, a back fence over which every resident of the motion-picture community bent an ear, it was sometimes difficult for Mr. Ince to account for where he had been. His standard explanation was that he had been hunting. But when a man goes Nimroding many times in succession and returns with no game in his pouch, his descriptions of scenery lack conviction.

I went hunting with Ince several times myself.

At that time I had a seventeen-room house in Westmoreland Park surrounded by two acres of the very best shrubs and equipped with two tennis courts and a swimming pool about the size of Puget Sound. I rented this place instead of buying it because I've always been like W. C. Fields, not wanting to own a lot of furniture and truck which eventually gets to own you. I had no use for the tennis courts or the swimming pool. I had begun to fancy myself as a horseman, riding near the Hillcrest Country Club every morning before going to work.

The size of my rented establishment made it a natural receptacle for the overflow of fauna from the studio, particularly ducks. Mother was partial to ducks. So the studio kept my tennis courts and swimming pool overstocked.

Tom returned from one of his hunting trips empty-handed one evening and said he needed the best alibi brains could build.

"All you need is ducks," I said. "I am long on ducks and weary of the beasts. Go help yourself."

Tom took a flashlight and chased squalling ducks over two tennis courts and a new geranium bed until he had nabbed about eight. Then he hung them over a clothesline and took aim with his shotgun. Apparently no one noticed that Tom's trophies were so domesticated they couldn't have flown more than six inches.

CHAPTER 12

Funnymen at Work

IT COULD be that I have been creating the impression all along that nothing but nonsense went on at the Keystone studio.

Actually we did an enormous amount of work. The more comedies we made the more we learned about how to be funny. And one of the most important things we learned is that comedy is a serious business. We found out that we could not make our best pictures without solemn and brain-beating preparation. A new theory of motion-picture economics smote us pretty forcefully. It was this: the more money we spent on the script, on writing the story, the less money it cost us to shoot the pictures when we put the actors to work. I thought that over and made motions to get all the work possible out of my writers. For one thing, I discovered that writing men are sad fellows on a full stomach. I set about abbreviating their lunch hours and ordered the commissary to short them on their rations no matter what they ordered.

As the end of the day came around, I would descend from my tower and take up a post in a large office near the foot of the stairs where the writers emerged from their roosts. As they passed my door one by one I would sing out greetings and invite them in for a drink. So far as I know there are no screen writers extant who can resist free drinking-liquor. Once I had them assembled with glasses in their hands, I would hold a story conference and keep them on the job for two to five hours past quitting time.

They caught onto me soon enough and an astonishing

rumor went around the Keystone lot. All the writers were on the wagon. It was a fragile wagon and they rode it only part of one day.

I have a letter from Vernon Smith, who was one of those writing men and who worked for me for thirteen years, both as a gag man and as scenario editor. Vern writes from New Orleans, where he has retired to put together his own book about show business. He begins by saying that I was a charming and magnetic personality in those days. Then he rears back and lets me have it with the truth.

"There was a Black-Irish streak in Mack Sennett that could transform him into the most disagreeable old so-and-so I've ever known. There were times when Sennett seemed to delight in upsetting everything and everybody in the studio for no reason at all except to get the black out of his system."

Vern recalls the time I stepped out of character and went high-brow. We were making a picture with Ralph Graves when—according to Smith—I called him into the rubdown room and said, "Vernon, our pictures are too cheap and sleazy. We've got to put more production into them. I want them dressed up so's they look better."

Smith said that, sure, boss, he could improve the sets and dress them smarter, but he wasn't prepared for what I had in mind.

According to him, I had joined the Hollywood Country Club, taken up golf, and become romantically interested in a Pasadena widow of social prominence.

"Now when we have flowers on the set," I said, "don't let Paul stick in those old paper flowers in that same old vase. I want real flowers. Roses! Have Lee call up and order two dozen American Beauties."

Smith swallowed hard and hurried out to obey orders. He knew, of course, that a two-reel Mack Sennett comedy with real American Beauty roses was fantastic. No one had ever dreamed of such a thing. One of the charms about Keystone pictures was the knockaboutness of the sets.

"And another thing," I said to Smith, "Ralph Graves is supposed to play the part of an artist in this picture, a real classy artist. I want him to *paint* classics. Get a classic of a cow for him to paint in the pasture scene.

"Then, when the farmer's daughter invites him home to dinner and he shows his art to her ma and pa, let him come up with some more classics. I don't want any of those dead ducks hanging by one foot.

"I know Paul hasn't got anything good in the prop room, so rent something from the museum. Something like 'Physic at the Well.' "

Smith explained to me that possibly the picture I had in mind was called "Psyche at the Spring."

They laid hands on all these things just like I ordered and put them in the picture. When I saw how out of place they looked in the first day's rushes I threw them all out and returned in a hurry to dead ducks and paper flowers.

Vernon Smith says this: "To an outsider the writing of a Sennett comedy must have seemed as fantastic as an explosion in a paint factory. But as a matter of fact those comedies were fundamentally sound in plot structure and characterization. Each comedian had a definite character and a definite range. The stories and the gags were custom-tailored to fit Ben Turpin, Harry Langdon, Billy Bevan, Charlie Chaplin, Mabel Normand, or whichever funny person the story was for.

"We never bought stories at any time from books or magazines or from outside writers. Every story that went on film was an original, written by the department. Mack Sennett supplied most of the basic ideas. Then he and I would kick these basics around until we were satisfied that we had the springboard for a good comedy. Then I would assign two writers to develop it. All they did was tell a story—no gags. They made no attempt to conform to any kind of pattern or even to stay within the limits of the footage required for two reels.

"When the story was complete I would climb up to the tower and tell it to the Old Man.

"When we decided that a yarn was good enough, it went to the gag room. This was a special room in a kind of tower of its own where we kept the scribes locked up. They didn't like to be interrupted. They had bribed the carpenters to make the top step of the staircase one inch higher than all the other steps so that anyone who entered was likely to stumble and fall on his face. To my knowledge, the Old Man never tripped once. He often caught the gag men asleep, working cross-word puzzles, or doping out the horse races.

"A gag conference consisted of about six gag men, the Old Man, and myself. There was no orderly procedure. The story was attacked from all angles by everybody. Anyone who thought up a funny situation would not only tell it but act it out at the same time. One gag would suggest another and often two jokesmiths would combine their gags into one routine.

"If a stranger had walked in, falling on his face, of course, he might have thought he was in the violent ward of an insane asylum. One of our best young men was Frank Capra, now a distinguished Academy Award-winning director. He was an action boy. When he wanted to get over how funny a plumber could be, lying on his back under a kitchen sink, he would sprawl on the floor and make like a plumber.

"When Felix Adler demonstrated a scene about a near-sighted farmer who milked a rubber glove instead of a cow, he came equipped with glove and milk.

"But there were times when the gag room was as dreary as a mortuary at midnight. Then you would see Jack Javene with his head down massaging his scalp, the Old Man slouched in his chair with his hands over his eyes, chewing tobacco. Harry McCoy would be at the drinking fountain swallowing aspirin and Earl Rodney would be pulling up his pants and stuffing his shirt-tail in and out. These gestures are very useful to writers when they are trying to think."

The writing of these stories was not cheap by any means. The average cost of a Keystone story was $2100 and some came to more than $3500.

Rob Wagner, who later became a well-known contributor to The Saturday Evening Post, came to work while Vernon Smith was scenario editor. As you might suspect, Rob's brand of humor was several cuts too intellectual and satirical for our burlesque. He moaned around for weeks, unable to comprehend what he was supposed to do or to adjust himself to our method of working.

"Nothing makes sense," he would say. "This place isn't a studio, it's a madhouse."

Then, as Vern Smith recalls, Wagner ran up to him in the restaurant one day and claimed that his mind was clear.

"I've got it," he said. "These Sennett comedies are master-pieces of exaggerated human conduct. The characters represent all of us, rich, poor, educated, and ignorant alike. And our emotions and physical actions are enlarged to such proportions that we can see ourselves in comedy relief. It has just come over me that these comedies are art, a new and distinct form of humor, based on the fundamentals of human nature."

I wouldn't know about that. I've been denying all along that we knew anything about art, but those words of Rob Wagner's are musical to me, and I'm glad to put them into print. But whatever it was that we created, we played it by ear as we went along.

The story projects my writers and gag men sweated out were directed by various men. Hampton Del Ruth, Mal St. Clair, Frank Capra (after he had served an apprenticeship as a gagster), Dell Henderson, Pathé Lehrman, and others who went on to more serious works and became famous.

Del Lord, the champion pie thrower, became one of the fanciest operators. He had been a racing driver and he came to us as a stunt man. For nerve and invention Lord was about the best we ever had. His first performance for us was a whopper. He drove a car over a cliff, wrecking it in a smoky tangle of flame, and walked out grinning without a scratch on him. Then he drove a car at forty miles an hour off a Venice pier into the ocean.

Del then gave a performance on top of the old Detweiler Building in downtown Los Angeles. Fred Jackman, the greatest stunt cameraman of all time, had thin steel girders thrust across a court at least 250 feet above the pavement. When Del Lord began to run back and forth across these girders as casually as a child playing hopscotch, a crowd of more than two thousand openmouthed Angelenos gathered below and screamed for the police. The police arrived along with the fire department and ambulances and the crowd went screaming wild.

At the last moment before arrest and a strait jacket, Lord and Jackman dropped a dummy into the crowd, packed up their camera, and performed a well-known operation described as getting the hell out of there.

This was our kind of a man. I made him assistant to

Jackman, and then turned him loose as a director. Del immediately disappeared with a cameraman and a small pickup crew, hired a boat, and set sail on the Gulf of Mexico. All that man had to do was go somewhere and improbable things would happen in front of his hot lens. He returned with pictures of a whale and a shark in a death struggle, and then topped that with a sharply focused sequence never before photographed, the nuptials of whales.

It wasn't exactly our kind of material. Kessel and Bauman hollered like banshees. But after they had run the film three or four times for their own amazement, they offered it to the theaters and we made a great deal of money out of it.

It was Del Lord, even after he became a director, who drove the paddywagon in those Keystone Cop chase sequences on the city streets. Our specially built patrol car, often containing "Fatty" Arbuckle, Charlie Murray, Chester Conklin, Hank Mann, and up to as many as fifteen Keystone Cops altogether, was a monstrosity eight feet high. Del Lord's favorite place for stunts with this vehicle was at Eightieth and Figueroa streets. He would sneak up on this location when the accommodating Los Angeles Police Department was looking the other way and spread a barrel of soap on the pavement. When he approached this at fifty miles an hour, slewed his wheels, and slammed on his brakes, the results were gratifying.

The only Keystone Cops who suffered bruises and abrasions from working with Del Lord were those with faint hearts who leaped out of his careening wagons, racing automobiles, or pier-jumping contraptions ahead of time. When they stayed with Del they always lit safely.

Del himself was injured only once. This was when he flipped backwards down a staircase of fourteen steps and missed his landing spot. He moaned and apologized for several weeks about that.

"Anything I can't stand is a damn accident," Del said.

When Del became a director he perfected his own special technique. He shot pictures backwards. He was convinced that the best way to make a motion picture was to photograph a climax, then start at the beginning and try to work up to it.

For instance, he began a picture one time, shooting the last scene first, of course, showing the beautiful Madeline

Hurlock as a fortuneteller. There was no sense or purpose in having Madeline a fortuneteller, but Lord liked to challenge himself with such predicaments.

He shot his way out of this one well enough with Billy Bevan and Andy Clyde. He started them on a train ride. When the conductor found they had no tickets and no money he put them to work in the diner. A customer ordered fish. The train crossed a river over a high trestle. Bevan stuck out a fishing pole and naturally caught a fish.

For this caper they were kicked off the train, along with their fish. Being hungry, they cooked their catch and started eating it. Then they found an important document in code inside the fish. What else would a Mack Sennett actor find inside a fish? Now Mr. Lord knew what to do with Madeline Hurlock and the fortunetelling scene. They took the document to her, she decoded it, and they all lived happily ever afterwards.

Logical? My patient reader, have you forgotten how those scenes flew? Sequences were shot so fast, often at twice normal speed, and edited so sharply with close-ups and action and gags coming so rapidly, head over each other's heels, that no one had time to think whether they made sense or not.

In addition to becoming the best pie thrower in the world, and the bravest stunt man, Del now wanted to be the world's champion comedy director—and he became exactly that. When we began to release our films through Pathé we were on a percentage deal at last and we stood to make or lose depending on how funny our pictures were. The days when the theaters would buy anything new that moved were soon over. With this in mind I announced a competition among my directors for a diamond-belt-buckle trophy and bonuses of $1500 and $2000 to those who made the highest percentage scores over certain periods. I had a belt buckle made up glittering with fine diamonds with a big comedy mask in the center, surrounded by a sterling plaque engraved with these words: "World's Most Famous Comedy Director."

As an afterthought I sent the buckle back to the engraver and had him insert the words "MACK SENNETT" in letters twice as big as the rest.

Del Lord won the diamond comedy belt buckle so many times in succession against such talented competitors as Eddie

Cline, Roy Del Ruth, and Harry Edwards that the game began to get silly. But the pictures began to get livelier and faster and everybody got fatter.

The first winner of my world's champion award showed that Del Lord could do more than stunts and chases. He created a little two-reel film called *Hubby's Quiet Little Game*, which became a minor motion-picture classic and was the forerunner of the family situation television comedies, as in Danny Thomas's *Make Room for Daddy*, *I Love Lucy* and *My Favorite Husband*.

We built a Toonerville Trolley during the Del Lord era and made comedians Arthur Stone and Andy Clyde corporation executives in charge of a small railroad in competition with a bus line. Our locomotive was a scandal to the boilermakers. It was a swinging, creaking, puffing, falling-apart contraption powered by an Essex mobile engine. We actually ran that thing back and forth between Los Angeles and Phoenix before annoyed farmers put the law on us.

The trick in this picture was a scene in which a little train was about to have a head-on collision with a big train. At the last moment the little train took flight and soared over the big train and back onto the rails, as neatly as a steeplechaser clearing a rail. Jackman and Lord worked that one out with cartoons. They had separate drawings by the hundred made for each move and shot them one frame at a time.

One of the cartoonists who worked on that film pleaded with me for weeks to make a full two-reel cartoon picture. Both Del Lord and I thought the man was addlepated and tedious. We had to get rid of him. I don't remember this cartoonist's name, but I'm sure it was not Walt Disney.

Madeline Hurlock, the beauty who worked in so many of Del Lord's pictures, will recall the afternoon when he instructed her to lie on the ground and permit a lion to put his paws on her chest. Del was persuasive.

"It's just an old kitty, Madeline, just tame old tabby. 'Twon't hurt you, honey," he argued.

"I believe you, Del. I believe every word," Madeline said. "But I don't understand exactly how you want me to play this scene. You wouldn't mind running through it for me, would you?"

Del reminded me of this incident just the other day and he said it was the stunt that frightened him more than anything else he ever did. Madeline had him and he was forced to lie on the ground and permit a mangy lion to nuzzle him.

"You're a blazing idiot—sir," said Madeline Hurlock. "I just wanted to see you do it. I never was afraid of lions."

Miss Hurlock was quite a gal in those days and she still is. After being brave and beautiful for us she quit pictures to become Mrs. Robert Sherwood.

Like every other talented person who ever worked for me, and this with no exceptions, Del Lord finally left the Sennett menagerie to make more money elsewhere. Turpin, Arbuckle, Langdon, Keaton, Murray, Swanson, Chaplin, and even Mabel eventually flew my roost.

Some of these people wound up happily, some of them in bitter disappointment. Only two come to mind with enormous bank accounts today, Charlie Chaplin and Harold Lloyd.

The big pictures soon came, and an industry, not just a fly-by-night carnival on flickers, was around the corner from Edendale in Hollywood.

D. W. Griffith made his first spectacle, *Judith of Bethulia*. Famous Players made *The Prisoner of Zenda* with James K. Hackett. For a while the most solvent companies preferred the classics. Universal made *Uncle Tom's Cabin*, *Robinson Crusoe* and *Ivanhoe*.

William N. Selig released *The Adventures of Kathlyn* in fifteen episodes. And on its heels came *The Perils of Pauline*. Jesse Lasky's brother-in-law, Samuel Goldfish, teamed up with Cecil B. DeMille and changed his name to Sam Goldwyn. Dustin Farnum made *The Squaw Man*. Adolph Zukor created Paramount.

The big glamour stars were J. W. Kerrigan, Crane Wilbur, Carlyle Blackwell, Maurice Costello, and King Baggot, until the arrival of the screen's first great profile, Francis X. Bushman. John Barrymore made his first film, *An American Citizen*, and Mary Pickford signed a contract for $104,000 a year, and soon was making $5000 a week.

Motion pictures were big business from now on.

CHAPTER 13

How To Throw a Pie

WHEN I started these recollections, I opened up with some remarks that might be taken as unbecoming and even downright immodest. I claimed that it had been a long, tired time since any citizens had been rolled in the aisles of a motion-picture house or had been doubled up with laughter while watching television comedians. I was implying, of course, that my own comedies truly murdered the people.

Don't get me wrong. It wasn't me, the Old Man, who was so funny; it was the comical people I had around me. I called myself "King of Comedy," a solemn and foolish title if there ever was one, but I was a harassed monarch. I worried most of the time. It was only in the evenings that I laughed.

I sat in a heavy, creaking rocking chair in the rear of my screening room at Keystone and examined our dizzy productions with a hard eye. When there was anything to laugh at I rocked back and forth with the contented rhythm of a broad-beamed Percheron in a bareback riding act. I seldom needed to say much to my writers, gag men, and actors. They watched the rhythm of the rocker. When I was in full gallop, they assumed that everything was as ridiculous as it should be. If I didn't rock and roar as the rushes went on the screen, everybody took it for granted that the work of art under eye was no good. Then we'd shoot scenes over again.

My main contribution to motion-picture comedy seems to have resided in my boiling point. I was equipped with a natural, built-in thermostat. It turned out that when I got up a full head of steam over a film and began to roll and spout, millions of movie-goers were likely to react the same way. I was a reliable one-man audience.

Since I did produce the Keystone Comedies, it turns out that I have been credited with considerably more inventiveness than I actually possessed. For instance, historians of the drama put me down for the creation of what was once a distinguished facet of cineplastic art—pie-throwing. I'd be glad to claim this honor, if I could claim it honestly, since a pie in the face represents a fine, wish-fulfilling, universal idea, especially in the face of authority, as in cop or mother-in-law. Also, those sequences in which we started building from the tossing of one pie, quickly increasing the tempo and the quantity until we had dozens of pastries in flight across the screen simultaneously, were wholesome releases of nervous tension for the people and made them laugh. But honor for the pie is not mine. It belongs to Mabel Normand.

Mabel was always shown on the screen as a comely girl, usually poor and unfashionable, whose fate was to find herself surrounded by ruffians, villains, and amiable boobs such as Ben Turpin, Ford Sterling, or 285-pound "Fatty" Arbuckle. As our story would begin to release doses of our stock commodity, pandemonium, Miss Normand would invariably be caught in the middle.

But one afternoon in Edendale we were having trouble shooting the simplest possible kind of a scene. Ben Turpin had to stick his head through a door. Since Mr. Turpin's eyes were aimed in all directions, we thought the scene would be funny. It wasn't.

"Don't look into the camera," I instructed Ben. "This is the kind of quick scene we throw away, casual-like."

Turpin stared at me, or approximately at me, with the affronted dignity of a Wagnerian soprano ordered to conceal her tonsils.

"Shoot the eyes! Shoot the eyes!" he squalled. "What do millions of people go to movies for?"

If Turpin had ever seen the Mona Lisa he could have explained an ancient mystery. He would have claimed she was about to break out laughing at him.

Ben squinted, peered, and mouthed, but still the scene

was not comical. Suddenly it was one of the funniest shots ever flashed on any motion-picture screen.

Mabel, who had nothing to do with this sequence, had been watching. She was sitting quietly, minding her own business for once, when she found a pie in her hand. It was a custard pie.

Miss Normand was not startled. At Keystone you were likely to find anything in your hand from a lion to a raw egg. You were as likely to meet an ape on the sidewalk as Gloria Swanson. If you were unwary you were likely to get a shock treatment in the seat of the trousers, mustard in your make-up, or a balloonful of water on your head. We lived our art.

As it turned out, the projectile in Mabel's hand was neither a joke nor an accident. Two carpenters were having custard for dessert. Mabel sniffed, and was inspired.

She weighed and hefted the pastry in her right palm, considered it benevolently, balanced herself on the balls of her feet, went into a windup like a big-league pitcher, and threw. Motion-picture history, millions of dollars, and a million laughs hung on her aim as the custard wabbled in a true curve and splashed with a dull explosion in Ben Turpin's face.

No one expected this memorable heave, least of all Turpin. The grinding camera, going sixteen frames to the second, was full on him. When the custard smote him, Ben's face was as innocent of anticipation as a plate. His aplomb vanished in a splurch[1] of goo that drooled and dripped down his shirt front. As the camera held on him his magnificent eyes emerged, batting in stunned outrage in all directions.

Worse luck for scholars, I don't remember the name of the picture in which the first custard was thrown. The date would have been sometime in 1913. But if we failed in later years to understand the long words laid on us by heavy-duty professors who explain our art to us, we knew a good thing when we saw it, seized upon pie-throwing, refined it, perfected its techniques, and presented it to the theater as a new art. It became, in time, a learned routine like the pratt-fall, the double-take, the slow burn, and the frantic leap, all stock equipment of competent comedians. When the Turpin pie

---

[1]*Splurch:* A technical and onomatopoetic word coined by Mack Sennett; applies only to the effect of sudden custard in the puss.

scene was shown that night in a screening room we saw at once why it was funny.

It was funny, not only because a pie in the face is an outrage to pumped-up dignity, but because Turpin received the custard without a flick of premonition. Non-anticipation on the part of the recipient of a pastry is the chief ingredient of the recipe. And it takes an actor with a stern artistic conscience to stand still and innocent, never wagging an eyelash, while a strong man takes aim at him with such ammunition.

If you don't run with show people you may find this incredible, but it is a fact that many actors are frustrated because they never had a chance to display their integrity and facial control by taking a pie. Franklin Pangborn, for instance, a gentle comedian and a fine artist, pined for many years to receive a custard. When he finally worked for me, we had to write in a scene for him in which he got splurched. Frank did well, too, but he said being pushed backwards into swimming pools while wearing top hat and cutaway was more in his line.

We became scientists in custard. A man named Greenburg, who ran a small restaurant-bakery near the studio, became a throwing-pie entrepreneur. Our consumption was so enormous that this man got rich. After several experiments he invented a special Throwing Pie, just right in heft and consistency, filled with paste, and inedible. He lost most of his eating customers when he began to sell them throwing custards by mistake.

Del Lord, my ace comedy director, soon became the world-champion pie tosser. And "Fatty" Arbuckle, who in spite of his suet was an agile man—the kind of fat man known as light on his feet—became a superb pie pitcher. Arbuckle was ambidextrous and had double vision like a T-formation quarterback. He could throw two pies at once in different directions, but he was not precise in this feat. The Christy Mathewson of the custard was Del Lord.

"This is a delicate and serious art," says Mr. Lord, "and not one in which amateurs or inexperienced flingers should try to win renown. Pie-throwing, like tennis or golf, which depend upon form, requires a sense of balance and a definite follow-through.

"Actually, you don't throw like a shortstop rifling to first base. You *push* the pie toward a face, leaning into your follow-through. Six or eight feet is the limit for an artistic performance.

"You must never let the actor know when you're going to give him the custard in the choppers. Even the most skillful actor, José Ferrer or John Gielgud, for instance, finds it difficult to conceal anticipation.

"The wisest technique is to con your victim into a sense of security and then slip it to him.

"In my day, when I was the acknowledged world-champeen pie heaver, I developed a prejudice for berries with whipped cream. After the actual whomp in the face, the berries trickle beautifully down the actor's shirt and the whipped cream be-splashes his suit. This is muddy, frothy, and photogenic."

Soon after we discovered that a pie is as theatrical a device as Bette Davis's handkerchief or Cyrano's nose, we made a picture called *The Great Pie Mystery*. Pies were thrown every time the heavy would try to do dirt to the girl or the comic. Pies came from everywhere and the audience couldn't see who was throwing them. Our pay-off gag was that the fellow who began telling the story in the first scene was throwing the pies.

We also invented a way to throw pies around telephone poles. We did this by having an expert fly caster out of camera range atop a stepladder. After a little practice he could let fly with rod and reel and make a pie do a figure eight before it hit a guy in the face.

As I was saying a while back, we demanded at least some kind of motivation in our pictures. Always the improbable, never the impossible. The introduction of pie-throwing was no stumbling block at all to our scenario writers. They simply inserted a restaurant or a bakery into the scene whenever it seemed like a good idea to fling a pie.

In speaking of the impossible, one of our most notable laugh-making scenes was one in which we had Charlie Murray tied to a steam boiler in a basement. The boiler actually expanded before the audience's eyes. Now that would be impossible, but that is how the boiler would *seem* to a man who was tied to it.

This rudimentary notion seems to be beyond the capacity of movie makers today. With my boys it was merely the beginning of a laugh sequence. They went on from the expanding boiler and had the *whole house* expand.

There are four kinds of laughs in the theater: the titter, the yowl, the belly-laugh, and the boffo, according to Mr. James Agee, poet and motion-picture critic.

I don't want to create the impression that the titter, the yowl, the belly-laugh, and the boffo were purely mechanical affairs, even when the switcheroo was as charming a device as a tastefully flung pie. Neither my rocking-chair responses nor the genius of my thinker-uppers in the gag room was responsible for all the fun. The Keystone studio was a university of nonsense where, if an actor or actress had any personality at all, that personality developed in full blossom without inhibition. Two of the most special performers who ever came my way were Harry Langdon and Ben Turpin, both prime comics, and as different in outlook, philosophy, and abilities as men could be. Like most of our people—it was some years before we employed the already famous—they came to us from the knockabout stage with no money and no fame.

Harry Langdon came from a small-town vaudeville act in which his specialty was helpless frustration with a balky automobile. Frank Capra, who had progressed from gag man to director, wanted Langdon as soon as he set eyes on him. Harry had a kind of dough-faced baby innocence about him, combined with malice, that delighted Capra. Harry Langdon actually was as innocent as an infant. He had his routines, well learned in vaudeville, and he could do them on demand, but he seldom had the mistiest notion of what his screen stories were about. Like Charlie Chaplin, you had to let him take his time and go through his motions. His twitters and hesitations built up a ridiculous but sympathetic little character. It was difficult for us at first to know how to use Langdon, accustomed as we were to firing the gags and the falls at the audience as fast as possible, but as new talent arrived, we found ways to screen it and to cope with it. I thought for a while Langdon was as good as Chaplin. In some of his pathetic scenes he was certainly as good.

Langdon was an oddly gifted fellow. He drew cartoons for *Judge* and *Puck*, was an expert designer, and curiously handy at carpentry.

On screen he resembled Chaplin in one kind of appeal. He was always the small figure of frustrated good will beset and bewildered by a cruel world of hard rules and economics. But Chaplin, who could be as pitiful as a kicked spaniel or as forlorn and brave as he was in that wonderful scene in which he ate his shoes in *The Gold Rush*, was a man. He was adult. His impulses were often venal. He chased girls with pretentious gallantry and they never took him seriously. He gave you to know, though, that, if ever a girl *had* taken him seriously, he might have made a fool of himself in her boudoir but he would have known exactly what to try to do. Langdon was infantile.

Ladies pursued him. He not only didn't know what was expected of him, he didn't even know they were after him. Everything from sex to money was college algebra to Langdon.

Like Charlie, Harry was a slow starter. Even after we learned how to use him—I mean, saw what his essential character was for screen purposes—we had to give him a hundred feet of film or so to play around in, do little bits of business, and introduce himself. The two were the same in their universal appeal. They were the little guys coping with a mean universe, and, since motion-picture audiences are seldom made up one hundred per cent of tycoons, heroes, or millionaires, a majority of people managed to identify themselves with these comedians. Charlie Chaplin, I suppose, carried out this appeal to the heights in the great pictures he made after he left me. But wonderful as Charlie was, or is, he didn't invent being a little man.

Being a little man was being laughed at and sympathized with long before Charlie, or Langdon, or Turpin arrived in the public eye. Like the fall of dignity, it is one of the essences of comedy. We didn't invent it any more than we invented those two other reliable stock characters, little David with his slingshot and little Cinderella with her pumpkin.

Langdon was as bland as milk, a forgiving small cuss,

an obedient puppy, always in the way, exasperating, but offering his baby mannerisms with hopeful apology. Frank Capra's enormous talents first showed themselves when he saw all this as something that would photograph. Chaplin was a waif, but an adult waif who thumbed his nose at anything.

Under Frank's easy guidance Harry soon became a Keystone star in two-reel comedies. His salary went up to several thousand dollars a week. Langdon became important and unfortunately realized it. Suddenly he forgot that all his value lay in being that baby-witted boy on the screen. He decided he was also a businessman. His cunning as a businessman was about that of a backward kindergarten student and he complicated this by marital adventures, in which he was about as inept as he was on screen. He was soon behind in alimony payments.

He decided that if Harry Langdon pictures could make so much money for Mack Sennett, they could make all that money for Harry Langdon. He heard about the wonderful grosses of big pictures like *The Miracle Man* and *The Birth of a Nation* and concluded that this kind of enterprise was for him.

Other companies were always ready to grab my stars after they had been tested and proved profitable. Soon enough Langdon had an offer from First National. It was a wonder, too. First National offered him $6000 a week and 25 per cent of the net provided he would make six pictures in two years with a limit of $150,000 production cost per picture.

Langdon was delighted by these fat figures, hired Harry Edwards as director at $1000 a week, Capra at $750 a week, and Bill Jenner as his personal manager at $500 a week.

Then he forgot that all this outgoing money was actually his own, merely his advance from First National. He blew the entire $150,000 production budget before he got his first story written.

Poor Langdon failed wretchedly as a producer, and lived brokenhearted and in near-poverty around Hollywood for many years. He did his last work at Columbia, where he attempted to dance in a musical comedy. But working and rehearsing all day exhausted the little fellow. He went into a coma and died of a stroke after lingering for about eight days.

He was bankrupt and neglected, forlorn and forgotten. His shy charm and his gentle humor have yet to be matched on the screen. I wish he had stayed with me. He was a quaint artist who had no business in business. He was hurt and bewildered at the end and he never understood what had happened to him.

Ben Turpin, the cross-eyed man, was an artist too, but another breed of cat.

All comedians, as I keep saying, are sensitive, egotistical persons. They require audiences, applause, security, and reassurance. Some are tender and some are tough. Some are both, but the combination of clown-poet-intellectual is a rare bird and occurs only once in a lucky generation, as in Chaplin.

Turpin came to us from the circus and the vaudeville stage. One of his demands on the studio as soon as his face became known all over the world was that we take out an insurance policy with Lloyd's of London which would pay him one million dollars if his eyes ever came uncrossed. It took only the simplest examination by an honest oculist to assure Lloyd's their money was safe. Ben's eyes were permanently fixed and so were his notions.

This skinny, strutting little man with a Polish piano player's mane of hair and a neck like a string was obsessed by money and by the conviction that he couldn't be funny after 5 P.M. He had a five-o'clock quitting time in his contract. When the bell rang he left no matter what it cost the studio.

Mr. Turpin had several wives. I was not acquainted with all of them, but he brought one to the studio and introduced her around. She was the one who was stone-deaf.

"Mr. Sennett," he said, "I want you to meet my wife. I got the old bag in trouble and had to marry her."

The deaf Mrs. Turpin smiled graciously and acknowledged the introduction.

Ben went on to find Mabel Normand.

"Mabel, I want you to meet the wife," he said. "She used to be a tattooed woman in a honky-tonk. Don't have anything to do with her. She's a blackmailer and a dope smuggler."

Mrs. Turpin beamed fondly on Ben and was delighted to meet his friends.

We paid Turpin $1500 a week at the height of his powers. He invested all his money, bought apartment houses, and became a rich man. He always saved a few dollars a week by personally doing the janitor work at all his apartment houses.

He seldom drove an automobile—a frantic thought at that: who knows how many directions he would have tried to drive at once? He preferred to save money by traveling by streetcar. As he would enter the trolley, he would draw his wrenlike physique up to full strut and squeak at the top of his voice:

"I'm Ben Turpin! Three thousand dollars a week!"

Before taking a seat he would treat the passengers to a 108.

A 108 is an acrobat's term for a comic fall which only the most skillful athletes can perform without lethal results. One foot goes forward, the other foot goes backward, the comedian does a counter somersault and lands flat on his back.

I've seen Turpin perform the 108 not only on streetcars but on concrete sidewalks—if there was an audience handy to whom he could announce himself as three-thousand-dollars-a-week Ben Turpin.

Turpin was an emotional little man, especially under the influence of money or the bottle. Once when we had leased a special train to take a company to Lake Tahoe, scheduled to leave at seven in the evening, Del Lord found Mr. Turpin hitting crescendo in the throes of a crying jag. On such occasions Turpin demanded the attentions of his attorney, his business manager, and his priest.

When Del arrived at the roaring Turpin establishment, Ben had decided that he was all right, but that for reasons obscure to everyone else, his wife (the deaf one) was dying.

Since Mrs. Turpin was blooming with health, Del dismissed the lawyer and business manager, took the priest home, and called up Tommy Lofthaus, chief of the Los Angeles Motor Patrol. Mr. Lofthaus was a good friend because we often gave his cops jobs on off-duty days.

Turpin arrived at the station under full siren, delighted with his police escort. He dashed into his drawing room,

belted down a scotch and soda, and went through the entire
train announcing himself as Ben Turpin, $3000 a week. He
performed a 108 in each car.

We got him to Lake Tahoe in fancy fettle, but Turpin
immediately became victim of a new terror. We had a scene
in which the giant Kalla Pasha, wearing a black fur suit,
worked interchangeably with a live bear which closely resembled him. The script called for Turpin to hop into bed
with the fur-bearing Pasha. Ben winced and keened over this
idea, said it was frightening enough to send a valuable actor
to the looney bin just to think of getting into bed with Kalla
Pasha, let alone a dangerous, man-eating critter. Anyway,
Turpin complained, he had no faith whatsoever in the integrity or the human kindness of anybody connected with
Keystone and Mack Sennett. He was dead sure he was being
framed and would wind up in the embrace of the bear.

During this tantrum our bear got his teeth into his train-
er's arm and almost chawed it off. This upset all of us to some
extent. The accident was particularly dismaying to Turpin.

As things came out, we had to do away with that bear as
a safety measure, but it seemed a shame to waste him. We put
the warm corpse in Kalla Pasha's bed and inserted Mr. Turpin.
Ben's histrionics made a notable scene for a few seconds. He
never forgave us.

It is honorable to give credit where credit is due. It was
Mabel Normand who connived the bedding of Ben Turpin
and the bear.

Turpin seldom invited guests into his home. On the few
special occasions when he did you knew immediately how you
stood with him the moment you entered his parlor. Unless
you were an extremely welcome guest you never got to see his
furniture. He kept every piece draped with white cloths which
he removed only as a delicate compliment of friendship.

Ben could fall, tumble, and prank with the best of my
roughnecks, but his special and universal appeal was, of course,
like Langdon's and Chaplin's, the appeal of all undersized
gents who stand up against Fate anyway. Ridiculous to everyone, yes, but never to himself. In Von Stroheim breeches
and monocle Turpin reduced Von Stroheim and all domineer-
ing Prussians to absurdity. With cross-eyes batting with pas-

sion he could lie on a tiger-skin rug and make the heaving sultriness of Theda Bara (or all pretentious love-making) a silly joke.

The thing was, he seemed to take himself with utter seriousness. You never felt sorry for him no matter how you laughed. You had to see that Mr. Turpin was very, very brave.

This was true also of Buster Keaton. Keaton carried out comic courage to its ridiculously logical absurdity. He never batted an eye or changed an expression, no matter what catastrophes threatened him. "Fatty" Arbuckle brought him to me. The two worked funnily together for several pictures. But these films were so hilarious that Keaton was immediately swamped with offers of more money than I could pay him.

He went to Metro-Goldwyn-Mayer, where he became, in my opinion, the greatest comedian the greatest studio ever had. His pictures eventually cost $200,000 to make and always brought in at least a couple of million dollars—a long cry from our cut-rate productions. Keaton married Natalie Talmadge, sister of Norma, Metro's biggest star at that time.

I fondly claim Buster Keaton. We could have done improbable things together. But the Great Stone Face was cut out for larger works than we had to offer. He was one of the first to set the pattern that kept me in trouble the rest of my life: start with Sennett and get rich somewhere else!

Ben Turpin died rich and having fun. After his retirement it was his hobby to direct traffic at the intersection of Santa Monica Boulevard and Western Avenue. With eyes crossed and arms flailing he engineered some of the most outrageous automotive jams in the history of congested Los Angeles.

He yelled to every motorist, "Ben Turpin, three thousand dollars a week!"

Discovering Charlie Chaplin

MABEL NORMAND and I went un-steady. Days and evenings added up to weeks during which my mother saw more of my girl than I did.

It was not always my fault. I often had to work late in the screening room, in the cutting room, or in long sessions with our writers and gag men. Pathé Lehrman missed no chances to tell Mabel that I had been out with other actresses. She responded by ignoring me when I called her and by encouraging Pathé's gossip, true or false. Lehrman would bring me word that Mabel still considered me the house-dick type. "In your best washed and polished job, she says you look like a Hoboken store detective," he said.

I don't blame Pathé too much. He was in love with Mabel himself. If I had known that at the time I might have been able to fix him. But I didn't know it. I thought he was on my side.

Mabel was as unpredictable as April. When she was happy there was sunshine. When she was sullen there were clouds and lightning. She did as she pleased whether I liked it or not. I tried to amuse her with expensive presents, but by the time I could afford to buy them she no longer set store by furs and diamonds from me. Her salary quickly went from $150 a week to $1500, then to $3000. At the height of her career she earned $5000 a week and received 25 per cent of the net profits of her pictures.

Late in 1912 I suggested that she join me and Mother on a trip to New York. I said I had some important deals to put over which wouldn't take long, after which we could do the town, see all the shows, and have a big fling in the fine restaurants.

"And ride over to Staten Island?" Mabel asked.

"That's a fool idea. We won't have time for that," I said.

Today I know the importance of ferryboat rides over diamonds, but when I was a young man I had not got the hang of this wisdom.

There was a roof garden called the American Theater at Forty-second Street and Eighth Avenue with a vaudeville show put on by William Morris, Sr., who founded the great theatrical agency which now has so many branch offices that its clients claim it is a convenience to be able to go broke simultaneously in Hollywood, New York, London, and Paris.

The agency is first-class, but William Morris's theatricals forty-two years ago were on the second-rate side. Mabel and I saw top-drawer vaudeville at Oscar Hammerstein's Victoria at Seventh Avenue and Forty-second Street and looked at Mr. Morris's offering as an afterthought. We caught one act called "A Night in a London Music Hall," which was more hilarious than anything at Hammerstein's. A "little Englisher," as Mabel called him, duded up in a frock coat, played the part of a drunken spectator in a box. He seemed about forty-five years old. He got into the act on stage, of course, and took part in a knockabout comic fight with the other English actors. The most striking effect of his make-up was an enormous red nose.

"Feller's pretty funny," Mabel said.

"Think he'd be good for pictures?" I said.

"He might be," Mabel said. "Isn't this the man you were asking Hank Mann about?"

I leafed through the program and found his name. Chaplin.

"I don't know," I said to Mabel. "He has all the tricks and routines and he can take a fall, and probably do a 108, but that limey make-up and costume—I don't know."

I filed a note to keep this comedian in mind because I'd been having trouble with Ford Sterling. Sterling was our star male comedian and he had become so popular in the theaters that I had to pay him $250 a week. Kessel and Bauman pleaded with me that this was an impossible sum for a Keystone Cop, even the chief cop, because those quick two-reel features were not sold on a percentage basis, as all pictures are sold now, and there had to be a limit to their cost. I thought of Charlie Chaplin as a possible addition to the cops in case I couldn't settle with Sterling.

When I returned to the studio I looked over the rushes and the current pictures with a hard eye to see if there was any way I could cut a corner or a salary. In this frame of mind I was watching a new picture one night when I spotted a skinny, pale-faced young man who I thought was doing everything wrong.

"That guy a schoolteacher or something?" I asked. "He hasn't got any notion how to be funny. How much do we pay him?"

One of the boys slipped out of the screening room, went over to the bookkeeping department, and came back with the information that we paid this actor $50 a week.

"Fifty bucks," I bellered. "Jumping Jehosephat, we can get comedians for that kind of money. Fire that guy first thing tomorrow morning. Don't even let him get on the lot. What's his name?"

A film editor looked at the back of an envelope where he had made a scribble and told me. Harold Lloyd.

The name meant nothing and I let him go. It is true that Harold was only nineteen years old then, but he was far from being the hopeless actor I thought he was that unfortunate night in the screening room. He had been on the stage since the age of twelve and was just about to become a great comedian. He began his series of wonderful pictures with my competitor, Hal Roach, in 1914, and went straight on to make his classics, *Grandma's Boy*, *Safety Last*, *The Freshman*, and *Speedy*.

It comes to this: if I had had the good sense to keep Harold Lloyd on the lot, and develop him, as we did for so many others, and discover what he could do, we would never have needed another leading comedian at the Mack Sennett studio. If I had recognized his talents at the right time I wouldn't have searched my memory the next day for the name of that obscure British comic Mabel and I had seen in New York.

Since I now live across the street from the Hollywood Roosevelt Hotel, I frequently go there for lunch. So does Harold Lloyd, world-famous man, millionaire many times over, and distinguished Past Imperial Potentate of the Shrine. If there is anybody around for an audience Harold always wags me over and tells the story of how I fired him.

I laugh, but I never thought that tale was half so funny as Harold thinks it is.

Ford Sterling was a circus, stock-company, vaudeville, and musical-comedy comedian from La Crosse, Wisconsin. We had worked together at the old Biograph Studio on Fourteenth Street and he was now my ace comedian in such pictures as *Dirty Work at the Laundry* at that top salary of $250 a week. I knew he was unhappy and wanted more money, but I didn't know how unhappy, or how much money, until he climbed up the tower after quitting time one evening and said he was leaving.

"You can't do this to me, Ford," I said. "And you can't do it to Bauman and you can't do it to Kessel. They will break my head and pull your legs off. We can't let you go. If it's just a matter of a little more money, how does $400 sound?"

I thought this sudden raise would shock Sterling into staying with us.

"Sorry, Mack, but I have to go."

"Ford, you're the best. We are going to make you the greatest. The blue sky's the limit. You'll be the biggest star the motion pictures ever knew. As for the dough, we'll keep raising you until you have to hire stevedores to tote it home in bales."

"How much will you raise it?"

"Ford, we'll make you a fantastical offer with an ironclad contract and no options. Seven hundred and fifty a week."

Sterling leaped from his chair, grabbed his hat, threw it out the window, and yipped like a cowpoke on Saturday night.

"Well, now, good. I'm glad you're going to stay with us. You'll never regret it," I said.

Ford peered out the window to see where his hat landed before he turned back to me.

"Why, no, Mack, I didn't say I was going to stay. I was
just celebrating knowing I'm worth $750 a week. I'm leaving
as soon as my contract expires, and I might remind you that's
a matter of a few weeks."

The certain departure of Sterling put me in a desperate
fix. We claimed to do the improbable always, but it's impossible to run a comedy studio without a leading comedian.
It meant a stoppage of production, a falling behind our
schedule of two short pictures a week. It meant howls from
Bauman and Kessel that I couldn't keep the help happy. I
thought things over in dark brown.

I asked Mabel to come up. "We have to do something
fast," I told her. "We need a leading comedian and I haven't
seen a new funnyman in sight for months."

Mabel suggested that Chester Conklin, Hank Mann, and
"Fatty" Arbuckle were certainly funny.

"As a matter of fact, my good fellow, there have been
modest occasions when I have been slightly amusing myself."

"Mabel, you don't get it," I said. "You're our feminine
star and the cutest trick there is. Conklin and Mann and
Turpin and the other boys on the lot are the top dogs in
their line of work. But they're all specialists. What we need is
a *leading* comedian."

"Hank had somebody in mind," Mabel reminded me.
"Feller he used to work with on the Sullivan-Considine circuit. What's his name?"

"It's that same guy we saw playing a drunk in a box in
William Morris's show in New York, isn't it? What *is* his
name?"

Mabel and I went to dinner at Baron Long's. We tried to
remember the details of the Fred Karno show and the routines
of the small Englishman in the box. We couldn't remember
much, but in the end I thought I'd better take at least a small
chance. I telephoned my New York partners and asked them
to find an Englishman, name unknown, something like "Chap-
man" or "Champion," who had played a drunk scene in *A
Night in a London Music Hall.*

Kessel and Bauman checked the New York booking
agencies next morning and sent the following telegram to Alf

Reeves, manager of the Karno troupe, then playing at Oil
City, Pennsylvania:

> PLEASE ASK MAN WHO PLAYED THE DRUNK IN THE BOX
> AT THE AMERICAN THEATRE TO GET IN TOUCH WITH
> KESSEL AND BAUMAN, LONGACRE BUILDING NEW YORK

Some accounts say that Kessel himself went to Oil City
to approach Chaplin, but my recollection is that Kessel
thought this low-level talent scouting was beneath his dignity. More than likely he sent one of the young men in his
office. At any rate, we found Charlie Chaplin.

According to Kessel, Chaplin was startled by the idea of
acting in motion pictures, which he had never considered, but
at the same time he was diffident and cautious.

"Oh, the flickahs," he said.

But his interest was solid when our man mentioned
money. At that time Charlie was making $35 a week, at the
top $50. We offered $125.

Alf Reeves came in the dressing room and translated the
dollars into terms Charlie could clearly understand.

"That will be twenty-five quid in our money."

Charlie reached for a pen.

Chaplin had to finish his tour for Sullivan-Considine, but
the routing brought him West by way of Kansas City and
Seattle and eventually to Los Angeles. I called on him backstage and was astonished. What I had seen in New York was
a deft, experienced, knockabout, roughneck, middle-aged comedian of the English music-hall type. In Los Angeles I met
a boy. Chaplin was only twenty-four years old.

Our conversation was stilted. Charlie addressed me respectfully as "Mr. Sennett," asked when he would start to
work, and that was that. He reported to the studio in
December 1913.

Chester Conklin, who had joined us only a short time
before Chaplin arrived, recalls having lunch with Charlie
his first day on the lot.

"He was a serious little fellow, very curious, always listening and observing and saying practically nothing except to
ask a few pointed and professional questions. He watched
everybody all the time.

DISCOVERING CHARLIE CHAPLIN 153

"That first day when we had lunch, he said, 'Mr. Sennett has given me a contract for $125 a week. That's more money than I ever saw before. I'm going to save it carefully and very soon I shall be able to return to England with a tidy bank roll.'

"Chaplin was lonely and humble when he started. He knew nothing at all about pictures. When he first saw himself on the screen he was all bowled over.

" 'It cawn't be. Is that possible? How extr'ordin'ry. Is it really me?' he said.

"He had a rough time at first. The main comedians with us then were Mabel, Arbuckle and his wife Minta Durfee, Mack Swain, Harry McCoy, Edgar Kennedy, Charlie Murray, Charley Chase, Slim Summerville, Hank Mann, and Al St. John.

"Boss, you gave that scared little Englishman a dressing room with 'Fatty' Arbuckle and Mack Swain, the hardest-boiled giants we had. For weeks he was scairt to change his clothes in their presence."

We rushed Charlie into a one-reel picture called *Making a Living* as fast as we could. There was trouble immediately. Chaplin worked in his own costume from vaudeville, an Oxford-gray cutaway edged with black tape almost to his ankles, a checked waistcoat, a bat-wing collar, and a polka-dot tie. He wore a tall silk hat, a monocle, and a "way-down-East" droopy mustache.

Chaplin was almost lost in the shuffle when Lehrman tried to put him through our fast paces. Virginia Kirtley, Alice Davenport, Minta Durfee, Chester Conklin, and Pathé himself went into their routines like sprinters taking off from their marks. Chaplin was confused and plaintive. He couldn't understand what was going on, why everything went so fast, and why scenes were shot out of chronology. He and Pathé Lehrman wound up in a major row, with Chaplin so embittered that I had to lay him off for a week to force him to follow instructions.

The first Charlie Chaplin motion picture, his debut on any screen, was released February 2, 1914. Later we sent it out under various titles, such as *A Busted Johnny*, *Troubles*, and

Doing His Best. No matter what we called it, the film was a flop.

Chaplin's music-hall costume was wrong—funny on stage with British comedians, no good on the screen with Chester Conklin playing a Keystone Cop. Pathé Lehrman was technically a sound director, but he worked Chaplin too fast. Chaplin didn't know what he was doing, and we didn't know what to do with Chaplin. Bauman and Kessel raised hell.

"We just got our little company in the black," Bauman squalled at me. "Now with this silly cheap comedian you picked out of nowhere, you're plowing us under the red."

I stuck up for my decision to put Charlie Chaplin in motion pictures. "The trouble is," I said, "we haven't got his character right yet. We haven't got his timing right, either. Or his make-up and costume. We've had to figure out those things for every other comedian on the lot, and we'll have to figure for this one. Give me a little time and I wouldn't be surprised if Charlie Chaplin doesn't turn out to be a fair actor."

For the record Minta Durfee (Mrs. Arbuckle) was Charlie Chaplin's first leading lady. Mabel Normand refused the assignment.

"I should say not, Mack," she told me. "I don't like him so good now that I've seen him."

We knew scarcely anything about Chaplin's background. Not a great deal that is accurate is known now. He was born in London April 16, 1889, the same year that Thomas A. Edison invented motion pictures. His father, Charles Spencer Chaplin, after whom Charlie was named, was part French, part Jew. It is believed that his mother, Hannah, was part Irish and part Spanish. Both mother and father were British music-hall performers. Charlie's half brother, Sidney, who later joined Charlie as an actor, giving us nothing but pains in the neck, was four years older. He was Hannah's son by a former marriage to a bookmaker named Sidney Hawkes. Charlie was taught to soft-shoe dance, sing, tumble, fall, and do pantomime before he was five years old. The family was always hard-up. The father died a drunkard, his mother's mind failed, and Sidney sailed for Africa, leaving Charlie Chaplin, aged about ten, a waif on the London streets.

Sidney eventually returned with a small stake, spotted half brother Charlie's talents, and hired him out to the stage at a small profit to himself. Apparently Charlie played every kind of singing, dancing, and comic role in the repertoire of the provincial music halls. He worked in a one-act play called *The Painful Predicament of Sherlock Holmes*, produced by Charles Frohman, and fell in love with Marie Doro, William Gillette's leading lady. He is also reported to have been in love with Lucille La Verne, who later played on Broadway in hillbilly character parts. When Sidney joined the Fred Karno Company he brought his half brother along with him and launched Charlie on the adventure which pointed to Hollywood. Charlie was seventeen years old at the time.

Some of the titles of the Karno gems will give you a fair idea of Chaplin's training. They include *Saturday to Monday*, *The Dandy Thieves*, *A Tragedy of Errors*, *Jailbirds*, *The New Woman's Club*, *Home from Home*, *Early Birds*, and a sketch called *Mumming Birds*, which developed into *A Night in a London Music Hall*.

Charlie never wore a costume or played a part in any of these acts even remotely suggesting the haberdashery of the tramp he made famous in pictures. He wore black capes and slouch hats and worked in mellerdrammers. He played juvenile delinquents, and he was often made up as a burlesque dude. As a matter of fact, some reporters claim that Charlie became a dude himself at nineteen, had a fancy apartment with Turkish trimmings, and wooed pretty actresses. It seems that he had no such success in the amorous department then as he enjoyed in maturity.

He was not new to the United States when Mabel Normand and I first saw him in 1912. He had played most of Europe with the Fred Karno company, had worked with the Folies Bergère, and had toured America between 1910 and 1913. His first American show was not the now-celebrated *A Night in a London Music Hall*, but a revue called *The Wow Wow's*, in which he competed for New York's applause with trick dogs, tumblers, trapeze artists, and cockney singers. He was finally promoted to the leading comedy part in *A Night in a London Music Hall*, succeeding brother Sidney. The climax of this confection occurs when the intoxicated, red-nosed

comedian, who has been heckling the actors from a box, falls
onto the stage and engages in a wrestling match with a
"Terrible Turk."

As I was saying, in this act Charlie revealed most of the
trade skills of the music-hall people. He could fall, trip,
stumble, somersault, slap, and make faces. These were stock-
in-trade items which we could use. I did not see then, and I
do not know anyone who claims to have seen then, the sub-
tleties and the pathos of the small, hard-pressed man in a
dilemma which a few years later were known as the genius
marks of Chaplin's art.

Charlie's second picture was called *Kid Auto Races at
Venice*. It was released February 7, 1914, five days after his
first film, *Making a Living*. It was directed by Pathé Lehrman,
who acted in it mainly because no one else on the lot was
enthusiastic about taking a chance with the new boy from
London. It was released on the same reel with a documentary
film called *Olives and Their Oil*.

Our plots, if you will patiently call them plots, were
usually no more than incidents inspired by a fire, a house
being moved, or a crowd. We sent Lehrman, Chaplin, and
cameraman Frank D. Williams down to Venice because we'd
read in the morning papers that some exciting automobile
races were under way there. We had no story. We merely
cherished the hope, and not too bright a hope in view of
Charlie Chaplin's previous failure, that if we turned the little
fellow loose to get in the way of newsreel cameras and racing
automobiles, Williams might be able to photograph something funny. That was all we had in mind.

Actually something of world-wide importance had already
taken place a few days before, at the studio.

Chester Conklin was there, so let him tell the story:

"It was a rainy day. We tried to start a picture called
Mabel's Strange Predicament and got soaked. The muslin
drapes we had strung over the hotel entrance scene were
dripping like dishrags. Then it came down in so many buckets-
full to the square inch that the Old Man couldn't even find
sand for us to shovel or carpentry work for us to mash our
thumbs with.

"Some of us hid out in 'Fatty' Arbuckle's dressing room and started a game of pinochle. Sterling and Arbuckle and I were cursing each other over the score and hoping the rain wouldn't let up so's we wouldn't have to go back to work being funny. The rule was that if the rain didn't stop by one o'clock, we could go home.

"It was Chaplin's dressing room, too, so eventually he drifted in. All the boys were competitive and glad of any chance to cut each other's throats, but we had begun to feel sorry for the Limey.

"He had told me a day or so before that he was going to quit motion pictures as soon as he could. 'I'm going to get out of this business. It's too much for me. I'll never catch on. It's too fast. I can't tell what I'm doing, or what anybody wants me to do,' Charlie said. 'At any rate, I figure the cinema is little more than a fad. It's canned drama. What audiences really want to see is flesh and blood on the stage. I'm not sure any real actor should get caught posing for the flickahs.'

"I told him to stick it out. I told him he was going to be something very big in motion pictures. I lied like hell. I didn't think any such thing. I can't claim I had the foresight to see Chaplin's future. But I have as tender a heart as the next roughneck and I couldn't help trying to cheer up that doleful Englishman. His criticisms of movies were nothing but whistling in the dark. Charlie was humiliated and needed encouragement. I talked him out of quitting.

"When Chaplin came in, we invited him to take a hand, but he wouldn't join the game.

"Truth is, Chaplin always declined anything that threatened to cost money. He was willing to let you buy him a drink at the bar, though he took his Scotch-and-soda by the thimbleful, never drank much at any time, but I guess he had not spent much time in London pubs where he would have learned that it was up to him to knock for the next round. We used to match for our lunch checks. Charlie avoided paying for any lunch except his own until we framed him. We wrote numbers on slips of paper, put them in a sugar bowl, and held a drawing. It was a crooked drawing. All the numbers were the same and Mr. Chaplin was out of pocket.

"Charlie ambled about the room looking pale and worried. Arbuckle's trousers were hanging on a chair. That isn't quite right. Those pantaloons covered anything they hung on. They sprawled over the chair like a circus tent with the center pole knocked down. Charlie fingered the pants.

" 'Mind?'

"Arbuckle didn't mind. Charlie got into the pants. He was a sight and we laughed at him. Poor guy, I guess that was the first time anyone had laughed at him since he closed his music hall act. He flip-flopped across the room and found Charlie Avery's coat. Avery was a small man and the fit was snug, with the tails jutting out a little, like a shabby-genteel sparrow. Charlie picked up a derby hat that belonged to Arbuckle's father-in-law, and clapped that on. He had a little trick with the hat he'd learned in the pantomimes. He tilted it from the rear and made it wabble on his head.

" 'Boy, you got something there. Looks like just what you need,' somebody said.

"Charlie fumbled his way out of the dressing room, walking with a splay-footed shuffle that we had never seen before, and went over to the make-up department. He returned with some crepe hair he grabbed off the bench, and started experimenting with it under his nose. He trimmed it with scissors, found a small black tuft he could wiggle, and stuck it on his lip with spirit gum. He found a thin bamboo cane somewhere and began to do tricks with it. We'd never seen anything like it. The cane seemed to come alive in his hand. It *gestured*. He tipped his hat with it. His starched cuff came loose, slid down the cane, and shot back to his wrist.

"I don't know whose brogans he got hold of, Ford Sterling's, I think. They were over-size. The rain slackened then and Charlie jogged over to the hotel lobby set and made like a drunk. He got his foot caught in the cuspidor. His cane betrayed him and tripped him up. The mustache wiggled like a rabbit's nose. A crowd gathered.

"We helped him out. A couple of people pretended to be a honeymoon couple going to bed. Charlie blundered in, tittered, tipped his hat—from the rear—spun around and made an exit hopping around a corner on one foot.

"Want to know something? Chaplin is lefthanded. Most people don't know that. As he took that exit he made it look

Yes, this is I, shall we say, "some years back," when it still bothered me to be called "The Old Man." I thought the mustache made me look rakish. Once I also dyed my hair. It turned green.

Motion-picture comedy was born here in bedlam and beauty. It all started in 1912—the Keystone Cops, the custard pies, the Bathing Beauties, and Charlie Chaplin. Upper right, under the "M" on the roof, is the tower where I soaked and worried in the oversized tub. The site at 1855 Glendale Boulevard is now occupied by the National Van Lines.

Photos by George F. Cannons

Leap for life from a mock plane perched on a water tank in the Glendale hills. The angles of the three cameras gave the illusion of frightening height. I am directing, second from left on the ground. Below, director Del Lord was the master of getting automobiles into incredible situations. He expected all actors to be acrobats and to enact scenes like this as part of a routine day's work.

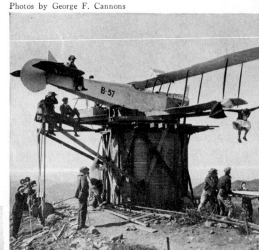

How to saw a woman in half—lengthwise. This is Marie Prevost in trouble, above and below, in a spoof called East Lynne with Variations. The others are Bobby Dunn, Heinie Conklin, with Ben Turpin to the rescue.

George ("Fat") Lobeck has just enjoyed the accolade of Sennett success, a custard pie in the face. World-champion pie thrower was Del Lord, who considered his technique an art. Below is Phyllis Haver, who joined us when she was barely sixteen and soon left to become a dramatic star. With her, inevitably, Ben Turpin.

The front gate of the studio and a safari of girls and touring cars. In the 'teens and early twenties we shot as many pictures outside as we did on the lot. There were always the city streets, and there was always Ben Turpin.

Photo by George F. Cannons

Burlesque is satire with a bed slat. Here Harry Langdon and the girls were kidding "The Sea Hawk." We called our drammer The Sea Squawk. At right is Jack Cooper and Alberta Vaughan in Smile Please with Harry. He was a confused, funny, gentle little man who ended sadly.

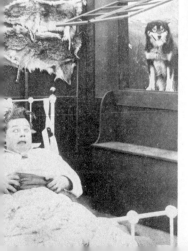

Roscoe ("Fatty") Arbuckle was fat, fast, and funny, a 285-pound acrobat who looked like a cynical baby. He turned a somersault and became a star.

Phyllis Haver, Charlie Murray, and Heinie Conklin, above, could poke fun at anything, even at Salome. They called this masterwork Salome vs. Shenandoah. At right is Madeline Hurlock, a famous Sennett Beauty, now Mrs. Robert E. Sherwood. Such pictures would usually be captioned ". . . with Billy Bevan, and friend." This was no friend.

Photo by George F. Cannons

In 1924 my clowns hurled automobiles off the cliffs of Santa Monica with commercial abandon. Al St. John is the convict and the picture was called Surrender or Else!

Our stars had to get run over by trains, leap from bridges, and risk their necks for laughs. This is a scene from An Innocent Villain, about 1915.

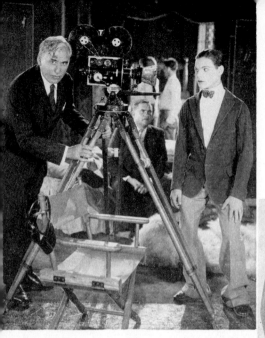

Left, an early motion picture, the early Mack Sennett, and Eddie Quillan. The cameras and I changed through the years. Eddie always seemed to look the same. Below, Gloria Swanson—she was so pretty I put her under contract the first time I saw her—in an early Keystone film with Bobby Vernon and a character actor.

Below, "Always the improbable, never the impossible," was the studio motto. Well, an ape might steal the steering wheel of a Tin Lizzie and run it into the Los Angeles River. George ("Fat") Lobeck is the damp actor in the derby.

My Mabel Normand, from a miniature by Kepec. She was as unpredictable as a spring morning and she was in love.

One of Mabel's famous scenes in The Extra Girl was the sequence in which she led a lion around the lot under the impression that she was taking a dog for a walk. Here she discovers her mistake. Below, left, Mabel about 1920, entering the old Hollywood Hotel, and right, in Suzanna, one of her best, just before she became involved in the William Desmond Taylor case.

Left and below, a wistful Mabel Normand in two other scenes from The Extra Girl. Louella Parsons and Hedda Hopper are in agreement about this: Mabel was a great actress.

The great Chester Conklin, wearing the sign, is the man who encouraged Charlie Chaplin to stay in pictures when the new and bemused English actor was about to give up. At the typewriter, Vera Steadman.

Left, reducing authority to absurdity was a standard formula. On Patrol, starring Jim Donnelley, Kalla Pasha, Mildred June, and Kewpie Moran was a reducing exercise of 1922.

Phyllis Haver again—not the first of the Mack Sennett Bathing Beauties, but soon, for revealing reasons, the best known.

The incomparable Kalla Pasha. Ben Turpin couldn't tell him from a bear.

Bathing Beauties in these risqué costumes shocked some people before 1920. The actors above are Billy Bevan and Eddie Gribben. Below, Eddie Cline is directing for a typical publicity still. The girls never went near the water. Mabel was jealous of all of them.

Photo by George F. Cannons

Photo by George F. Cannons

Once, in a scene like the one above, the sawdust caught fire. It delighted us and I kept the accident in the picture for laughs.

Above, She was a high-school girl named Jane Peters. I discovered her and changed her name to Carole Lombard. The lovely at left began as a Bathing Beauty and soon became a star under the name of Toby Wing.

Smick-smack beauties like Anita Barnes, above, started at $3.00 a day. But I made them world-famous by having $250-a-week cameramen photograph them. Below is Ford Sterling (in uniform), the first real comedy star in motion pictures. When he left me, he was succeeded by a timid and inexperienced little Englishman named Chaplin, whose first pictures were failures.

Bing Crosby was singing with a band when I put him in pictures and was astonished to find out that he could act. The blonde with Franklin Pangborn is Toby Wing, the cop is Bud Jamison, and the girl in Crosby's arms is Babe Kane. In 1925 a young and unknown actor appeared briefly in Sennett pictures.

The scene above is from The Gosh Darn Mortgage, and the actor leaning in the doorway is Charlie Farrell. And remember beautiful Thelma Parr, on Farrell's arm?

You can see, at left, how I felt when Ralph Edwards trapped me into appearing on his television show, "This Is Your Life." With me are Phyllis Haver and Jack Mulhall, who forgave me for once blacking his eye.

as if the door smacked him full in the face. We were watching his right hand, of course. Everyone does that unconsciously. He caught the door with his left and fooled us.

"Mabel and Ford and Hank and Avery and Arbuckle and Minta Durfee were laughing at Charlie. We didn't notice the Old Man had come down from the tower and was standing in the rear. All of a sudden we heard him.

" 'Chaplin, you do exactly what you're doing now in your next picture. Remember to do it in that get-up. Otherwise, dear old England is beckoning.' "

And there it was. Charlie Chaplin's tramp costume was seen first in *Kid Auto Races in Venice.*

One of the legends about Chaplin is that he tangled with Ford Sterling when he arrived at the studio and that the two comedians fought it out to the death. Sterling lost the battle and departed, leaving Chaplin in command as top comic. As I've already said, the truth is that we brought Charlie in because we already knew that Ford Sterling was quitting. As a matter of fact, Sterling was thirty-two years old and a major star when twenty-four-year-old Charlie entered the scene. Ford did not consider Chaplin a competitor.

Ford not only gave Chaplin a leg up by contributing a pair of Size 14 shoes that became as famous as the Seven League Boots or Cinderella's slipper, but worked in two pictures with him. These were *Between Showers,* with Sterling, Chester Conklin, and Chaplin, directed by Pathé Lehrman, and *Tango Tangles,* which I supervised with Sterling, Arbuckle, Conklin, and Chaplin.

If Charlie did not become a major star with his first handful of pictures, there were a number of reasons why. He was working with, and at the same time against, seasoned and jealous experts. In his first one-reeler he was up against Chester Conklin. In his second he had to cope with Pathé Lehrman, who also directed and who gave himself the best camera angles. In his third his competition was Mabel Normand, Hank Mann, Chester Conklin, and Al St. John. In his fourth, Sterling and Arbuckle. In his fifth, Arbuckle and Minta Durfee, and in his sixth, Sterling, Arbuckle and Conklin.

Never again in all his pictures, from *Making a Living* in 1914 to *Limelight* in 1952, did Charlie Chaplin face up to such competition.

He worked in eleven pictures with Mabel Normand, the greatest motion-picture comedienne of any day, and they got along fine.

After Mabel saw what Charlie could do in his new costume and tramp character, she changed her mind about "that Englisher." She not only wanted to work with him but wanted to help him. Charlie knew nothing about screen acting. He did not know how to behave in front of a camera, or why he was directed to move left or right in order to match a scene shot the day before. He was baffled by instructions to react to someone off camera—someone who would be inserted in the next day's shooting. Mabel patiently explained these and other simple techniques to Charlie, who had rebelled when Pathé Lehrman gave him orders. He despised Lehrman and he had reasons. Pathé was intelligent, glib, quick with a gag, and he knew how to make a picture, but he was tough, impatient, careless of actors' safety, and incapable of understanding that Charlie Chaplin was not an automaton.

Mabel and Charlie had much in common. She was as deft in pantomime as he was. She worked in slapstick, but her stage business and her gestures were subtle, not broad. Lehrman was not the man to appreciate what happened when Charlie, while being dragged heel-first on the sidewalk by a cop, reached out and plucked a violet. Mabel—and millions—understood perfectly.

She often invited him to her dressing room to encourage him and to talk things over. Aside from that, being invited to Miss Normand's dressing room had practical advantages. She had the only quarters equipped with a stove.

They actually studied French together. Whether Chaplin ever became fluent I do not know. My conversations with him were carried on in basic English because what we had to talk about always involved either a comedy situation or dollars. But Mabel continued her lessons for years and became facile. She was one of those persons with an ear for the "tune" of any language or any kind of idiom. I imagine her grammar was atrocious, but she spouted French effortlessly.

Mabel's and Charlie's inspiration for becoming linguists was Max Linder. Max was the celebrated French comedian whose pictures for Pathé Frères in Paris had influenced me as long ago as when I was working for Biograph and Griffith on Fourteenth Street. And there is no doubt that his style had a considerable impact on Charlie Chaplin's development as a comedian.

Mabel and Chaplin rejoiced when Monsieur Linder came to Hollywood with drums beating, but Max was a failure. Charlie Chaplin was the big little man in comedy and Linder eventually returned to Paris, disappointed.

Mabel and Chaplin were under the impression that Linder spoke no English. They admired him as an artist, which he was, and decided they should pay their respects together. So they studied French. Here are some of the phrases they learned preparatory to calling on the master:

Number One: "Good morning, Mr. Linder, the sky is gray; it is covered with clouds."

Number Two: "Open your umbrella."

Number Three: "The pen of my aunt is in the other room."

Number Four: "Where is the concierge? I want a room with a bath."

With these and other phrases patly memorized Miss Normand and Mr. Chaplin called on Monsieur Linder.

Mabel opened the conversation with Number One: "Bonjour, Monsieur Linder, le ciel est gris; il est couvert de nuages."

Linder bowed gravely and showed them into his drawing room.

Chaplin's gambit was Number Four: "Où est le concierge? Je désire une chambre avec une salle de bain."

"C'est bien ça, monsieur," Linder said, bowing them to a divan.

Miss Normand tried Number Three: "La plume de ma tante est dans l'autre chambre."

"C'est là, certainement," Linder responded.

"Ouvrez votre parapluie," said Chaplin, remembering Number Two.

"Magnifique," said Monsieur Linder, staring at Mabel and Chaplin with what must have been considerable awe.

"And a most delicate attention, *mes amis. Absolument* the most amazing French I've ever heard in my life. But please do me the favor of speaking English. I am trying so hard to savvy your doggone difficult native lingo."

Mabel was the only person at the studio with whom Charlie Chaplin ever played jokes. It became a habit of theirs to walk arm-in-arm on Wilshire Boulevard until they came to a congested intersection where a policeman had stopped traffic. When they were sure they had an audience, Charlie would scream, do a somersault and a fall, and writhe on the sidewalk in a frothing fit.

Mabel would take his head in her lap, stroke his brow.

"My poor darling husband," she would cry. "He'll be all right in a moment, if none of you does anything to frighten him. He is completely insane and escaped from the asylum this morning.

"Only I can induce him to return."

The pair would then get up and stalk solemnly away.

Three or four blocks further on Mabel and Charlie would reverse roles. Mabel would topple to the pavement, jerk in spasms, stiffen, and scream in unknown tongues.

Charlie would explain to the crowd which quickly gathered.

"Do be very patient and very quiet," he would say to the policeman and the bystanders. "My wife is a homicidal maniac, but perfectly harmless when she is with me. I am taking her to the hospital now."

Charlie and Mabel appeared together in his third picture, *Mabel's Strange Predicament,* one reel of nonsense based on an incident. Charlie in his new tramp costume waddles into a hotel lobby, searches his pantaloons for a nickel to make a phone call, finds he had no nickel. Mabel trips in, made up to be winsome, leading a fashionable dog. Naturally Mr. Chaplin stumbles over the leash and becomes entangled with dog and Mabel. During the scuffle he gets his foot caught in a brass cuspidor.

As I recall it, that is as detailed a synopsis as we worked with when we shot the picture. But Charlie also tripped over Pathé Lehrman and became so embroiled in debate with his director that I had to move in and take over the production. Also in that picture were Harry McCoy, Alice Davenport, Hank Mann, Chester Conklin, and Al St. John. It was a magic thing for the newcomer to establish himself at all against that kind of competition.

In his two pictures with Ford Sterling, Chaplin was not the star, but showed he could hold his own. *Tango Tangles* was off-the-cuff and without make-up. We took Chaplin, Sterling, Arbuckle, and Conklin to a dance hall, turned them loose, and pointed a camera at them. They made like funny, and that was it. In *Between Showers*, with Chaplin, Sterling, Conklin, and Emma Clifton, a one-reel epic unwinds about what happens when Charlie and Sterling try to help a pretty girl over a puddle.

Now we were learning how to use an actor who was on his way to becoming an artist. Still, Charlie was considered an odd-ball by my team of professional slam-bangers. They considered him cheap. He wasn't cheap. He simply didn't enjoy drinking or gambling. He was lonely and *liked* to be lonely. He walked the streets at night peering at things and people. He lived in a shabby hotel and he stayed in it until long after he became worth a million dollars a year.

A friend who visited him in his small room recalls that Chaplin was innocent about money. He had a small, scuffed trunk tightly strapped and locked, which he opened cautiously to show his friend. The top tray was stacked with slips of green paper.

"These are most of my checks from the studio," Charlie said. "I'm saving them up, as you see, most carefully. As soon as I have twenty thousand pounds I shall quit movies and return to England."

Chaplin's friend was experienced. He explained that checks were not the same as money, certainly not Mack Sennett checks, and that any vouchers signed by me should be cashed on the day of receipt.

"My God," said Chaplin.

He became a steady customer of banks.

By the time Chaplin had made a dozen one- and two-reel pictures, we knew what a great find we had. And Charlie himself was sure of something: he no longer wanted to be directed by Pathé Lehrman. He had watched and listened and asked questions, and learned from Mabel Normand. Chaplin was still shy and inarticulate and I do not know that he ever found a way to say to me why he thought he was different from other comedians. But he knew it.

Late in April 1914 he received screen credit as a director and writer. The plot had him follow a married woman from a park to a hotel and into her bedroom. Her husband, the enormous Mack Swain, finds them there and throws Charlie out. But that night the lady walks in her sleep—into Chaplin's room, where else? Charlie now becomes gallant and attempts to lead the wife back to her husband. The husband misunderstands, takes Chaplin by the seat of his pants, and throws him out into the rain.

It was called *Caught in the Rain* and released May 4, 1914. He had come part way. But you will note that he did not create his pathetic clown, his universal "little man," or the rhythms which reminded critics of ballet, the first time he tried.

The Chaplin pictures began to make money, not a great deal, but a good profit. We were happy. Ford Sterling had been adequately replaced, Mabel Normand had a new partner, and Chaplin was delighted with himself on screen. I raised his salary to $250 a week.

When *Caught in the Rain* was shown in our screening room we had an unusual audience. Every director was present. I sat in my big rocking chair to see what would happen. I could hear Dell Henderson, Del Lord, Pathé Lehrman, and my other comedy makers suck in lungfuls of air, getting ready to let loose jeers and catcalls.

Instead they applauded from the first scene. My rocking chair went into action and stayed at full gallop.

With Chaplin launched I could turn my attention to other pressing affairs. Mabel, for instance. And Mother. Mother had begun to have some oddly expensive ideas.

And it was time for the Mack Sennett Bathing Beauties to make their entrance.

CHAPTER 15

They Had Such Lovely Legs

I USED to know a widow in Glendale who inherited a fortune from her spouse, a hard-fisted Milwaukee brewer. Her tears, and the ink of the probate judge's signature, were barely dry when she moved to California and began to solace herself with culture in wholesale batches. She went in for Art, especially Greek and Roman statues. Pretty soon her front hall and drawing room were populated with so many bronze and marble replicas of young men with muscles that her establishment looked like the locker room of one of Dean Cromwell's track teams.

She also had cupids. These were in plaques and friezes, the kind of little boys Aldous Huxley once described as "cherubs condemned to the perpetual inspection of each other's behinds."

The widow's collection was dusted and polished by an aged colored woman of the Mammy type who had bathed and fetched up several generations of boys, including a half dozen of her own by various husbands. I wondered what she thought of Art, so I asked her a question.

"Nellie, doesn't a conservative, churchgoing girl like you get upset by all this nakedness?"

Nellie looked at me with a watermelon-wide grin.

"Gracious no, Mr. Mack," she said. "Nekkedness ain't no treat to you and me, is it?"

Well, I did create the Mack Sennett Bathing Beauties. The Beauties accomplished even more than Miss Annette Kellerman toward unshrouding the American girl from several yards of heavy wool and letting her be herself in swimming. But I enter a demurrer when it comes to being recorded in popular annals as the man who *invented* nudity. Some people seem to believe that. The subject comes up to embarrass me every now and then.

A few years ago I was proud to be the guest of the French Government at the annual film festival in Cannes. They showed some of my early comedies, *Love and Dynamite, She Sighed by the Seaside, Hoboken to Hollywood,* and *Caught in a Cabaret* with Charlie Chaplin and Mabel Normand. They laughed at the pictures and called upon me for a speech.

I stumbled to my feet. According to an interpreter who claimed he could understand me, I began my address with: "Ladies and gentlemen, and you people of France——"

This drew an even bigger laugh than the pictures. Then the French got around to what the French often have in mind. They took me to the beach and showed me a hundred or so of the most beautiful women in the world in Bikini bathing suits.

"You're the inventor of the bathing beauty, Monsieur Sennett," they said. "How does this strike you?"

I yawned. The French were amused by such sophistication. Then I explained. "You've gone too far," I said. "This leaves nothing to the imagination. I'm sorry I yawned but I did it because I'm tired and sleepy and nothing here wakes me up. A charming girl getting on a streetcar revealing a neat ankle in nylons is much more exciting."

I recall a trip to Paris some years ago when some local show people thought the proper entertainment for Mack Sennett would be a visit to the Café Cent Belles Poules on the Rue Blondel. When the door was opened not less than one hundred heavy-chested, long-legged girls wearing exactly nothing started toward me. I took my foot in hand and retreated faster than the Hessians at Trenton. There is neither charm nor fun in such a spectacle. I got out of that place fast, mortified.

Let me tell you how the Mack Sennett Bathing Beauties started, and why.

In 1914 I had some of the smartest and most expensive press agents purchasable working for me to sell my pictures, grab free space in the newspapers and magazines, and get my name spelled right. One of the best publicists I ever had was the late Harry Carr, who later became a distinguished columnist for the Los Angeles *Times*. But even with this kind of talent we had difficulty inducing editors to accept pictures of Chaplin, Turpin, Conklin, Arbuckle, Keaton, and the rest of our funnymen. News editors were not enchanted when our boys came in with expensive art of clowns with tired walrus mustaches and droopy-bottomed pantaloons.

One morning as I went through the *Times*, in my tub, I noticed a three-column picture on Page One of a pretty girl who had been involved in a minor traffic accident. The picture made the front page for two obvious and attractive reasons. The young lady's knees were showing.

On Page Four was a one-column cut, probably six or eight years old, and doubtless dug up from the morgue, of President Woodrow Wilson.

I called in the staff. "Boys, take a look at this. This is how to get our pictures in the papers. Go hire some girls, any girls, so long as they're pretty. Especially around the knees. Take a good look."

When we had the girls, we posed them with our comedians. Some genius at Keystone—I think it was Jimmy Starr, now motion-picture editor of the Los Angeles *Herald & Express*—had the pictures shot so that the comedians could not be cut out.

The results were highly satisfactory. Mack Sennett pictures began to get more space in the press than all the studios in Hollywood combined.

The next step was obvious. "Get those kids on the screen," I told our people. "Sure, I know they can't act, but they don't have to act. Put them in bathing suits and just have them around to be looked at while the comics are making funny."

Our wardrobe department supplied what it thought was appealing in the way of bathing suits. They sent over high rubber shoes, black cotton stockings, dark blue bloomers, and voluminous tunics with tatted neckpieces and ballooning sleeves.

I howled in dismay and told them to junk all that stuff

and design some bathing suits that showed what a girl looked like. The whole studio turned conservative on me in one of the most unexpected upheavals since the San Francisco earthquake. Even the comedians complained I was risqué. But I went ahead and put the girls on film in the most abbreviated suits possible forty years ago. When the studio received hundreds of letters of protest from women's clubs I knew I had done the right thing.

Like the first Keystone Cops, the names of the first Mack Sennett Bathing Beauties are still in dispute. I can name three for sure, Marie Prevost, Evelyn Lynn, and Cecile Evans. Then came, at various times, Phyllis Haver, Carole Lombard, Juanita Hansen, Virginia Fox, Irene Lentz, Sally Eilers, Madeline Hurlock, Lucille Miller, Natalie Kingston, Jacqueline Logan, Julia Faye, Vera Steadman, Gloria Swanson, and hundreds more.

Phyllis Haver was not one of the original Bathing Beauties, but she was blond and smick-smack and charming. For a whole generation of Americans I imagine she represented the Bathing Beauty. She was in town the other day and had some quaint memories of those days:

"I was fifteen and said I was sixteen when I came to Keystone, straight out of Manual Arts High. Roy Del Ruth interviewed me on the lot and took me up to the tower.

"Mack, so far as I remember, you said only two sentences. 'Let's see your legs, Phyllis. Hmmm, you'll do.'

"I started at twelve dollars a week, like everybody else, with a three-dollar bonus for working after four o'clock. But I became a leading lady in three days because you had some wild scene in which a girl had to be tied to a burning post. Being new and expendable, I was elected. That made me a leading lady and upped my salary to twenty-five dollars a week.

"Remember the flu epidemic? Your mother made everybody on the lot wear a bag of asafetida attached to a little string around the neck. And as for costumes being considered risqué, why women didn't even have bosoms in those days, not on the Keystone lot, anyway. According to the Keystone style, all the girls had to bind their bosoms like mummies and wear waistlines halfway down to their knees. There must have been at least a hundred and seven Bathing Beauties making twelve dollars a week at that time.

THEY HAD SUCH LOVELY LEGS

"When you paid me that big fat salary of twenty-five dollars, and gave me feature billing, William Randolph Hearst had just started in the motion-picture business and he sent for me. I was amazed when he offered to pay me $750 a week to leave you and join Cosmopolitan Pictures. I ran home to Mother and told her I was about to be a rich and famous motion-picture star.

" 'Honey, we better think this over,' Mother said. 'You know darned well you have only three expressions, the "oooh," the "smile," and the "take it!" Baby, you can't act, and the best thing for actresses who can't act is to stay with Mr. Sennett.'

"Mother and I went up to the tower and talked it over with you. And you gave me $150 a week.

"I wasn't much of an actress. When you were shooting *The Extra Girl* I missed a call from the studio, stayed home two days when I should have been working, was replaced in the picture—and not even you knew the difference."

I have to interrupt Phyllis Haver here to remind you that, no matter what she says now, she was an excellent actress. When she left me in 1925 she went with Cecil B. DeMille and starred in a number of fine pictures, including *The Way of All Flesh*, *What Price Glory?* and *Chicago*.

More than that, Phyllis was a good talent scout and I wish I had taken her advice about an actor.

"Met a dead-pan boy with big black eyes," she told me. "He isn't a comedian, of course, but there's something compelling about this guy and it seems to me that you ought to put him under a little contract and find some way to use him."

I told her I already knew the boy she was talking about, Rudolph Valentino. He lived in back of Roth and Rossen's furniture store on Sunset and Gardner. One afternoon when I was driving the Fiat toward Beverly Hills, Rudy was standing on the corner. I gave him a ride and asked him how he was getting along. Rudy said he didn't think he was making much progress in pictures, but that a new one had just been suggested which he thought might do him some good.

"Trouble is," Valentino said, "I can't pronounce the title. It's the 'Four Horsemen of a long word I can't say.' "

I told Rudy I didn't know anything about that story but that it sounded like there might be a good part in it for him.

Let me jump several years ahead of the Bathing Beauty times to complete my Valentino anecdote. Rudolph Valentino did, of course, star in *The Four Horsemen of the Apocalypse*. When it was finally released there was doubt among distributors and theater managers about whether a long religious picture could possibly make a dime at the box office. I, too, was an exhibitor by then. I had the old Mission Theater, in downtown Los Angeles with Jesse Crawford at the pipe organ, and admittance prices jacked as high as the traffic would bear. I wanted big pictures with world-famous stars, certain to be profitable, and I took no chances on new players or on pictures with "messages."

My mother heard about *The Four Horsemen*.

"Run that picture, Mike," she said.

I protested. I even protested two or three times, but Mrs. Sinnott was firm. On her command I opened *The Four Horsemen of the Apocalypse* at the Mission and I forget now how many months it played—close to half a year, I believe.

I said to Mother, "This is the first time you ever interfered in my business. And you made us a great deal of money. But why did you do it?"

"Why, Mike," Mother said, "it wasn't a matter of *business* at all. This was religion."

One more note on Rudolph Valentino. I suppose even today's cool kids in junior high school who've never seen a Valentino picture have heard about him as the great sheik of the twenties with Vaselined black hair, the tango gigolo of the silent screen, a lugubrious symbol of an era of cloud-cuckoo nonsense. Actually he was a shy, gentle boy. He came to America from Italy to be a gardener, worked in dance halls, and became a movie star.

When Valentino was at the height of his hothouse fame, the sixteen-year-old daughter of a friend of mine pleaded with me for months to introduce her to him. Who can resist a sixteen-year-old girl? So one afternoon I took her to call on Rudy at his home on Whitley Heights. Valentino and the child had a long walk and a private talk in his garden. I asked her on the way home what their conversation was about.

"He told me to work hard in school," she said.

The most famous actress who was ever a Mack Sennett Bathing Beauty was, of course, Miss Gloria Swanson, and I have a story about her. Miss Swanson says it isn't true.

"It makes a better story my way, Gloria," I said. "And anyway, the way I tell it I don't fancy it up much. You going to be a story killer, of all people?"

Here it is.

It begins when an assistant came up to the tower office to tell me that there was an attractive girl on the lot asking for a job. I wasn't fascinated by this approach. Pretty girls came by the dozen every day. But I looked out of the window, clapped an eye on this one, and hurried down.

She said her name was Gloria, that she had worked for Essanay in Chicago, and that she was ambitious. She had a cute nose and beautiful eyes. The Swanson eyes are indeed magic and beautiful. It isn't a trick of make-up that beams them at you from the screen.

I went overboard. "Gloria, I think you have a good chance to succeed in this business if you're willing to work hard and learn, and start from scratch."

I had an ex-elephant tender on the lot. His name was Wallace Beery. We had tried him in various kinds of roles without much success until someone dressed him up as a Swedish servant girl and photographed him. The strong-armed, scowling Mr. Beery in this guise was so outrageously ridiculous that we soon had a profitable new comedian on our hands.

As I talked to Gloria Swanson, Mr. Beery struck various nonchalant and disinterested poses, leaning on posts, tying his shoelaces, examining the sky for weather prophecies, all the time edging closer to Gloria Swanson and me. I saw Gloria cut those eyes at him several times.

"Okay, Miss Gloria Swanson, you're hired. Report at nine o'clock tomorrow morning ready for work, and I'll have a little contract ready for you."

I was excited about the possibilities of this new actress. When nine o'clock arrived and she did not report, I presumed she had lost her way in the studio and couldn't find me. I sent secretaries out to look for her. She finally came in, looking tired, at eleven o'clock.

"Good afternoon, Miss Swanson," I said.

"Mr. Sennett, I'm awfully sorry, just awfully sorry."

"What happened? Where were you? And by the way, you look entirely different."

"Mr. Sennett, I just couldn't make it. Even after all those wonderful things you said, and the promise of a job, and a contract. Last night I drove up to Santa Barbara with Wallace Beery and got married."

Miss Swanson assures me that she was married to Wallace Beery before she applied to me for a job, but I like my story better.

Gloria appeared as a Bathing Beauty in only a few Mack Sennett pictures. Her dramatic talents and her beauty were so outstanding that even on the custard-pie lot we recognized them at once and gave her acting parts as soon as we could. Even so we were comedy merchants. Miss Swanson played her first lead with Chester Conklin, known at the studio as "Mr. Droopy-bottom" in a picture called *The Pullman Bride*.

I know a man who claims that all inanimate objects are perverse. He says things deliberately hide from him. I believe this man has discovered an important new natural law. My tobacco, my reading spectacles, and my most important business papers are all perverse and plot together against me. But I found my specs and three pieces of paper the other day.

One was Gloria Swanson's first Hollywood contract, signed by her and by me. It is dated May 29, 1916, and employed her to work for Keystone studio for the six months ending November 28 at sixty-five dollars a week. It contained an option clause raising her salary to seventy dollars a week for the six-month period ending May 28, 1917.

Next to this was my contract with Wallace Beery, dated October 30, 1916, employing him as an actor and director at fifty dollars a week with options raising him to one hundred dollars a week on January 30, 1917. But a note attached to this, dated October 30, 1917, reminds me that I fired Mr. Beery as of that date. I don't know now why I let Beery go. More than likely it was a matter of inventory—too many comedians on the lot at the same time. At any rate it was only a few months later that he hit his stride as a star with other studios—at $10,000 a week.

Along with these mementos there pops up a letter which I shall quote in full:

"Dear Sir: Mrs. Gloria Swanson requests me to advise you that she will discontinue her services with the Keystone Film Company. Yours very truly, Milton K. Young."

The date of this letter from Gloria's agent is September 19, 1917. Mrs. Beery left me for Cecil B. DeMille and Paramount. One year later her salary was $20,000 a week. I hated to see her go, but as I said at the time to Abdullah as he slapped me around in the tub, "Boys, I can pick 'em."

"Boss, you can lose 'em, too," Abdullah said.

Some of the Bathing Beauties became famous dramatic actresses, some married millionaires, some ended in tragedy, and one is reported to have become the bride of a notorious Chinese river pirate.

One of the unlucky girls was Marie Prevost. She was an exquisite little thing with big brown eyes, auburn hair, and a provocative figure. She added excitement to hundreds of Bathing Beauty scenes and was for a long time as anonymous as Gloria Swanson and Carole Lombard when they did the same work. But Marie soon developed into a suave and skillful actress who could perform such deft scenes with a mere look or a slight gesture that she was obviously out of place among my roaring pie throwers. Ernst Lubitsch called her the most brilliant young comedienne he'd ever seen and picked her for the star of *The Marriage Circle*.

Her tragedy involved the sinister threat which haunts all American women today—calories. At the height of her career she took on weight. Her neat curves became heavy and overblown. She died suddenly and mysteriously and alone. The headlines said: "Mystery Shrouds Sudden Death of Marie Prevost, Sennett Beauty." It is my understanding that the police were never able to determine exactly what had happened, but however her death came about, it is my opinion that it was inspired by a broken heart.

It was Sally Eilers who brought a young girl named Jane
Peters to Keystone. She was a scamp and madcap, much like
Mabel, and we were so struck by her personality that we put
her under contract. She began at $50 a week and was soon
raised to $400. I never got to know this girl very well—she
stayed with us only a short time—and the only important thing
I recall about her now is advising her that Jane Peters was not
a particularly good theatrical name. I had her change it to
Carole Lombard.

Bebe Daniels was a Mack Sennett girl over my objections.
Her mother, Phyllis Daniels, was wardrobe mistress at Keystone and her small twelve-year-old daughter used to frolic
around the lot. When I heard that the child had charmed
several of my directors into giving her Bathing Beauty parts, I
threw up my hands like a pious Irishman and ordered them to
cease and desist. The enterprising Miss Daniels thereupon
looked up another performer I had dismissed from Keystone.
At the age of thirteen she began to play leading roles with
Harold Lloyd.

Ruth Taylor was born in Grand Rapids, Michigan, later
moved to Oregon, and everyone told her she ought to be in
pictures. She was blond and gay and pretty and "you ought to
be in pictures" meant only one thing in those days: as soon as
she finished high school, she headed straight for Hollywood
and Mack Sennett. I had 20/20 vision and the good sense to
hand her a contract and a fountain pen as soon as I saw her.
Little Miss Taylor was not only an actress but a diarist. I think
the most accurate account of what it was like to be a Mack
Sennett girl is in this selection from her notes:

"Jan. 4th. I kept thinking all day how lucky I was to get
on here at Sennett's. It's the best of all. Started in the 'Puppy
Love' series today with Eddie Cline. He is a grand director to
work with. We have the most fun of anybody on our set, everybody laughs all the time.

"Jan. 7th. Great great great. They took up my little option.
Am I happy! I am learning so much here and it is so much
fun.

"Jan. 18th. You certainly have to go in for everything if
you're aiming to be a comedy queen. Started taking horseback
riding lessons today. Mr. Sennett said I should. Madeline Hur-

lock is riding with me. She is so beautiful she takes my breath away. I wonder if she will become a great dramatic actress the way she wants to. I hope so.

"April 18th. I fixed 'em on the set today. I made up like a colored mammy and not one of them knew me when I walked on the set!

"May 14th. Who do you think came to see us today? Mabel Normand! Why, I can't hardly believe it yet. Mabel Normand herself. She looked thin and she has been ill but she was all they told me around here she would be. Everyone acted like the queen had come.

"June 19th. Started another picture today. It seems I just go from one picture to another and I'm getting ahead beautifully. I'm happy.

"June 29th. Worked on retakes on the Ben Turpin picture. I'm sorry the picture is ending. Ben has been a riot. He's the funniest man in the world. He has had everyone on the set laughing all the time.

"July 8th. I think with another year of Sennett training I will be ready for features. Lots of girls who worked at Sennett's have gotten a great break when they leave Mr. Sennett. Look at Gloria Swanson. And right now there is Phyllis Haver starring in 'Chicago'—and Marie Prevost in a picture called 'On to Reno.'

"Aug. 2nd. Had my first swimming lesson at the Hollywood Athletic Club today. Not that I have to have it for pictures because it seems a Sennett girl never goes near the water, at least I haven't, but Mr. Sennett says it is good for you. Mabel Normand was a swimming champ.

"Aug. 21st. Worked all day and mother and I went to Madeline Hurlock's for dinner and to the theatre. I like to be with Madeline because she talks about so many interesting things. I expect if anybody overheard us they would hardly think we were Sennett girls.

"Nov. 19th. Went to the opening of 'What Price Glory.' Marvelous picture. Phyllis Haver was sensational. Another Sennett girl makes good.

"Dec. 4th. Started a picture. Eddie Quillan, Madeline Hurlock and I are to be featured. Madeline and I are a good contrast. She is so tall and dark and I am little and blond.

"Jan. 20th. I am going to leave Sennett's. I want to get out and try my luck at features.

"March 9th. My last day with Sennett. Went to the studio in the afternoon to check my wardrobe. Everyone wished me luck as a free lance and seemed to mean it, bless them. I know my training and experience in comedies will help me in features. Said good-bye to Ben Turpin and we cried. How grateful I am to him for his help and kindness. On the last Sennett set I saw there were 10 new bathing girls. They looked eager and happy and beautiful. Mr. Sennett says Carole Lombard and Sally Eilers are the pick and they will be great stars some day.

"March 10th. I wish Madeline would get away from two-reelers now, too. I missed being with her today. I think it is time for her to leave."

They all left, one way or another. Miss Taylor did not depart like Gloria Swanson to overnight fame and an enormous weekly salary. She had a number of wretched days before she found work. But about this time another young lady named Anita Loos published a best-seller called *Gentlemen Prefer Blondes* and when the time came for this to become a motion picture the sage Miss Loos insisted upon a clause allowing her to pick the blonde. The search for an actress who could read the immortal line "Diamonds are a girl's best friend" with poise and conviction was long and desperate. But one afternoon the late Mal St. Clair, the director, came wearily to the end of the long waiting line of hopeful blondes and there was Ruth Taylor.

"You just might do," St. Clair said. "Any experience?"

"Yes. With Mack Sennett. For years."

"If your test comes out the way I think it should, you're Lorelei."

And she was. You have to see the magnificent Miss Marilyn Monroe in the same role today to get an idea of how good Ruth Taylor was. She married a millionaire and lived happily ever after.

Trying to remember all the wonderful girls who made our funny pictures beautiful is like trying to recall the names of every bud in a hothouse. There was Virginia Fox, now Mrs. Darryl F. Zanuck; Irene Lentz, now the world-famous Metro-

Goldwyn-Mayer fashion designer; Carmelita Geraghty, now the wife of the distinguished producer Carey Wilson; Marian Nixon, now married to William A. Seiter, the director; Marjorie King, whom John Gilbert courted, now wife of Phil Plant, the millionaire and former husband of Constance Bennett; Ruth Hiatt, formerly a queen of the Western that-a-ways, with Ken Maynard; Olive Borden, who starred with George O'Brien; and Vera Reynolds, the "perfect flapper," who went on to dramatic stardom with Cecil B. DeMille.

I have been asked a number of times how I selected pretty girls for motion pictures. I don't know. So far as I am able to find out, Flo Ziegfeld never knew either. That is to say, there are no rules. The stories you read in newspapers and magazines, always illustrated with photographs of directors or producers measuring lovely women with tapelines, are the routine fabrications of press agents. A pretty girl is *not*, thank God, a compilation of statistics.

What I looked for was charm. If you try to pin me down for a definition of charm, I'm stuck again. But I think any all-American male with reasonably good eyesight knows what I mean.

The only absolute rule that we had about the beauties on the Mack Sennett lot was that if some comedian were going to help some girl get ahead in the acting profession by dating her he got fired. Six-foot Blanche Payson, the policewoman, was on hand to enforce this law.

CHAPTER 16

Poetry in Slapstick

THERE WERE NO Mack Sennett Bathing Beauties in the Chaplin films. The ladies did not arrive in Edendale in time for us to display them in the first dozen pictures with our new boy.

Except in one two-reel comedy, *Dough and Dynamite*, we omitted pie-throwing in Charlie's films. *Dough and Dynamite*, later released as *The Cook* and as *The Doughnut Designer*, was his twenty-ninth motion picture. It was a hit at the box offices and Charlie's first personal triumph as a comedian. His name was important after this picture.

We were also sparing in the use of one of the prime tricks of the comedy trade, now the main thing in Westerns. We seldom used chase sequences with Chaplin. He was not the man to take violent part in those looping pursuits through city streets with fast cameras trained on running cops, wild automobiles, and hairbreadth escapes. Chaplin was often—almost always—a fugitive, but he was a *furtive* fugitive: he hid and peeped.

He was not scornful or unappreciative of our methods. On the contrary, he was as tough and spry a slapstick actor as the next villain. He is agile today. In his latest picture, *Limelight* (seen at a trade showing in Hollywood but not yet released to the public), he performs a tremendous fall from a theater stage through a bass drum in the orchestra, and he was sixty-three years old when he shot that scene. But on the whole I think he was correct in omitting our three main trademarks, the Bathing Beauties, the chase sequences, and the pies.

Anything that diverts the camera's eye from Chaplin himself is likely to be a waste of celluloid. His style is intimate, not panoramic—the one-shot instead of the crowd scene. We understood that early in the game.

He was certainly not unaware of the Mack Sennett Bathing Beauties. No one on the lot ignored *them*. Mr. Chaplin had first-rate eyesight and understandable ambitions. He pined for several interesting girls. I remember one evening at Baron Long's when he developed a powerful attachment to a small blonde, courted her with quaint sayings, did imitations for her, and pursued her across the room in full cry. As he embraced her, the young lady gave out with such passionate yelps and wiggles that Charlie thought he had made an unconditional conquest.

It turned out that he had backed the girl up against a hot radiator.

As he went along with us, Chaplin used the familiar slapstick framework—he never discarded it altogether at any time —but he began to develop the character and the tricks that eventually made his tramp a celebrity. To begin with, he and Mabel Normand became a team.

In *Mabel at the Wheel*, Charlie's tenth picture and his second with Mabel, he experimented with his costume for the last time. He went back to the long frock coat and high hat and pasted two wisps of hair on his chin in addition to the mustache. The story involved Charlie on a motorcycle competing with Harry McCoy in a racing automobile, both of them sweet on Mabel. In this picture, and in many others to come, Chaplin was not adverse to dishonesty. He ties up Mc-Coy to get him out of the race and Mabel has to drive the car instead. Then Charlie greases the track, causing Mabel to drive off in several wrong directions and lose the contest.

I directed that one, and Miss Normand acted in it.

In *Caught in a Cabaret*, which Charlie is credited with directing, he is a phony, impersonating a duke in order to make love to Mabel. From then on, always under my supervision and with stories cleared by me and the scenario department, he received screen credit as writer and director for every picture he appeared in with the exception of *Tillie's Puncured Romance*.

I use the word "writer" loosely. Chaplin's literary style embraced the roughest, briefest possible outline. He improvised the action, the business, and the gags as he went along. I understood this method. I always instructed my writers, "Don't write it, tell it."

Jokes have been made for years about Hollywood producers (all alleged fugitives from the cloak-and-suit trade, of course) who cannot comprehend even the basic English in which most popular fiction is written. Therefore, they employ readers and storytellers to recite them. The fact is there are no illiterate producers. But if a writer, an actor, or a director has a good story, that story, as a motion-picture possibility, is many times more effective when told than when written.

In his seven- and eight-reel pictures I suppose Chaplin put more on paper than he did at Edendale, but I understand that even then he wore few pencils to the nub.

In *The Fatal Mallet*, with Mabel and Mack Swain, Charlie showed that he could work roughhouse action, and take part in it himself: we all got hit on our heads with bricks and mallets. Miss Normand did some outstanding acting as she watched these proceedings as if they gave her a severe case of ennui, but the picture ends with Mr. Chaplin kicking Miss Normand in the *derrière*. As I was saying before, Chaplin was working up to it even then, but it was a long time before he abandoned cruelty, venality, treachery, larceny, and lechery as the main characteristics of his tramp. Chaplin shrank his tramp in gradually diminishing sizes and made him pathetic—and lovable.

In *Her Friend the Bandit* Charlie played an impostor who goes to a party at Mabel's home and doesn't know how to behave in society. The comedy spins on Chaplin as a fake with bad manners.

In *Mabel's Busy Day*, the picture hangs on Charlie's getting drunk in a saloon and stealing hot-dogs from Mabel, a poor girl who operates a small stand. He bankrupts her.

In *Mabel's Married Life*, he plays the part of Mabel's husband, comes home drunk, and gets defeated in a boxing match by a dummy. Mack Swain, Charlie Murray, Hank Mann, Harry McCoy, Alice Davenport, Alice Howell, and Wallace MacDonald were in this, a large cast for a one-reeler, but

Mabel prevailed. She stole the picture by mimicking Chaplin.

In *A Gentleman of Nerve*, which Chaplin wrote and directed, Charlie and Mack Swain sneak through a hole in the fence to see an automobile race. After Charlie gets several innocent people arrested, he winds up as a thief—stealing sips of refreshment through a straw from a bystander's pop bottle. It was one of his funniest pantomimes.

When he wrote and directed *His Trysting Place*, he preceded W. C. Fields by many years with scenes in which he got laughs by being mean to a baby. The film ends with Mabel Normand batting him unconscious with an ironing board.

Charlie depicted himself as an unfaithful husband in *Getting Acquainted*. He gets his comeuppance when Mabel, the girl he is chasing, betrays him to the police.

Chaplin acted in eleven pictures with Mabel Normand. I directed him in nine and found him easy but unpredictable. He would agree to a scene as I outlined it, then discombobulate me by doing everything some other way.

Including *Caught in the Rain*, the first Keystone picture for which he received screen credit for "writing" and directing, Chaplin wrote and directed twenty-two of the thirty-five films he made in Edendale. From then on, of course, he wrote and directed everything in which he appeared—forty-two features in all, including *Limelight*, which hasn't been released, but excluding *A Woman of Paris*, in which he acted in one scene only.

He hadn't perfected, or thought through, what he was going to be as a screen comedian, but in his performances Chaplin did, at twenty-five, point directly to his big pictures.

Burlesque, for instance.

All Keystone comedians dealt in burlesque. We made fun of a number of things, including *Uncle Tom without the Cabin*, *East Lynne with Variations*, and *The Battle of Who Run*; Theda Bara, Rudolph Valentino, William S. Hart, and Von Stroheim. Chaplin joined in and burlesqued Hollywood actors in 1914. In *The Masquerader* he chased women, spoiled scenes, disguised himself as a girl, and fell in a well, all for the purpose of kidding our own business. We chose "Fatty" Arbuckle, Minta Durfee, and Charlie Murray to help him. (This picture is also known as *Putting One Over, A Picnic,* and *The Female Impersonator.*)

Late in 1914 newspapers, magazines, and Arthur Brisbane created a flurry of popular interest in mankind's Stone Age origins. Our response with Chaplin was two reels called *His Prehistoric Past,* in which Chaplin played a thin-muscled cave man in a derby hat.

When he had money to spend and more time to shoot, Chaplin developed irony and satire, they say. Satire, of course, is burlesque without bed slat.

The Chaplin tricks and capers were Chaplin's own, from the whimseys to the acrobatics. But Hank Mann had already leaned against a burning building and nonchalantly lit his cigarette from it when Charlie scratched a match on a bald man's head in *The Rounders.* The difference was, Chaplin's gesture seemed quaint.

In *Twenty Minutes of Love* he invented a scene which in various circumstances he used many times later. He becomes romantically affected while watching a young couple make love in a park. Chaplin responds by embracing a tree. Only one other player I can think of—Mabel Normand—could have turned that absurd bit of business into laughter plus pathos.

In a scene with Mack Swain at a restaurant counter Chaplin improvised a sequence in which he reaches for a napkin, becomes entangled with Swain's beard, winds up using Swain's soup for a finger bowl.

These were simple things, we're inclined to say, but then they weren't so simple. They were the first signs of a complicated pattern. This was how Chaplin started to become Charlie Chaplin.

Late in October the studio fell behind its quota of films for New York. Rain began to fall, and I had to go to Catalina Island to do a picture with Mabel. I left the studio to make a Conklin-Chaplin two-reeler as fast as I could to quiet Kessel and Bauman. Conklin and Chaplin had no complete story on paper.

"Never mind that," I said. "Take the boardinghouse set. The two of you can't miss. You're bound to think of something. Just get me two reels as fast as you can."

Chester and Charlie worked out a situation in which they

were both on the make for the landlady. This vague plot line faded after a few takes. Chester said, "Looky here, Charlie, you're going to get credit as writer and director of this pastry, haven't you got a story?"

Charlie said that chasing a landlady was the only idea he had. From there on he was stuck.

They left Edendale by streetcar that night, close to desperation. Then the trolley stopped at an intersection where many people got on and off and Mr. Chaplin's nose began to twitch. A savory aroma smote him. Across the street was a large bakery. Chester and Charlie peered at it and spotted a sign in the window: "Boy Wanted."

They turned to each other and said the same words at the same time: "This looks like our story."

Next morning at Edendale they commandeered all the property men, painters, and carpenters they could lay hands on and built a bakery set. When the flats were up, Conklin and Chaplin put their heads together and cast themselves not as pastry cooks but as strikebreakers. They gave a small girl the role of a customer, sent her in to buy a loaf of bread, and planned to have her return it with a complaint that the dough was not well baked.

I returned from Catalina at this point and made a suggestion.

"If you'd put a stick of dynamite in that bread and blow up the bakery, I think you'd have something, boys."

We exploded the bakery with trick camera work and splattered dough for miles around. The picture was released as *Dough and Dynamite* and was Chaplin's best up to that time.

Late in the summer, with the Chaplin-Normand films selling briskly, I battled with Kessel and Bauman for permission to make the first full-length, or six-reel, motion-picture comedy.

My partners pointed out to me, correctly, that such a picture would not only cost in the neighborhod of $200,000, but demanded a star whose name and face meant something to every possible theatergoer in the United States and the British Empire. Not even Mabel Normand, who was certainly widely known and, more than that, was the only feminine comedy star so far established in motion pictures, had a great enough name to carry such an investment. Certainly not Chester Conklin. Absolutely not Charlie Chaplin.

On top of that, I was reminded, no one had ever made a six-reel comedy. Under any circumstances the venture was a gamble.

"Not a gamble with Marie Dressler," I said.

Kessel said yeah, maybe not with Marie Dressler, "But we ain't got Marie Dressler. You might as well think about Weber and Fields or Lillian Russell."

"Happens I know Miss Dressler," I said. "We're old friends. Knew her well when she played in *Lady Slavey* in Northampton.

"Also, everybody and his grandmother are whistling and singing 'Heaven Will Protect the Working Girl.'"

This was the song which Miss Dressler made a hit when she sang it in her stage play, *Tillie's Nightmare*.

Even Adam Kessel could hum "Heaven Will Protect the Working Girl," though he may not have agreed with it.

"So all right," he said. "You named a name. And you named a hit tune, which I would point out nobody can hear on the screen, but what are we going to do when Miss Dressler names her price?

"And just by way of idle curiosity, you got a story for Marie Dressler? You been writing a masterpiece for Marie Dressler while you ain't been making the pictures we need here in New York?"

"Oh, story," I said. "Well, of course. That's the least of it."

The upshot of these long-distance telephone and Western Union arguments was that I was allowed to make a play for Miss Dressler. When I approached her, it turned out that Marie had wondered what had become of the boilermaker who came backstage with a letter from Calvin Coolidge. She was delighted to learn that the Mack Sennett who made funny pictures was the same person. She pined to be a movie actress and she would work for what she considered a reasonable salary.

Miss Dressler's reasonable salary was $2500 a week.

I'll omit the arguments I had with Bauman and Kessel

when I put Marie Dressler under contract at that figure to make the first six-reel motion-picture comedy—with no story. I had my way. The celebrated Miss Dressler arrived in Hollywood, leased a magnificent house, and went on salary from the moment she stepped off the train in Pasadena.

I called Craig Hutchison, our scenario editor, up to the conference bathroom in the tower and said to him, "Where's the story?"

"What story?"

"The Marie Dressler story, of course. And her salary started this morning."

"I need to sit down," Mr. Hutchison said.

I told Craig he and I had better get to work that evening. We met at the old Van Nuys Hotel downtown and had a brace of cocktails. No wisdom flowed during dinner. We drank several bottles of beer. After apple pie and ice cream we were still not inspired. We had four scotch highballs. We broke up about 1:30 A.M.

"Boss, I'm afraid we didn't get much done," Craig said as he left.

We tried Echo Park without benefit of beer.

This went for something more than a week. Finally I called in Hutchison and Hampton Del Ruth for another conference. "You boys are coming with me to the hotel and we're not leaving until we get a story," I told them.

I had a case of champagne sent up, locked the door, and put the key in my vest pocket.

"Have all the champagne you want, boys, but we don't leave this room or eat until we get the story for Marie Dressler."

Thus inspired, we got an idea by 2:00 A.M., with three bottles of Mumm's left over. It was Mr. Hutchison who had the moneysaving notion of using the story line of Miss Dressler's stage hit, *Tillie's Nightmare*.

We outlined that on not more than two sheets of hotel stationery, had it typed in the morning, and sent it up to the boys in the gag room with orders to make with the funny business.

To support Marie Dressler as the country girl, I threw every available player we had into the cast: Chaplin as the city slicker; Mabel Normand as Chaplin's confederate in shady deals; Mack Swain as Marie's father; Charlie Bennett as her rich uncle; Chester Conklin, Minta Durfee, Edgar Kennedy, Charlie Murray, Charlie Chase, Phyllis Allen, Gordon Griffith, Harry McCoy, Alice Davenport, Wallace MacDonald, Alice Howell, and the whole battalion of Keystone Cops.

Inspired by this cast, much the largest and the most notable ever put together for a screen comedy, Hampton Del Ruth and the entire department took a slim idea from Miss Dressler's stage play and turned it into *Tillie's Punctured Romance*.

As the villain of the piece, Chaplin is working the farm country for suckers. He meets Marie Dressler (Tillie) when she conks him on the head with a brick.

Charlie dazzles Tillie and induces her to steal her father's money and run away with him to the city. There they meet Mabel, Charlie's partner in crime, who becomes jealous and knocks him down.

Big scene: Tillie intoxicated in a café doing absurd dances. Charlie steals her pocketbook and escapes with Mabel. Meantime Tillie's rich uncle is reported dead and she becomes an heiress. Charlie returns, fascinates Tillie again, and marries her.

They buy a vast home and enter society. They give a ball, dance the tango together, trip, fall, and raise a ruckus. In the midst of this the rich uncle—not dead at all—returns. Chase sequence: cops, an automobile on a pier, collisions, boats upsetting, and Tillie in the water.

Both ladies now turn against Charlie Chaplin. They embrace while Charlie shrugs. The cops take him off.

That was the story. It was issued just ahead of D. W. Griffith's *The Birth of a Nation* and is still running today in various parts of the world—the oldest of all full-length motion picture comedies.

It took forty days to shoot *Tillie*, much more time than we had given to any picture before. There were two reasons for this:

With Bauman and Kessel crying at me as if they were starving I had to continue the steady flow of two short comedies each week. This meant that I never had my *Tillie* cast all working together on any given date. One or two of them were constantly out of the picture acting in a two-reeler.

The other trouble involved Miss Dressler herself. No matter that this was her first motion picture, she was a great star, this was her own story, and she was still inclined to remember me as an awkward boilermaker from Northampton.

In the midst of a comic scene I had planned carefully beforehand, Miss Dressler would say:

"No, Mack, that's wrong. Now this is the way we're going to do it."

I was the head of the studio and I was supervising this particular picture, but neither of these things influenced Marie Dressler. My arguments didn't influence her either.

"Okay, Marie, you do it your way," I'd say. And I would leave the set.

Usually a sweating messenger would arrive within an hour. Miss Dressler, who didn't know a camera angle from a hypotenuse, always threw the company into a swivet when she took over.

"Mack, there's just a little technicality here you can help me straighten out," she'd say.

"Sure, sure, Marie, call on me any time."

Dressler got along well with Charlie Chaplin, although she was a hefty woman and overpowered him physically in their love scenes. She had only one complaint about Chaplin.

Chaplin wore a celluloid collar in *Tillie* as part of his rig. Marie called me over one afternoon after I'd hurried out to solve a small *contretemps*—a matter of the whole company being near mutiny after one of her directorial efforts—and said:

"You know Mr. Chaplin's neck? And the celluloid collar around it? Well, Mack, I do not mind the same celluloid collar sixteen days in succession, but I'm a mite squeamish about that same piece of decaying banana on the same collar for the past sixteen days.

"As a matter of fact, Mr. Mack Sennett, if the banana is not removed, I shall enact you the goddammedest vomiting scene in the annals of the drammer."

On the whole Miss Dressler's engagement for *Tillie* was a pleasant and profitable experience all the way around. The picture was an instant hit and made money. It launched Marie Dressler as a motion-picture actress and made her a star. And we all had fun when we were not quarreling. Miss Dressler's husband and business manager, Charles Dalton, a big, red-faced, redheaded man, enjoyed Hollywood life more than any-body. Mr. Dalton was a bottleman of great prowess. He knew many people everywhere and had important political connections. He liked to tell the story of his visit to the White House when Teddy Roosevelt was President.

When the President and Mr. Dalton were having lunch-eon together one day, Dalton entertained him with so many tall and funny stories that the President decreed an award.

"Crack a bottle of champagne," he told the butler. It was done and Dalton's tales continued to flow.

Then there was an interruption. His secretary came in and reminded the President that it was past time for his appoint-ment with a delegation from the Women's Christian Temper-ance Union of Ohio.

Mr. Roosevelt shoved the champagne bottle and bucket under the table with his foot, pulled the tablecloth down to cover it, and had the good ladies shown in. He charmed them and promised them his abiding interest in their affairs.

When the highly pleased Temperance ladies were shown out, the President dived for the floor, rescued the bottle, and said to Dalton:

"I *was* dry all the time they were here."

Tillie starred Marie Dressler, but it possibly benefited Charlie Chaplin more than anyone else in it. After this picture every producer was after him. I posted guards to keep agents from approaching him on the lot. I was not cordial to Winnie Sheehan of Fox when he came to Edendale and asked to meet Chaplin. But there was no way to isolate Charlie from all con-tact with other people who wanted to make money on him. He played in only two more pictures under the Keystone label, *Getting Acquainted*, with Mabel, and *His Prehistoric Past*, with Mack Swain.

Bauman and Kessel agreed to an offer of $400 a week to hold Chaplin. I raised it to $750 on my own recognizance.

Charlie didn't argue, but he declined. It was obvious that he had an offer far better than that. Unless I was prepared to lose him I had to come up with something spectacular.

Now: the rumor runs, and all motion-picture histories that I have examined say that I let Charlie Chaplin go because I did not appreciate him enough to pay him the money he deserved. The fact was this:

When $750 was not enough I asked Chaplin what salary he thought would be right. He declined to mention a sum. I then made a decision on the spot and offered Charlie Chaplin half my kingdom.

I mean precisely that. I owned one third of the Keystone studio (soon to become the Mack Sennett Studio) and I offered to split my share with Chaplin if he would stay with us.

That is to say, my tender to Chaplin was one sixth of Keystone.

When he turned that down I had no more chips to raise the bet with.

Chaplin went to Essanay, the "Bronco Billy" Anderson Studio in Chicago, for $1250 a week. He worked for Essanay one year and made fourteen films, including the classic picture, *The Tramp*, the first comedy with a doleful ending. He left Essanay for Mutual at $10,000 a week and a bonus of $150,-000, or a total of $670,000 a year.

It now cost $100,000 to produce a Chaplin two-reeler, more than most features at that time, and he took his time about making them.

I did not know until recently, when I looked up the records, who Chaplin's first leading lady at Essanay was. The picture was *His New Job* and the leading lady was the girl with marvelous eyes named Gloria Swanson.

Chaplin dropped Miss Swanson after one try, in favor of a beautiful blond stenographer named Edna Purviance. Gloria made her one Chaplin picture in Chicago. She came straight to Edendale where Wallace Beery and I put her under contract at the same time.

The rest of the Chaplin story is his, not mine.

Until long after he packed his baggy britches and left Edendale there was no comment in the press about his political beliefs. I knew him only as a comedian.

When he worked for us sound had not arrived in pictures (Al Jolson's Vitagraph voice was still thirteen years off-stage), so I did not know then that Charlie was a musician. He had learned to play the cello backstage in his Fred Karno days. It is true that he composed the themes for *The Gold Rush*, *The Great Dictator*, and *Monsieur Verdoux*.

One of the last conversations I had with him took place in 1931 on the sidewalk in front of Musso & Frank's restaurant on Hollywood Boulevard. Chaplin pinned me and recited the entire plot and action of a picture he was planning to make. I was hungry and wanted to get away. I knew what Chaplin was up to. He was using me for an audience. He wanted to see if his story would set my rocking chair in motion.

But I had no rocking chair on the curb and I wasn't happy about being a sounding board. He made the picture he described to me and it was great—*City Lights*.

Thinking all this over, I wonder if in all the history of the world, giving the kings and captains and heroes and celebrated women their full due—I wonder if there was ever a single person so beloved and so well known to millions of people everywhere as that baggy-pants tramp invented by accident one rainy day in Edendale.

As for Charles Spencer Chaplin, I am not at all sure that we know him.

CHAPTER 1 7

Date for a Wedding

MABEL and I set a date.

It took me long enough to get around to it, but I finally said the words: "Mabel, let's get married."

We had quarreled and fought and broken up and patched up so many times during the past six years that I wasn't sure what Mabel's answer would be. I wasn't sure that Mabel would take the question seriously. I said it seriously enough, probably scowling, but I wouldn't have been surprised if Mabel had laughed.

She put her hand on the table.

"I've been wearing the ferryboat ring long enough to deserve that question at last, Mack," she said. "You mean it?"

"I was afraid to say it," I said.

"Were you afraid of me?"

"No. Yes. I don't know."

"Are you afraid I'll say yes?"

"I'm afraid of that, too."

"My good man, that's possibly the most sensible remark you ever made in your life. Imagine! Us! It scares me too. You want me to say yes?"

"That's what I want, Mabel."

"All right, sir, here we go. Yes."

It was June 1915.

"Let's go, then," I said.

"Where?"

"It's getting past office hours but I know a man who will

open up the marriage license bureau. I know a priest. Come on, Mabel."

"Whoa, there, Great Man, not so fast. You can cast me in a picture with a snap decision and I'll take it. But if I'm going to be leading lady under a lifetime contract I want everything that goes with the part.

"Meaning orange blossoms, a wedding gown and a honeymoon, damn it."

I argued. I gave logical reasons. I told Mabel how busy I was at the office, how many problems we had now that we had lost Charlie Chaplin. I pointed out that we were grown-up citizens. I said that trousseaux and long honeymoons were outdated foolishness for old-fashioned young people.

Mabel said no, and she said, damn it, no orange blossoms, no wedding.

"I'll buy you the handsomest wedding ring this side of Paradise, first thing tomorrow morning," I said. "There'll be a stone in it so big and shiny you'll have to wear smoked glasses to look at it."

"I have the ring," said Mabel. "When I get married—and give me your wandering attention—I'm *going* to get married this time, so don't try to squeeze out of it. But there's going to be a trousseau."

I had to agree, as men have always had to agree. We picked a date three weeks off, made our plans, and decided to tell no one.

It was possible, of course, for Mabel Normand to order all the trousseau finery she wanted without attracting even slight attention. She often spent more than five thousand dollars at Madame Frances's or at Lady Duff-Gordon's in one afternoon's shopping spree. She had a karakul coat, a Russian sable, a silver fox, a mink, a moleskin, a white ermine, and a chinchilla. The chinchilla cost twenty thousand dollars.

She owned a collection of pendants, necklaces, chokers, tiaras, brooches, bracelets, and pins, some of which I had given her, many of which she had bought herself. At one time she had these baubles insured by Lloyd's of London for $250,000.

It was routine office procedure at the studio for Mabel to sign a chit for an advance of five thousand dollars on her salary to buy a new emerald clip. Los Angeles merchants brought things like that, jewelry and furs, to her house, and displayed them for her in the evening. Mabel was always sorry for them and seldom sent any salesman away without making some purchase.

Once she went out ermined and jeweled in a Rolls-Royce, grew bored at a party, failed to find her chauffeur, and returned home in a milk wagon.

She could no more resist these toys than a child with a dime can resist a gumdrop counter. And they were toys. Once she had them, she set little store by them. As I think I said before, she must have given away more than half of her suits and evening dresses and hats before she wore them.

I saw I had to humor the girl. After all, if she could splurge up to five thousand dollars on silks and trinkets merely because she was going to a dinner party, it was unreasonable to expect her not to primp for her own wedding.

And Mabel could have ordered up a dozen trousseaux without anyone suspecting that she was going to become Mrs. Mack Sennett.

She began to order things the next morning. She set the date, July 4, 1915.

If any young men in my acquaintance are thinking about falling in love with actresses I can advise them that the world holds no more delightful, passionate, and sincere women to fall in love with. But the enterprise is not precisely the way it has been described in romances.

There are not so many high-flown moments of tasting champagne from evening slippers and scattering roses in boudoirs as young men would like to imagine.

Actresses are not, as some cynical fellow said, a third sex, but they are not schoolteachers, either. Most professional girls, from the schoolmarms to the M.D.'s, are inclined to give up their careers, or at least put careers on a half-time basis, in favor of marriage. Actresses in any bracket, from burley-cue strip-teasers to dramatic stars, are dedicated to their trade. They may compromise, but they won't temporize.

More than that, they are businesswomen. They may be bad businesswomen, but there they are with names more famous than most corporations. Industries, investments, and executives revolve around them and they know it.

The worst predicament of all is to fall in love with an actress with whom you are in business.

At the time Mabel and I became engaged that June, she was unhappy with the Keystone Studio. She considered herself a great star, which indeed she was—she was unique—and she quarreled with me about getting away from the slapstick boys. She thought that she could play longer and deeper and more romantic parts than we were giving her in the quick one- and two-reelers we turned out on our assembly line.

For instance, we got a tip one day that the city of Los Angeles planned to drain the small lake in Echo Park. When the Water Department boys arrived to unplug the pond, we were there with a camera crew trained on Mabel and a screen lover in a rowboat. The heavy in this comedy, jealous of the boating sweethearts, opens a valve, the water spurts out in a torrent, and the boat sinks swiftly to the muddy bottom of the ex-lake.

We threw in some trick photography here which made it appear that the lake was draining at a Niagaran rate and that the rowboat went down faster than McGinty to the bottom of the sea.

It was taking advantage of situations like this that kept Keystone alive. Audiences were astonished by the apparent expense of such a spectacle—which had cost us nothing.

We sent Mabel out frequently to take part in any public event we thought might be sensational. She once spent more than two days waiting for a wrecking crew to topple a 120-foot-high brick chimney. When the chimney fell, we shot flashy pictures of it, cut back and forth to Mabel and Ben Turpin, and put a hundred-thousand-dollar spectacle on the screen on terms highly satisfactory to Bauman and Kessel.

That is how we got along and made money. Now Mabel began to complain that she was a better artist than an innocent bystander.

Mabel never complained when her salary wasn't paid. Sometimes we had double armfuls of cash on hand, sometimes we were corporately broke. Our methods of collection from the exchanges was inefficient. On top of that Bauman and Kessel still kept an eye on Belmont Park and Hialeah: when they bet on the wrong horses somebody's salary went in hock. It was usually Mabel's.

Mabel didn't complain, either, about Bauman and Kessel's manipulation of various companies bearing her name. They had at one time or another Normand Pictures, Inc., Mabel Normand Productions, the Mabel Normand Company, Normand Films, Inc., and the Mabel Normand Comedy Studio. They raised cash with these corporations, put out several pictures under the names of each, and let them die. There was nothing unethical about their operations. It was simply necessary all the time to finance and refinance in order to keep going.

It had become possible to get advance cash from exchanges and exhibitors on the mere announcement that a new Mabel Normand comedy was in production. We played that angle straight. We kept Mabel working simultaneously in as many pictures as possible. It was not unusual for her to be toiling in six comedies at the same time.

With the departure of Ford Sterling and Charlie Chaplin we had relied on Mabel more than ever. We were soon helped out by the appearance of a new comedian.

One afternoon when Mabel and I were in my office, disagreeing, a tremendous man skipped up the steps as lightly as Fred Astaire. He was tremendous, obese—just plain fat.

"Name's Arbuckle," he said. "Roscoe Arbuckle. Call me 'Fatty.' I'm with a stock company. I'm a funnyman and acrobat. Bet I could do good in pictures. Whatcha think?"

With no warning he went into a feather-light time step, clapped his hands, and did a backward somersault as gracefully as a girl tumbler. And that was how the famous and later notorious Roscoe ("Fatty") Arbuckle introduced himself to motion pictures.

Mabel played in scores of pictures with Roscoe and liked him well enough. He was a good guy all the time we knew him and a fantastic athlete. Once we took him to Tía Juana to see the bullfights. The *toreros* laughed at the 285-pound fat man and claimed that all his stunts in motion pictures were fakes performed by doubles. After the fights Arbuckle challenged them to a foot race around the arena. I thought he was about to disgrace himself, of course, but he beat the fastest *torero* by ten yards without breathing hard.

At any rate, funny as Arbuckle and Ben Turpin were, Mabel knew that she was a more subtle kind of artist and more important. She begged for—correction, she demanded in concert pitch—bigger and better pictures.

I explained corporate finance. I might as well have tried to explain the queen's knight's opening to a hopscotch kindergartner.

"Ah, the great Napoleon," Mabel would say. "Come off the high horse, Gineral. You don't know what you're talking about. You're a bathhouse Johnny at heart."

We were in the midst of this running argument when, with my usual good timing, I asked Mabel to marry me.

It is my observation that getting engaged to a girl is no way to end a quarrel.

I accused Mabel of being temperamental. She flung back at me that I took her for granted. She said that I was always experimenting with new talent, building up other comedians, and giving brand-new, unknown girls bigger chances than I gave her. She also said, and she said this bitterly, that my personal interest in the new girls, their faces and figures, was a whale of a lot more than the head of the studio needed to show.

"Hmmm—pretty nice," she would say when a new girl arrived. "Pretty nice for you. What'll I be hearing next?"

I denied everything. It was difficult to explain that my preoccupation with the new girls was merely the prudence of good business practice. Mabel declined to believe that it was necessary to interview these actresses at dinner parties or at their homes in order to perform money-making judgments about their values on the screen.

While all this was going on, Mabel befriended a young actress she had known in New York. She took her into her own apartment when she first arrived in Los Angeles, brought her to the studio, and saw to it that we gave her a small contract.

One evening I had a date with this actress to talk about her next role. After dinner we went to her apartment. It was a moonlit Southern California evening and the warblers were twittering in the shrubbery, a most romantic setting. I leaned on her upright piano, muttering bass notes, while she played a little night music.

The living-room door flew open and there was a quick stab of high heels across the hardwood.

Mabel walked up to us, stopped, put her hand to her forehead, stared for an instant, then turned and fled.

She said not one word.

Silence from Mabel was more eloquent than *The Charge of the Light Brigade*. She was quiet only when she was desperately hurt and angry. I had seen the quick moisture in her deep brown eyes and the slight quiver of her mouth.

"Wait," I called out. "This is not what you think. I can explain."

Every innocent man always thinks he can explain.

Mabel went down the steps and I went after her, yelling for her to wait and listen. Her car and chauffeur were at the curb, but she was not in the car. I caught a glimpse of silky legs as she flashed around the corner and headed up an alley. I plodded after her as hard as I could go.

Mabel was faster than a frightened kitten. She put one hand on a board fence, sailed over it, and disappeared into the shadows.

I had to walk around the fence to pick up her trail again. Then I heard her heels on a sidewalk. She beat me to her apartment on Union Street and I heard a door slam as I raced through the entrance hall.

I banged at the door, rang the bell, and finally put my shoulder to it, breaking the lock. Mabel was kneeling on the floor at the hearth of her marble fireplace. Her jewel box was beside her. She had a hammer in her right hand.

As I ran to the middle of the room and stopped in astonishment, she scooped a handful of diamonds into a pile on the marble and raised the hammer to smash them.

I'm a slow thinker, but there are times when I'm a lightning calculator. I saw that Mabel was about to destroy *les pièces de résistance* of her gems.

"Not a cent less than $30,000 worth," I said under my breath. I knew because I had bought most of them.

Then I sprawled on the floor and grabbed Mabel.

"Don't *do* that," I yelled. "Honey, we can make up like we always do, *but you can't make up those diamonds!*"

I tried to take her in my arms. I might as well have been holding a china doll. I kissed her. It was no good. She did not resist, she simply did not respond. She was withdrawn and hurt and her lovely brown eyes looked at me without recognition—but with a look I recognized: the look of a small, trapped animal.

Finally she said, "I'm tired, Mack. So desperately tired. Tired of everything. You'd better go. Please stay away. I'm so tired."

I fumbled in my pocket and found the little chamois bag containing my mother's diamond. I went over and dropped it in her lap.

"Only if you really need it," Mother had said.

I really needed it.

Mabel did not look up. She did not open the bag.

I had to join a camera crew early the next morning to begin directing a comedy sequence with Weber and Fields, the famous vaudeville team, on the street. I had taken over the supervision of their picture because in our eagerness for new star names we were making the almost unheard of investment, at that time, of five thousand dollars a week for their salary.

I had Joe Weber and Lew Fields in a taxicab in a collision with a wagonload of hay. The hayload topples and the comedians are almost smothered inside the cab.

I was calling out instructions through a megaphone when I was outyelled by a competing voice.

"Read all about it! Movie star desperately ill! All about Mabel Normand!"

I grabbed a paper. The headlines were two inches high. A sensationally written story, based on no fact, said that Mabel Normand, the famous Mack Sennett Beauty, was dying.

Joe and Lew looked at me. I looked at them. Nobody smiled. They understood and they knew I understood.

Mabel was staging a thriller to get even.

I had no more comedy in me that morning than the last act of *Romeo and Juliet*. But I had to stand on that street corner all day directing funnymen while the newsboys screeched about Mabel. I was sure that the next yell would be "Read all about Mack Sennett!"

Mother did all she could. She went to Mabel with small objects she had had blessed by the Holy Father on a recent trip to Rome, but Mabel wouldn't talk. She merely said she was tired.

I was not allowed to see her. She abandoned her apartment and lived for several weeks with Minta and Roscoe Arbuckle because that was the last place I would look for her.

When actresses cannot be appealed to as women, sometimes you can make a flanking attack through their careers. I stopped trying to explain myself to Mabel and sent word to her that I agreed completely with all her plans for future pictures. I told her that we would avoid sinking rowboats and toppling chimneys from now on. We would make the kind of pictures she deserved. More than that, she would not even have to work in the same studio with the slapstick, pie-throwing comedians.

I bought a piece of property on Sunset Boulevard several miles from Edendale, built a small studio on it, named it "The Mabel Normand Studio," and handed her the key. Away from the stage I created a small park with a little building containing beautiful dressing rooms for Mabel Normand.

Mabel thanked me calmly and said she was ready to return to work.

"Then it's all right between you and me?" I asked.

"I didn't say that. Let's discuss the picture I'm to make in the new studio. You have something in mind?"

I had something in mind. After the success of *Tillie's Punctured Romance*, the first full-length comedy feature, I had had less trouble than before in convincing Bauman and Kessel that a six-reel picture starring Mabel would be a hit. I threw all my personal assets behind the picture.

Even so, we were unable to start for a long time. Mabel's headlined illness was a phony we never discussed, but now she was really ill. She suffered from sinus troubles and a hacking cough which made it impossible to begin the new picture for many weeks.

When we did get under way, it was with a director and cast picked by Mabel herself. We argued about Dick Jones, who I thought was too young and too much of a stunt and slapstick man to direct a full-length picture, but I was letting Mabel have her way about everything. Jones became the director. She picked George Nichols to play the part of her foster father; Laura LaVarnie as a society woman; Lew Cody as a millionaire playboy and a rascal; Minta Durfee as the conniving sister of the society dame; and Wheeler Oakman as the handsome hero.

We began the picture in August 1916, and took eight months to shoot it. It was a simple story, no more than the adventures of the pretty daughter of a Western prospector who comes to New York as a Cinderella, inherits great wealth, and is pursued by the rascally villain. But it was held up week after week by accidents and troubles.

There was a scene, impossible to show on the screen today under the Production Code, in which a squirrel runs up Mabel Normand's leg and Wheeler Oakman retrieves it. The squirrel was supposed to be controlled by invisible piano wire, but it bit Mabel on the ankle.

In the midst of the picture Dick Jones and I had trouble about money. Some of the backers who had helped me lay out my share of the investment failed to come through in time. Dick thought he wasn't going to get paid. He remembered what Tom Ince and I had done to fetch Bauman and Kessel into line when we hid all our film in safety-deposit boxes. He did the same thing with three reels of the current production.

But in the end we came through with a film that I knew was a handsome and funny production, by far the best thing ever done with Mabel Normand. It gave scope to her whimsical talents for the first time.

We had no name for the picture until the last reel had been shot. Just before we sent the six reels off to New York in April, I discarded all the fancy ideas we had tried to tag on this simple comedy and named it *Mickey*.

Then I called in Harry Williams, who was well known both as a song and story writer, and paid him a large fee to write a title song to be played by theater orchestras. He wrote the song "Mickey," still a standard, and still a favorite with barbershop quartets.

Harry was a professional craftsman. He did his work superbly, on time—and dry. "No good idea ever came out of a seltzer bottle," he used to say.

I waited for applause from New York. *Mickey* meant more to me than any picture I had ever made. I had used up all the cash I had and all the cash I could borrow to fulfill my end of the deal. I had put almost a year's work into the film and close to $125,000 of the company's cash.

Kessel and Bauman sent word that *Mickey* was a failure. No exchange was willing to release it. No exhibitor wanted to show it.

I took the train to New York, set up showings of *Mickey* in screening rooms, and called on all the executives of the film industry.

No smiles greeted me anywhere. *Mickey* was no good and would not be shown in any theaters. Bauman and Kessel reminded me that we were stuck for close to half a million dollars.

I was as concerned about that as any man would be, but when I had been turned down and outargued all over town, I took the next train back to the coast to see the person far more important to me than any sum of money or any motion picture.

I was met at the studio with the news that "Fatty" Arbuckle had received a better offer and was leaving me to work for another studio.

"Oh well," I said.

Then I called on Mabel. She told me that she had signed a contract to make pictures for Sam Goldwyn for the next five years.

CHAPTER 18

Where Was St. Anthony?

I WAS NEVER a complicated fellow. When Mabel walked out on me I was as distressed as any man when his girl gives him the gate—as a matter of fact, Mabel threw the gate at me. But I don't recall spilling hot tears under the willows, or baying at the moon, or having nightmares that would interest a Viennese dream reader. I was busy at my profession of inventing nonsense to make people laugh.

Hard lines were being written for day after tomorrow. Curious things were about to happen. But even when they came along, as staggering as they were, the part I had to play was always the same. I was that slapstick producer who dealt in snickers.

I liked my work. There isn't a happier, more satisfactory life in the world than being serious about comedy. I think it is as respectable to make the people grin as it is to make them pray. I resented any interruptions while my wild men and I sought targets for the next custard pie.

I understand that President Eisenhower now runs the world only twenty-three and a half hours a day. He takes thirty minutes off to think. That's more than most of us take in a lifetime. But when I could think—between japes and shouts at the studio—I realized that Mabel Normand was no longer a little girl from Staten Island. She was a mature woman. And even a junior country-store philosopher knows that a mature and beautiful woman never blames herself for anything: she blames another woman.

I had done all I could for Mabel in *Mickey. Mickey* was

a glittering surprise, wrapped up like a package on Christmas morning—and what happened?

Mickey was a failure.

What did Mabel think about that? She had picked her own director, Dick Jones, and her own cast. She had made *Mickey* in her own brand-new, personal studio. She had done her finest work, and during the shooting of the film she had been enthusiastically convinced that this was her best, the complete answer to her acting ambitions.

But the picture was a flop and that was that.

My fault. I did not know why it was my fault, but it had to be. Someone has to be guilty of a grievous mistake when Hollywood's most charming comedienne finds her most fetching picture gathering layers of dust on layers of dust in the vaults of the exchanges and no man willing to show it.

I was unable to communicate with Mabel in any way. She would not see me. My phone calls were rejected. My flowers were not accepted. The laborious hand-written notes I composed late at night were returned unopened.

She talked with my mother, of course. That is to say, Mother pleaded with her. For the first time in her life Mrs. Sennett was baffled. She called on St. Anthony repeatedly, but the good man had apparently moved away from Southern California.

My course now was clear enough. Since I could not influence Mabel on any personal basis whatsoever, it was up to me to make amends and fight my fight through the same medium that had brought us together. I made plans as fast as I could to help her professionally and to work out a way for her return to her own studio, where she belonged.

I got little sleep. I was involved in a number of the important maneuvers which changed a toy into a world-wide industry and eventually turned Hollywood into a citadel.

The big, expensive feature picture, best identified as the kind of films Mary Pickford, the Gish girls, and D. W. Griffith now began to make, was fighting its way clear of the jerky one-reelers which had dominated our business. It had all begun with a Kinetoscope peep show on Broadway in 1894. But now there were more than seventeen thousand motion-picture theaters in the United States. Theaters, exchanges, and producers were still hamstrung by the legal claims of the old Patents Company. The Patents Company finally died under a United States Supreme Court decision in 1917, but there were revolutions before that.

Early in 1915 I went to La Junta, Colorado, to meet D. W. Griffith and Thomas H. Ince in the parlor of the Harvey House. We emerged with the Triangle Film Corporation, which we announced with the loudest brass and drums we could hire press agents to beat. We had famous names, great stars. We had my old baritone adviser, De Wolf Hopper; Raymond Hitchcock, who had fired me from *King Dodo*; Joe Weber and Lew Fields, Dustin Farnum, Billie Burke, Louise Dresser, Mary Boland, Sir Herbert Beerbohm Tree, Sam Bernard, Willard Mack, Louise Glaum, William Desmond, Eddie Foy, Frank Keenan, and the most valuable property in motion pictures, William S. Hart.

Now I made a change in Edendale which I looked forward to as the highest point of my life. I took down the huge sign which announced the Keystone studios and replaced it with a much bigger sign. It said:

MACK SENNETT STUDIO

It didn't make me happy. As Miss Billie Burke says, by the time you get your name up in lights you have worked so hard and so long, and seen so many names go up and come down, that all you can think of is, "How can I keep it there?"

The Triangle Film Corporation was incorporated for $2,500,000 at $5.00 a share and became a brisk speculator's item on Wall Street. Quotations went steadily up.

Bauman and Kessel spotted an athletic young actor at lunch one day in the Knickerbocker Hotel Grill, waved a contract under his nose, and sent Douglas Fairbanks West to make pictures for Griffith. Griffith was unhappy about Douglas Fairbanks, whom he did not appreciate, but he set about contriving a picture called *The Lamb* for the acrobat. He wrote the picture himself, but gave screen credit to his *nom du cinéma*, "Granville Warwick."

Triangle made its bow on Broadway with a splash and a

boom. We charged $2.00 a seat for the opening at the Knicker-
bocker Theater. We showed Fairbanks' first picture, *The
Lamb*, Tom Ince's *The Iron Strain*, with Dustin Farnum; and
Mack Sennett's *My Valet*, starring Raymond Hitchcock.

I reminded Mr. Hitchcock several times that he had
failed to appreciate the dancing of a chorus boy named Sennett.

D. W. Griffith turned from Douglas Fairbanks to the vast
conception called *Intolerance*. Having proved himself as an
epic maker with *The Birth of a Nation*, he now had no op-
position, even from Bauman and Kessel, when he began to
spend twelve thousand dollars a day for actors, including
Erich Von Stroheim, Bessie Love, and Constance Talmadge.

He made a picture that covered three hundred thousand
feet of negative, cost $1,900,000, and took seventy-four hours
to run.

It was eventually cut to thirteen reels and was a magnificent failure at the box office. Griffith accepted all respon-
sibility. He bought the picture himself, on the installment
plan, eventually paying Triangle more than a million dollars.

I am still convinced that *Intolerance* was one of the most
magnificent motion pictures ever made. But it carried on four
themes at the same time and in 1916 moviegoers hooted it
down as difficult and "abstract."

It was with affairs like these that I was overwhelmed,
as one of the partners of the triangle, when Mabel Normand
ran away.

She went to New York and I followed hard on her heels.

I brought my lawyer, A. G. Butler, and through his offices
I finally had a talk with Mabel. I stuck to business.

"How much is Goldwyn paying you?" I asked.

"A thousand a week," she told me.

" 'Tain't enough," I said. " 'Tain't nearly enough. This
has got to be readjusted."

It was readjusted, eventually, after a series of arguments
with Goldwyn, and Mabel's salary was set at $1500 a week. I
still thought this was absurd.

Mabel was as uninterested in my financial assistance as
if I had done no more than tip a waiter. It came out later, as a
matter of fact, that she scarcely glanced at her salary check
from Sam Goldwyn. She threw the company's books out of

balance by losing, and not bothering to look for, nine checks for more than five thousand dollars each.

I tried again, and again, and again, to induce somebody to show *Mickey*. No one would show it.

During the time Mabel was in New York, the start of her first picture held up for several months during the arguments about money, she lived with Raymond Hitchcock and his wife, Flora Zabelle, at their home in Great Neck, Long Island.

Hedda Hopper was in New York at that time and knew Mabel well. Miss Hopper tells me that she thought then that Sam Goldwyn was in love with Mabel.

"I never saw anybody prettier or more don't-give-a-damn than Mabel Normand at that time. She used to ride surfboards behind fast motorboats in Long Island Sound, and rush in pink and glowing, her long, dark eyelashes fringed with white salt spray.

"Sam would be sitting in the living room waiting. He would rise to greet her. But she would merely wave her hand at him and dash upstairs to have a drink with her pal, Pauline Frederick.

"And she'd stay there. No matter how late Sam hung around—and he could hear the girls giggling and laughing upstairs—she wouldn't come down to see him."

Louella Parsons knew Mabel then.

"I made an appointment to interview her at lunch. And what do you know? She was scared of me! She went high-brow at me. She talked about books, about Sigmund Freud, and about Ethel M. Dell, and about poetry. It was getting to be a miserable interview.

"Finally I said, 'Golly I'd like a drink.'

"Mabel broke out laughing. 'Great cats, Louella,' she said, 'whyn't you say so before you spoke?'

"That broke the ice. We became warm friends and remained warm friends. And I got a good story.

"Yes, I think it's true that Sam Goldwyn was in love with Mabel, but I know she did not respond. She could imitate anybody, you know. Her comic imitations of Sam Goldwyn would put you in more stitches than an ambulance surgeon.

"I lived at 116th Street with my daughter, Harriet, and Mabel often visited us there. She spent money wildly for

people she liked, all sorts of fancy and wonderful things for
my little girl and me. Once I went to Europe and returned
with no gift for Mabel. She was as wounded and disappointed
as a little girl whose birthday has been forgotten.

"She was the most beautiful girl I ever saw in my life—
and a madcap.

"I know this, and I know it for sure: she loved one man
only."

At Keystone, now the Mack Sennett Studio, Mabel had
worked hard and done as she pleased. She was late for everything. She was at the heart of every prank. She called me
"Napoleon" and shortened it to "Nappy" in derision. If I
went to her dressing room, to be sure she reached the set on
time, she made fun of me, teased me, changed the subject,
pouted, and acted as if she had never heard of the picture
she was supposed to be working in. She would throw me out
and I would stalk to the set, scowling, to explain to the director that our star Miss Normand had a headache and would
be detained. But Mabel would have taken a short-cut and beat
me to the stage. There she would be, playing her part as if she
had been before the camera all morning and hadn't clapped
eyes on me for days.

She gave Sam Goldwyn and his directors and business
office people the same treatment. She never reported for work
on time. She sassed the executives, then sat on their desks
and twinkled her pretty legs, and made them laugh. She
paraded around the lot, tagged by a liveried chauffeur bur-
dened with an armload of mink and books, making like a
movie star.

More than halfway through one of Goldwyn's expensive
pictures she failed to show up at all one day. Next thing the
office knew about her was from Associated Press reports under
a Paris date line. She ordered the smartest clothes Parisienne
couturières could overcharge her for, danced with princes, and
flitted about the cafés.

She went to England and gave high-diving exhibitions on
the estate of a swanky member of Parliament. The newspapers
were flashy with the names of titled foreigners who wanted to
marry her.

Late one night after trying many times I got a transcontinental and transatlantic telephone call through and spoke to her.

"For God's sake, cut out the spree and come home," I said.

"Why?" said Mabel.

"I need you," I said.

"You had me," Mabel said.

She tinkled a champagne glass against the telephone receiver.

"I have a great new picture in mind for you, Mabel," I argued.

" 'S no good, Nappy," Mabel said. "My contract with Sam still has a long time to run."

"If you don't come home and work out that contract it will run forever," I complained.

Mabel laughed at me.

She was right. It wasn't any good.

When she did return there were stories in the newspapers about how she had dived into the ship's swimming pool *sans* bathing suit. I hear this gossip repeated about Mabel Normand in Hollywood to this date, but I've never believed it. Mabel was casual, foolish—anything you want to say in the framework of those terms—but in all personal things she never violated good taste.

She returned to Sam Goldwyn when she had had her fling and was ready. All told she made between fifteen and twenty pictures for Sam. Some of the best known ones are *The Venus Model*, with Rod LaRoque; *The Last Chance*, with Tom Moore and Herbert Rawlinson; *Peck's Bad Girl*, *A Perfect Thirty-six*, *Upstairs*, with Cullen Landis; *The Slim Princess*, and *Head over Heels*.

She insisted on working on a stage to the accompaniment of the loudest jazz syncopation the record library could provide. Other actresses, particularly such dramatic stars as Mae Marsh, Mary Garden, the opera star, Madge Kennedy, Marie Doro, Maxine Elliott, and Jane Cowl, were put in the proper mood by the sobbing of soft violins. Not Mabel. She wanted action. Wherever she was, there was action.

But this girl was a paradox. She liked jazz, but she read

Brander Matthews, the learned literary critic and contributor to the New York *Times*, Goethe, and Nietzsche. She washed these doses of culture down with large quantities of syrupy motion-picture-fan magazines, sensational novels, funny papers, and the *Police Gazette*. The *Gazette* was one of her favorites.

It was about this time in her pursuit of culture that she met a man named William Desmond Taylor. Mr. Taylor was a Paramount director and president of the Motion Picture Directors Association. He stood about six feet two and had a pale, drawn face which seldom changed expression. He was a man of unshakable poise, beautifully dressed, quiet, with courtly manners. He was well read, and took a kindly interest, in his aloof way, in Mabel's approach to knowledge.

Mr. Taylor will come on stage again.

Mickey had been on the shelf for more than a year.

I was in New York, still trying to interest some theater in screening what I thought was the best work we had ever done, and having no luck.

Late one afternoon while I was in the Bauman and Kessel office the owner of a small theater in Bayside, Long Island, came in with a problem.

"I'm stuck for a picture," he announced. "Some damn fool at the exchange has sent our film to somebody else. Unless I get hold of a feature right now our house is going to be dark tomorrow."

"*Mickey*," I said.

Bauman and Kessel shuddered.

But the Bayside theater owner snapped his fingers and stared at me.

"Saaaaay—*Mickey!* That's the Mabel Normand picture! That's the picture I read all about. That's the picture we've been waiting for. You mean you got a print here?"

Of course he knew all about *Mickey*. For almost two years Harry Carr, Jimmy Starr, and other bright members of the Edendale publicity staff had been putting out a semi-weekly bulletin to every theater in America. Mabel Normand and *Mickey*, with pictures, had been featured on Page One in every issue.

Here was an exhibitor who knew all about *Mickey* but hadn't seen it or heard what the exchanges thought about it. We loaded him with cans of film on the spot, took him in a taxicab to Pennsylvania Station at Thirty-fourth Street, and put him on the next train for Long Island.

When the Bayside theater opened Saturday afternoon with only a few one-sheets in the lobby to announce the film, that astonished manager had to cope with a line of people that angled around the block. By nightfall the police department had to lend a hand. Some customers arrived because they saw the crowds and thought there was a fire.

Audiences almost split that small theater open, rocking it with laughter, during the weeks *Mickey* played there.

The rest came gradually, but the Bayside success encouraged other theater managers. They booked *Mickey*, crossing their fingers for luck, and every time that picture opened it was a hit. *Mickey* is probably the greatest Cinderella story in the history of motion pictures. It is the only film I know of that sat in the ashes so long before making good. It moved on to Broadway, on to Chicago, Philadelphia, Boston, and the other great cities, and its openings were cheered and applauded everywhere.

"Ha!" I said.

I felt like a justified wizard. I hollered, "I told you so!" and "I knew it all the time!" I reminded everybody within earshot that Mabel Normand was the greatest comedienne in the world. There were days when I warmed up so much enthusiasm about Mabel and *Mickey* that I completely forgot that she wasn't under contract to me, either to make pictures or to get married.

Money rolled in so fast we had to hire educated men to count it.

Reporters interviewed me. Exchange executives looked at me with awe—well, anyway, respectfully.

I raised no objections at all when my typewriter boys put out stories about "Mack Sennett, King of Comedy."

Boys, it was good!

By comparison with modern motion pictures with sound and perhaps with color *Mickey* of 1916–17 seems absurd in some sequences. But the photography is sharp (according to a rule we had: comedy has to be *shown*; let the audience see everything; don't confuse 'em), the comedy scenes are hilarious, the chases are breath-taking.

And Mabel Normand is prettier than a speckled pup.

Mickey is still playing here and there. In the intervening years I lost all track of accurate box-office records and I do not own Mabel Normand's wonderful picture today. But trade-paper accountants tell me that *Mickey*, the picture nobody would look at, has grossed more than eighteen million dollars.

As soon as *Mickey* had caught on enough to show that it was going to be a hit and a personal triumph for Mabel, I left New York like a man shot out of a cannon.

I dropped nickels in a pay-station booth at the station in Los Angeles and demanded to speak to Miss Mabel Normand in her dressing room at the Sam Goldwyn Studios. Perhaps she didn't know who was calling. She answered.

"I got news!" I shouted. I probably didn't need a telephone.

"No news from you is good news to me," Mabel said.

"News about you," I said, swallowing hard. "We're in. I mean you're in. *Mickey's* a hit. A real hit. A smash. Opened at Bayside. Kind of an accident. But as soon as the audiences saw you on screen the election was all over.

"Best picture you ever made, everybody says. Mabel, I knew it all the time. You don't know how hard I've worked to get that picture shown——"

"Good for you, Nappy," Mabel said quietly. "It *is* a good picture. You always make good pictures. I'm awfully glad for your sake."

I was as deflated as an actor when the critics call him "adequate."

"Mabel, listen, please. Now don't hang up. Don't you see? That is the kind of picture for you. We've got it. You and me. I know what to do now, how to treat you, what kind of stories to give you."

"I'm due on the set," Mabel said.

"Mabel, *Mickey* is just the start. I've had the boys working on a new one for you, just for you. Nobody else can play it. Big picture, bigger'n *Mickey*. Bigger'n *Tillie*. It's a Cinderella story——"

"What other story *is* there?" said Mabel.

"—it's a Cinderella story about a girl in Brooklyn who delivers laundry and meets a handsome boy who's rich but whose family thinks she isn't good enough for him, and then of course in the end——"

"Truly, I think that sounds mighty fine, Nappy," Mabel said. "But there's no use discussing it. You know I still have a long time to go with Sam. 'By. Love to your mother."

I had Dick Jones set to direct the new picture, *Molly O*, but Mabel wouldn't budge. She gave Goldwyn hell, and upset his executives and directors, but she was loyal. Once when an influenza scare closed thousands of theaters throughout the country she walked into Sam's office and turned her handbag upside down on his desk.

"You'll need cash while the theaters are closed," she said. "Here are a few dimes from me."

What Mabel called "a few dimes" consisted of all her jewelry, all her Liberty Bonds, and all her cash—something over $85,000.

Sam got by without the loan. Sam always gets by.

If I had thought there was a remote chance of getting Mabel, I would have kept the script of *Molly O* in my desk until it aged as hard as the Rosetta Stone. I would have produced it from a wheel chair, fondling my beard.

But that screen play now stood the studio at $40,000, which represented a great many theater tickets at twenty-five cents a ticket, and my business partners were men who could do sums in their heads. They looked on *Molly O* as a personal foible of mine and had no patience with losing $40,000 because I had lost my girl. There was one thin chance left.

I went to see Sam Goldwyn with the desperate hope that I might be able to talk him out of Mabel Normand, at least long enough to make *Molly O*. I thought if I could get her for *Molly O* I could keep her forever.

I approached Sam with the proposition that I could do him a favor.

"Sam," I said, "you have Normand under contract, but

you haven't got any work out of her for a long time. She's a pretty expensive luxury, isn't she?"

"We have a number of stories in black and white for her, but they're only verbal yet," Sam said. "Mabel Normand is the most valuable property in Hollywood. But—if you want to make an offer——"

"I didn't bring my checkbook with me," I said.

"A handshake would do," Sam replied. "We're not ready to start production with Normand right away, so maybe if you would make a handshake to pay us $30,000, we could go into business together separately."

I can add too. Forty thousand dollars for preparing the *Molly O* story plus $30,000 to release Mabel from a Goldwyn contract makes $70,000. I knew Bauman and Kessel and my Triangle associates tolerably well by this time. Well enough to know they would cry "no" to such a deal.

I promised Sam to think it over. My prospects looked dark brown.

If Mabel couldn't, or wouldn't, do *Molly O*, who could?

That was not so hard to answer. There was one other actress. I made an appointment to a British-accented butler and hurried out to Pickfair and called on Miss Mary Pickford.

"You could do this story," I argued. "It's practically written for you. It's exactly the story you need."

"Let me read it," said Mary.

"It stands me $40,000 as is, Mary. I'll let you have it for that, if, maybe, you'd feel like throwing in a small profit for all the time I've spent——"

Miss Pickford sent the script back the next day with a firm "no."

Dark Figure Off Stage

No MATTER which way I turned there was a barrier between me and Mabel. I began to understand that this was not all my fault, and not Mabel's.

If I'd been a farmer, a mechanic, or an ironworker, and if she had been an average girl in an average town, we would have been married long ago. But ever since we met under the sponsorship of D. W. Griffith—in the beginning my university, now, amazingly, my partner—the compelling business of making motion pictures had always stood between us.

Now the industry was not a cheap-Jack carnival trick, but a growing giant. The giant threw its weight around in strange directions.

In 1918 a young man from Indiana named Will Hays became chairman of the Republican National Committee. That same year Lewis J. Selznick picked up for little or nothing a newsreel organization, the World Film Corporation. The first newsreel star was H.R.H. Edward Windsor, Prince of Wales, now the Duke. Audience interest in H.R.H. taught publicists that the screen was as important as the national press in popularizing a personality. Will Hays, smart man, understood this and used the newsreels liberally to put over his candidate, Warren G. Harding, of Ohio.

William Fox saw that Hays knew how to get things done and offered him a job at $75,000 a year. Hays declined, but he became a firm friend of Hollywood and did us many favors in Washington. Hays became Postmaster General.

But motion pictures were in trouble, under fire from

churches, civic groups, and women's clubs for scandals and extravagances, and we needed more than a powerful friend. On January 14, 1922, Hays accepted an offer of $100,000 a year for three years to become the first head of the Motion Picture Producers and Distributors of America, Inc. My own company, Triangle, approved the contract through our representative, P. L. Waters.

One of the reasons we needed Will Hays was the "Fatty" Arbuckle scandal. On September 5, 1921, Roscoe gave a drinking party in a suite in the St. Francis Hotel in San Francisco. He was accused of attacking Pathé Lehrman's girl, Virginia Rappe, and Virginia died.

The Arbuckle tragedy smeared the front pages for months. There were allegations of perversion and savagery. Altogether the story was as wicked and as smutty a tale as ever came out of Hollywood—or Babylon. Arbuckle was tried in the San Francisco courts while the headlines roared. Two juries hung up. A third jury acquitted him.

It is hard to believe that Roscoe Arbuckle, the butt of our jokes and comedies at the studio, was as evil as some people say he was. His wife, Minta Durfee, who now runs a small shop in Hollywood, long ago retired from the screen (she was Chaplin's first leading lady) never believed that Arbuckle was guilty of meanness at any time during his life. But Roscoe had left me five years before the Virginia Rappe tragedy and I know nothing about the case.

I can add one sentimental note. Before Pathé Lehrman died some years later he made arrangements to be buried beside Virginia Rappe in the Hollywood Cemetery.

The Arbuckle debacle was the first sinister problem that confronted Mr. Hays. Soon there was to be another, closer to me.

All pictures became bigger and more expensive as the curiosity of dime-store girls and Park Avenue debutantes alike took relish in the private affairs of movie people, from their money to their morals. The Rudolph Valentino madness was nationally contagious. Mary Pickford and Douglas Fairbanks reigned as king and queen of Hollywood and entertained foreign princelings. Kids had two new heroes bigger than

Buffalo Bill or Happy Hooligan—William S. Hart and Charlie
Chaplin. George Arliss made *Disraeli*. Pauline Frederick was
seen in *Madame X*. Robert J. Flaherty produced the first
documentary, *Nanook of the North*. It was high noon for the
Gish girls, Harold Lloyd, Pola Negri, Charlie Ray, Milton
Sills (*The Sea Wolf*), and Wallace Reid.

Wally died a few years later, a victim of narcotics, and
that sad story was widely published.

All these things, not forgetting the newsreels, which were
now important short subjects in direct competition with Mack
Sennett and Hal Roach comedies, changed our industry
abruptly. They focused the sharp, curious eyes of hundreds of
millions of motion-picture goers on every gesture made in
Hollywood. It was like one big eye examining goldfish with a
reading glass.

This was the decade in which everybody quoted Sigmund
Freud, "Vas you dere, Sharlie?" and Tex Guinan's "Hello,
sucker!" . . . Bootleggers and hijackers, gunfire in Chicago,
and Marilyn Miller in *Sally* . . . the Florida boom . . . Gilda
Gray . . . Scott Fitzgerald's *This Side of Paradise*, which Mabel
liked so much . . . bobbed hair . . . the flapper . . . the Hall-
Mills murder . . . and the Leopold-Loeb murder . . . ouija
boards . . . the Shimmy . . . Al Jolson on a runway at the
Winter Garden entertaining show folks late Sunday nights
. . . Mae West . . .

"Twenty-four for Underwood" . . . Norman Brokenshire
and Graham McNamee . . . Paul Whiteman with eleven
bands . . . Georges Carpentier and Jack Dempsey in the first
million-dollar fight . . . scotch at $25 a bottle, gin at $18 . . .
Babe Ruth's twenty-nine home runs . . . Fred and Adele
Astaire a hit in London . . . the Prince of Wales on and off
horses in the rotogravure sections . . . Sophie Tucker, "Last of
the Red Hot Mamas" . . . Mary Pickford in *Daddy Long Legs*
. . . *Broken Blossoms* (a Triangle picture) . . . Marion Davies
in *When Knighthood Was in Flower* . . . Theda Bara and Pola
Negri . . . John and Lionel in *The Jest* on Broadway . . .
Abie's Irish Rose . . .

Ted Lewis . . . Elinor Glyn . . . Fred Waring . . .
Lenore Ulric . . . *Blossom Time* . . . Ramon Novarro . . .

the Great Ziegfeld . . . the first Atlantic City Beauty Pageant
in 1921 (we were ahead of 'em at Edendale) . . . Heywood
Broun and Alexander Woollcott at the Algonquin Hotel
Round Table . . . Big Bill Tilden . . . attacks on motion pictures by the Rev. Dr. John Roach Straton . . . tea dances
. . . meeting under the clock at the Plaza . . .

It was an improbable time. Every American was getting
rich and everybody felt safe. Even kings in Europe felt safe.

All kinds of things and forces were in motion in that
frenzied time in the early twenties, but none of us had crystal
balls.

Out at Baron Long's the band played "How Ya Gonna
Keep 'Em Down on the Farm" and "Let the Rest of the
World Go By." We all bought superheterodyne Victrolas and
listened to "April Showers," "I'll Say She Does," "Beautiful
Ohio," "Chicago," "Margie," "If You Knew Susie" (Eddie
Cantor knew her better), "Barney Google," "Hot Lips,"
"Ain't We Got Fun," "Aggravatin' Papa," "Three O'Clock in
the Morning"—and "Dardanella."

Anybody who can remember the words to "Dardanella"
is getting along, but who can forget the tune?

The twenties marked a high-water point for me. We made
big pictures, made big money, and thought it would last forever.

Miss Julia Benson, R.N., of 3921 Ingraham Street, Hollywood, received her nurse's cap from St. Vincent's Catholic
Hospital. Her first assignments, after her graduation, included
nursing a number of priests of the Roman Catholic Church.
It seems likely that Mabel heard about her through one of the
fathers. At any rate, Mabel suffered an attack of what was
called the Spanish influenza in 1919, and the smiling, efficient,
and deeply religious Miss Benson looked after her. She stayed
with Mabel for more than ten years.

"I found a little girl just over five feet tall, weighing only
ninety-nine pounds, in pigtails and a flannel nightgown," Miss
Benson tells me. "And that is how I thought of Mabel from
then on."

Mabel kept Miss Benson, not only as nurse, but as con-
fidante and companion, gave her clothes, took her on vacations,

slept in the same room with her, and introduced her to celebrities, not as her nurse, but as her friend.

Julia Benson says that Mabel never wanted to go anywhere farther than across the street without five hundred dollars cash in her handbag. Her smallest tip to waiters and porters was fifteen dollars. She drank occasionally, at parties, as everyone in Hollywood did, but while Miss Benson was with her she recalls that Mabel would go to extreme lengths to avoid smoking a cigarette in the presence of a child. Mabel and Julia made several pilgrimages to a monastery to kiss a relic of the True Cross.

"She talked about someone she called 'Nappy' all the time but you didn't come to see Mabel in those days and I didn't know who she meant."

She may have talked about me. I hope she did. But she didn't talk *to* me. Miss Benson believes that Charlie Chaplin was in love with Mabel, something I'd thought of myself, but only thought of. Plainly there was no truth to this.

The man she did talk about and see frequently was the handsome actor, Lew Cody. Cody was a Shubert star Thomas H. Ince brought to Hollywood. He was the first of the clothes-horse actors, beautifully shirted and tailored, and he became known as "The Butterfly Man." He was more than that. He was a kind man, as I found out years later, and I liked him, but at the time I wished him no better luck than broken legs. I was sorry I had cast him as the villain in *Mickey*, where he got to know Mabel so well.

The man Mabel Normand saw mostly was William Desmond Taylor.

She went with Taylor to talk about books and to argue about psychology, in the same spirit that she made friends with Earl Rogers, the great criminal lawyer, father of Adela Rogers St. John, whose life story is supposed to be the basis of *A Free Soul*, Lionel Barrymore's Academy Award-winning picture.

Taylor made good movies. He had directed Mary Pickford in *Captain Kidd, Jr., How Could You, Jean?* and *Johanna Enlists*; Betty Compson, Constance Talmadge, Dustin Farnum, Wallace Reid, Jack Pickford, Elsie Ferguson, and many other great stars of the day.

I knew Taylor only slightly. He was never in my home, nor did I ever visit his two-story stucco bungalow on South Alvarado Street. He was on the intellectual side and not exactly my style of man, not that I held that against him. He was a close friend of Marshall Neilan and Gloria Swanson and had been president of the Motion Picture Directors Association for three consecutive terms, so he was a figure in motion pictures; but not the kind of figure with which I had much in common. Taylor was the poised, sophisticated type you find in Hollywood today under the label "British actor."

I can't say now for sure that anything would have been different, that Mabel might have been better off, if I had known Taylor—that is, if I had known a few private facts about him. If any of the people whose lives were affected by him had been aware of his background, perhaps many things would have turned out differently. Who this man really was turns into the kind of tough and fantastic mystery story that Alfred Hitchcock handles so well.

But if I had known all there was to know I would not have been able to tell Mabel. Here is the sad truth:

The incident of the diamonds ended the love affair.

I had tried to recapture the girl, but the spark was gone. She looked on me coldly and refused to talk to me on the old basis. I was no longer a little boy sighing for a lost sweetheart. I was a man hard-pressed by the exigencies of a hard, fast business. When I negotiated with Sam Goldwyn for Mabel's return to my studio I spoke for my partners and our investors. I understood clearly—Mabel made it plain—that our only relationship now was that of actress and producer.

I was barely aware, until it was too late, of her friendship with William Desmond Taylor. But this man I hardly knew came out of the wings and walked onto a dark stage in a scene that affected us all.

It is a curious fact of being alive that things like this happen. A stranger you never heard of, never wanted to know, with whom you have nothing in common—and who has no concern whatsoever for you—can do something you are unaware of and suddenly change your life.

As for Mabel, she was not the only girl who found William Desmond Taylor interesting. A child actress named

Juliet Shelby made a hit on Broadway in *The Littlest Rebel* and came to Hollywood under a million-dollar contract with Realart Pictures. Before she was seventeen years old, she had contracts and investments which made her worth more than three million dollars. Her movie name was Mary Miles Minter.

Mary knew Taylor as a highly respected, conservative man, and it is no disservice to her to say that she fell in love with him. As a matter of fact, there are some pretty convincing, and overblown, statements by Mary Miles about her love for Taylor in the files of the Los Angeles District Attorney.

But I was concerned with a number of things aside from Mabel Normand's somewhat scatter-witted approach to culture, with Bill Taylor as tutor, and Mary Miles Minter's affection for this gentleman. Triangle was making money by the bale. D. W. Griffith's and Tom Ince's spectacular pictures were crowding the theaters. My comedies, issued under my own name at last, were going so well that profits skyrocketed a thousand per cent. I bought a theater, a yacht, played the stock market on tips from Diamond Jim Brady and Don Lee, took high dives into gold-mine speculations—and was unhappy. I was reconciled to losing Mabel—there seemed to be no chance of making up—but I was not reconciled to failure with *Molly O*, the picture I had prepared especially for her, which now threatened to cost me many thousands of dollars unless I could produce it.

When I called on Sam Goldwyn the second time to negotiate for Mabel's return, I would have paid him the $30,000 he asked—if I had had to pay it. But now the proposition was strictly business, so I went at it this way:

"Look, Sam," I said, "there's no getting around it, I know and you know I know that you're paying Normand a tremendous salary and losing money every day she is supposed to be making pictures for you and ain't.

"I know she's giving you trouble. How much did you have to spend to redecorate her dressing room because you brought Geraldine Farrar out and gave her a fancy boudoir and Mabel flung a fit and went into a tantrum when she heard about it?

"Cost you $2000, didn't it?

"Never comes to work on time. Skipped off to Europe in

the middle of a picture. Won't take anything seriously, including your own orders. That's Mabel, isn't it?

"We've been all through that at my place. I don't say we can *handle* her. Who can? But we raised her from a kitten and we know how to get along with her.

"You like her. You know she's great. She's a fine artist. She ought to be making fine pictures. Sam, for the last time, I'll make you an offer. No cash. No commitments. But if you want to get out of this deal with Mabel I'm willing to take her off your hands."

One of the longest speeches I ever made. One of the longest speeches anybody ever made without getting contradicted by Sam Goldwyn.

Sam grinned.

"You're right, Mack," he said. "Take her."

I'm a man who will accept all the credit he can get because I'm a man who always needs it. But I have to say that it wasn't my logic, or my shrewdness, that convinced Sam to let me bring Mabel home. When it comes to logic and shrewdness, or for that matter anything else that needs brains, the man hasn't come down the pike yet who can keep step with Sam Goldwyn. On top of that, for good taste and decency and for imagination and great motion-picture making, I am hard put to name even a small handful of men who can stand up to Goldwyn, or look him in the eye without looking up.

Sam knew that he had done all he could with Mabel, and for Mabel, and he knew several other things. I'd say that as of right now the Great Goldwyn is still leagues ahead of Hollywood in the knowing business.

What Sam knew then, and what I didn't know, was that Mabel's cheeks were no longer as round as apples. She was thin. She photographed without her old-time sparkle and bounce in recent pictures, not yet released, which I had not seen. She was unhappy and ill and she looked it. We were amazed and upset when she reported for wardrobe tests.

All those years of neglecting herself, of fun for fun's sake and ice cream for breakfast, of driving herself to be gay and amusing, had left a mark on a girl who after all was very small.

She was still beautiful. Her eyes still laughed. She wore magnificent clothes as if all the magnificent clothes-makers in

Paris had been born with her in mind. Fashion writers crowded
the studio to tell the world about Mabel Normand's newest
frocks and jewels. They described silver brocades, steel beads,
rhinestones like dewdrops, gold embroideries—I can remember
some of the phrases:

"Humming birds' wings and orchids" . . . "moonlight on
fallen snow" . . . "joyous youth and the Rue de la Paix" . . .
"clear water of a forest spring . . ."

For hoity-toity rhetoric read the poets in the fashion
magazines.

At that, they described Mabel. Only they didn't describe
Mabel inside, and neither can I.

Mabel was happy with the cast of *Molly O*, especially
happy with Dick Jones, who had made *Mickey*, as her director.
Both Dick and I had long talks about Mabel late at night in
the tower office. Mabel wasn't the same. She was ill.

I have been asked many times what picture I would re-
make of all the films issued under my name. The answer is
Molly O—if I could find the right girl to star in it.

Molly O cost something more than $500,000 and did not
come close to the incredible $18,000,000 gross of *Mickey*, but
it was a fine picture and eventually a hit. I had bought the
Mission Theater, a large, handsome house in downtown Los
Angeles, and we opened there in January 1922, with the famous
Jesse Crawford at the pipe organ and reserved seats at $1.60.

My troubles were now over. In spite of the exorbitant
cost of the script, of Mary Pickford's rejection of the story,
of my desperate campaign to get Mabel away from Sam
Goldwyn to play the lead—in spite of all these things, St.
Anthony had returned and everything was going to be all right.

On the evening of February 1, 1922, I had an appointment with Tom Ince and Al Lichtman to talk over national
and foreign distribution of *Molly O* and our other big pictures. I went to Ince's home early that evening, had dinner
with Tom and Al, and we talked business until past midnight.

At approximately eight o'clock that night William Desmond Taylor died with a bullet in his back.

CHAPTER 20

Murder

THE telephone in my bedroom jangled at four o'clock Friday morning, February 3. I ignored it. Finally, when it rang persistently, I floundered out of bed, stumbling in the dark, and barked, "Hello."

"This is Mabel."

"Who?"

"Mabel. Are you awake, Mack? This is Mabel. Can you understand me?"

It was the first time she had called me in two years.

"Oh. Hello, Mabel. I'm trying to get awake. Just a minute——"

"Mack, I have to hang up quickly. I think people are listening in. There's something awfully peculiar about Bill's death. Somebody shot him. Shot him in the back. He was murdered."

This was hard to take in. Up to that moment I had heard nothing about an accident with firearms—or a murder.

"Wait a minute, Mabel," I said. "I heard this afternoon there was a doctor there, wasn't there? Didn't he say Taylor died of a hemorrhage?"

"That's right. That's what they thought at first. Then they removed his coat and found out. There was a bullet hole. He was shot.

"And Mack—Mack, I'm in serious trouble. I was the last person seen with him."

I think there must have been a long pause here. I didn't know what to think or what to say.

Mabel was hysterical but quiet. When the chips were down she was always deadly calm, hanging on tight.

Now I understood what she meant by "people listening in." I could hear clicks and hums on the wire. Our conversation was being tapped. By the police, I assumed.

"I'll see you first thing in the morning," I said. "Let's not try to talk now. I'm sorry, and you know I'll do all I can——"

Mabel interrupted.

"There's nothing for you to do, Mack. Nothing at all. I've never brought you anything but trouble. I just wanted you to know. . . ."

Her voice trailed off.

I sat up the rest of the morning gulping black coffee and worrying.

I was sorry for Bill Taylor, but after all this man was a bare acquaintance, not a friend. I didn't go into mourning for him. And I was sorry for anything bad or uncomfortable that happened to Mabel Normand.

But she was either at William Desmond Taylor's house the night he was shot in the back—or she wasn't. There was nothing I could do about that.

She had courage. She could trot around the Sennett lot leading a lion by a string, pretending she thought she was walking a collie. She actually did that scene once and it was great. But, like most completely feminine women, she was terrified of firearms.

Those thoughts went through my mind, leading nowhere. What did strike me, and bowl me over, was the thought of another Hollywood scandal. This one involved the star of my new picture, *Molly O.* I knew exactly what would happen. Civic groups, churches, and women's clubs would condemn us again—and boycott *Molly O.*

"There goes a half million dollars," I mumbled, slugging at the coffee. "We're ruined. Mabel's career is ruined. The picture's washed up. And nothing to do but sit and take it."

Later in the day I learned that both Mabel and Mary Miles Minter had rushed to the Taylor house Friday morning. Both girls were concerned about letters they had written to Taylor and had tried to recover them. Many persons were allowed in the house after Henry Peavey, the butler, discovered Taylor's body. This was because the first doctor on the scene declared that Taylor had died of a stomach hemorrhage. No one suspected murder until several hours had passed. As a matter of fact, Peavey made his first call to Charles Eyton, general manager of the Lasky Company, Taylor's employer, instead of to the police.

Then Mary Miles Minter and Mabel met at Mabel's home. By now the cry of "Murder!" was being yelled by newsboys in the street. The girls talked in Mabel's bathroom with the water taps running full tilt. They thought police and detectives were listening everywhere.

They were.

Will H. Hays had begun to superintend Hollywood morals exactly two weeks to the day before the William Desmond Taylor murder. There was nothing he could do. The facts were the facts. And, as I expected, every reformer with a brick to toss took dead aim at Mabel Normand and *Molly O.*

Hollywood was drawn and quartered by everybody and the pieces thrown over every back fence in the nation. Rural parsons and big city bishops orated against us. If there was a public figure on the side of law and order who didn't hold us in loud contempt, that man must have had laryngitis in February 1922. It appeared certain that *Molly O* was sunk and along with it Mabel Normand and Mary Miles Minter.

Meantime the Los Angeles Police Department and District Attorney Thomas Lee Woolwine's office hopped aboard a number of theories and rode off in all directions.

The first person they talked to was Henry Peavey.

Peavey told the District Attorney that he had served Taylor's dinner in the living room and that Taylor was talking to someone on the telephone when Mabel arrived at about seven o'clock, Wednesday evening, February 1. He left Mabel and William Desmond Taylor together, spoke for a few minutes to William Davis, Mabel's chauffeur, who was waiting outside, spent the rest of the evening in a pool hall, went home, and came to work the next morning at his usual time, 7:30 A.M.

When he opened the front door he discovered Taylor's body on the floor.

Douglas MacLean, the comedian, who lived with his wife at 406½ South Alvarado, exactly cater-cornered from Taylor's house at No. 404½ South Alvarado Street, heard Peavey scream for help.

"Oh, Lord. Oh, my God, Mr. Taylor's dead! Help! Come quick! Mr. Taylor is lying dead in the front room!"

Exactly who responded first, and who called the police at last, I never found out. The MacLeans and Edna Purviance, Charlie Chaplin's leading lady, who lived one house away from Taylor, came in a hurry. Apparently Peavey then put in the call to Charlie Eyton. Then the doctor came—who he was I don't know—and said that Taylor had died of a hemorrhage.

Even the amateurs noted peculiar things long before the detectives began their examination of the premises. Taylor's body was lying stretched out on the floor with arms straight at his sides, neither his collar, his cuffs, nor his cravat rumpled. The living room was tidy, and there was no suggestion that a struggle had taken place. Everybody noticed, incidentally, that the room contained many photographs of movie stars, all affectionately autographed.

Mary Miles Minter wrote on her picture: "For William Desmond Taylor, artist, gentleman, Man! Sincere good wishes, Mary Miles Minter. 1920."

Mary Pickford's said: "To my nice director William Taylor, the most patient man that I know. With sincere friendship, Mary Pickford."

Mabel, who seldom put much more on paper than her indorsement on checks, merely scribbled: "With all the best, always, Bill, Mabel."

A few hours later, the police discovered a large bunch of keys in Taylor's pocket. They never found a door which any of these keys fitted.

On top of that, when the police finally took over, they found money and jewelry in Taylor's pockets worth more than $2000. There was a two-carat diamond ring on his finger, and in his vest pocket a platinum watch which had stopped at precisely 7:21.

The police found a handkerchief, a woman's handkerchief, with the full name embroidered on it. The name was Mary Miles Minter.

Upstairs in a cardboard box in Taylor's bureau drawer detectives found a filmy, feminine nightgown.

Peavey knew about that nightgown. He said he had come to work for Taylor six months before the murder and had seen the nightgown in the bureau in the same box at that time. Apparently Peavey had all the normal curiosity of a professional butler. He was able to tell the District Attorney that he was sure the nightgown had never been out of the box during his employment.

None of these clues pointed anywhere yet. But there was a second circumstance which might have revealed something, if about fifteen hours had not elapsed between the time William Desmond Taylor died and the time the Los Angeles police realized they were investigating a murder.

When the coroner took charge at last, he discovered that Taylor had been killed with a .38-caliber revolver. The bullet had entered the left side and had traveled upward until it lodged in the right-hand side of the neck. Taylor was wearing both a vest and a jacket.

The holes in the vest and the jacket did not match.

It looked, therefore, as if Taylor had been standing or sitting with his arms raised over his head. In this position, his jacket would have been tugged up so that the two holes would match.

This suggested a holdup. Someone had shot Taylor after forcing him to raise his hands. But nothing was missing. The cash and jewelry were still on his body. The house had not been ransacked. The living room was neat—and there was William Desmond Taylor, laid out on the floor as if in repose.

Arthur B. Reeve, the celebrated detective-story writer, was one of the ace reporters who took an interest in the Taylor shooting. He came up with some contradictory statements about the nightgown.

Mr. Reeve said that a former servant of Taylor's said that he had seen that nightgown, had been curious about it, and wanted to know if it was being used. He would take the nightgown from its cardboard box in the bureau, fold it in a certain way, and return it. The next morning, he said, he would look in the box and there would be the nightgown all right—but folded in an entirely different manner.

The nightgown was a headline sensation, of course. But like other clues in the wayward investigation of this murder, it eventually disappeared.

Peavey, the butler, went on to tell what he knew.

He said he came to Los Angeles from San Francisco and that he was originally from St. Louis. Peavey said he knew no motion-picture producers or directors, didn't know Tom Ince or me, but he could identify Marshall Neilan, the director, a close friend of Taylor. And he knew both Mary Miles Minter and Mabel Normand. As he recalled it, Mary came to Taylor's house only once, shortly after he started work. He recognized her from pictures in many of Taylor's rooms. Mary came to the house again the day after the murder, but did not go inside.

He had telephoned Mary once at Taylor's instructions, was unable to get her on the wire, and delivered a letter to her.

He said that Mary Miles Minter telephoned frequently, but that she didn't want to speak to Taylor.

"How is Mr. Taylor, Henry?" she would say. "The reason I ask you is because Mr. Taylor is just like a father to me. We've known him for a long time."

She left no messages, Peavey said, explaining she just merely wanted to know how Mr. Taylor was getting along.

Peavey said Taylor would not accept telephone calls from Mary, anyway. But he told his butler to take messages from Mabel and that he would always call her back.

He said he saw Mabel for the first time about four months before the murder, that he put through calls from Taylor to Mabel about a dozen times, that Mabel visited the house about four times.

Peavey told the District Attorney he thought William Desmond Taylor might have been in love with Miss Normand, but that he had no way of telling what Miss Normand thought of Taylor. Then he contradicted himself flatly by claiming he knew they planned to get married.

Later on Peavey went off the deep end with the statement to the police that he knew who had killed Taylor. He identi-

fied a man who was in the state penitentiary on the date the
crime took place. Peavey was no help.

Florabel Muir, the redheaded, distinguished Los Angeles
correspondent for the New York *Daily News,* was a young reporter working on a Los Angeles paper when the Taylor
murder story broke. Florabel reached 404½ South Alvarado
Street fairly early on the morning of February 2, before Taylor's body had been removed. She is under the impression today that it was Peavey who straightened out the corpse before
the police arrived, thus accidentally concealing the bullet
wound for several hours.

Frank Carson, Miss Muir's managing editor, and the late
Al Weinshank, circulation manager, were convinced that
Peavey was guilty and they went after the story, girl reporter
tagging along.

"They took me with them," Florabel says. "They went to
Peavey's place one night and sort of kidnaped him. Peavey was
an enormous Negro, but he was effeminate. He had a high
voice. In his spare time he used to crochet and tat. So we
thought we could frighten him into a confession and get a beat.

"We took him out to the Rosemont Cemetery and up to
the grave where William Desmond Taylor was buried.

"Al slipped away in the dark and threw a sheet over his
head. Suddenly he leaped from behind the tombstone and accused Henry Peavey.

" 'I am the ghost of William Desmond Taylor. You murdered me. Confess, Peavey.' "

As I get the story from Florabel, that scene in the cemetery with Al Weinshank bobbing around in a sheet and
muttering in sepulchral tones was a ghastly and lugubrious
situation.

Peavey's eyes were wide in the faint moonlight and his
mouth popped open a country mile. He struggled to get away
and roared out loud.

The boys thought they had him for sure. The effeminate
Negro who tatted and crocheted was bellering in high C and
the next step would be a signed confession.

"Then we realized that Peavey wasn't hollering from
fright," Florabel goes on. "That scene might as well have been

played by Ben Turpin and some of your pie throwers. Peavey
wasn't intimidated. He wasn't scairt. He was roaring with
laughter.

"We hadn't figured one thing. We'd forgotten that William Desmond Taylor spoke with the accents of a British
gentleman. Nobody knew that better than his own butler.

"And Al Weinshank talked like a guy from the streets of
Chicago."

When this angle failed to get a story for Florabel & Co.,
they took a tip from Ike St. John, husband of Adela Rogers
St. John, and began to investigate leads growing out of William Desmond Taylor's campaign against narcotics. Ike and
Florabel went out together, following the slimmest kind of
clues in the hope they might turn up something. For some
reason they went to the old Broadway Hotel, which still stands
near the Civic Center in downtown Los Angeles.

In a bedroom there they found the dead body of Earl
Rogers, the West's most famous criminal lawyer. But none of
their investigations brought them to the murderer of William
Desmond Taylor.

The New York *Times* revealed William Desmond Taylor's true identity two days after his death. His name was
William Cunningham Deane-Tanner. He was born in Mal-
lows, County Cork, Ireland, in 1877. His father had been a
colonel in the British Army.

He became an actor with the distinguished Sir Charles
Hawtrey (Billie Burke's discoverer) in *The Private Secretary*
when he was eighteen years old.

He married Ethel Mae Harrison, a member of the original
Floradora company, but abandoned her in 1908, after which
she obtained a divorce and married Edward L. S. Robins, of
the S. M. Robins company, which owned Delmonico's famous
restaurant. "Taylor" was the father of one child, Ethel Daisy
Taylor, nineteen years old.

William Desmond Taylor Cunningham Deane-Tanner
became vice-president of the English Antique Shop at 246
Fifth Avenue, between Twenty-seventh and Twenty-eighth
streets. He belonged to the Larchmont Yacht Club. One afternoon in 1912 he went to the Vanderbilt Cup Races on Long

Island, returned to town drunk, registered at the old Continental Hotel on Broadway and Ninetieth Street, sent to his office for six hundred dollars cash—and disappeared.

Dennis Deane-Tanner, his younger brother, served as a lieutenant in the Boer War and was also in the antique business. Four years after William Cunningham Deane-Tanner (or William Desmond Taylor) vanished, the younger brother also disappeared, leaving a wife and two children.

These were the curious people with whom Mabel's name was now linked—and linked with a golden chain. In William Desmond Taylor's vest pocket, attached to the platinum watch which stopped at 7:21, was a locket. It was inscribed "To my dearest," and contained a picture of Mabel Normand.

One week after the killing on South Alvarado Street the newspapers came up with another yarn. They quoted an informant in Denver—name never revealed—who said that Dennis Deane-Tanner was known in Hollywood under the name of Edward F. Sands.

Edward F. Sands was the butler whom Henry Peavey succeeded on South Alvarado Street.

Sands, too, disappeared. He had fled from Los Angeles when William Desmond Taylor returned from a vacation in Europe to find that his name had been forged to a number of checks. He lodged a complaint against Sands and Sands vamoosed. And so it was claimed by some people that Edward F. Sands lurked in the shadows while Mabel visited William Desmond Taylor on the evening of February 1, and murdered his own brother.

But can we believe that? If Sands was a thief and a forger (according to the charges filed against him by Taylor), why was none of the cash or jewelry in the Taylor house touched that night?

The only witnesses to what went on in the neighborhood of William Desmond Taylor's house the night he was killed were Mr. and Mrs. Douglas MacLean. They told an interesting story to the District Attorney.

CHAPTER 21

Detective Story

WHAT the MacLeans had to say, and the reports of every other witness, from Peavey's unreliable statements to Mary Miles Minter's heartbreaking testimony, concerned me deeply. Of course, I was not directly involved in the William Desmond Taylor murder investigation, which developed into the most sensational murder mystery of the times —but hold on a minute. I wasn't involved? I was involved to the extent of a half million dollars and the career of the woman I once wanted to marry.

The tragedy brought Mabel and me no closer. I talked to her briefly that Friday morning after she telephoned me. She told me little except that she would go to the District Attorney as soon as he wanted her and reveal all she knew.

"I'm sorry, Nappy," she said. "I've ruined the picture and cost you a fortune. I'm sorry."

"We'll make more pictures. This will blow over," I tried to assure her.

I wasn't convincing. I was certain that *Molly O* was as dead as William Desmond Taylor himself.

"We'll do *Suzanna*. And that'll be your best and your biggest," I said.

"Not if you never get *Molly O* off the shelf," Mabel said. "You'd better go now, Mack. Good-by."

I ran the studio, made pictures, argued a few exhibitors into showing *Molly O* in spite of the scandal, and kept close watch on the Taylor case. A murder mystery is not my style at all. I never read them. But if a man has $500,000 at stake he's likely to keep an eye peeled.

No charges had been made against Mabel Normand, but she was condemned and criticized on all sides as if she'd been indicted, tried, and convicted. I hoped that when her whole story was made public this senseless persecution would stop.

Before going on I think I should explain something about where the Taylor murder took place. It has probably struck you as odd that a motion-picture director, Edna Purviance, and the Douglas MacLeans were living in a courtyard instead of in Beverly Hills or Bel Air, where you expect to find movie people.

South Alvarado Street was fashionable in 1922. It was comparable to the part of Sunset Boulevard known today as "The Strip." There were night clubs, smart hotels, and restaurants. It was a convenient place for people who had famous names and made large sums of money. Mabel's home was on 3089 West Seventh Street, just twelve blocks from Alvarado, and Mary Miles Minter was on New Hampshire, also nearby.

Both Mary and Mabel were in a state of collapse. Mabel attended the Taylor funeral, which was watched by a morbid, shrieking crowd of more than ten thousand people in the streets. She fainted. The butler Peavey sat in the front row and sobbed out loud.

Now the police, the headline hunters, and the District Attorney's office, all of whom had come in late, made a rabble-rousing show of William Desmond Taylor's death. The newspapers tried in every edition to find some fresh angle as an excuse for mentioning the names of Mabel Normand and Mary Miles Minter. All of us in the motion-picture industry, even those who were so remotely associated with Taylor as to make investigation nonsensical, were questioned at length. All of us were made to feel that we were constantly watched and shadowed. I was bothered least of all because it was plain to everybody, even to the detectives who misplaced so much of the evidence that was available, that I had no light to shed on anything connected with William Desmond Taylor. I tried to attend to business. I tried to save *Molly O* and my $500,000 from the harpies and the fanatics. I told Mabel to tell the police every shred of facts she knew that might have any bearing on a solution.

Meantime Doug and Faith MacLean went to Mr. Wool-

wine's office and described what they saw on the night Taylor
was killed.

Doug had known William Desmond Taylor only casually, had never worked in a picture for him, and neither he nor
Faith MacLean had peered out their windows across the way
to spy on visitors. This was MacLean's story:

"We have dinner at 7:00 o'clock. Mrs. MacLean was always anxious for me to be on time on account of the servants.
That night I was five minutes late. I know that because I
looked at my automobile clock. As I came up through the alley,
I honked for Christina. She came to the door and I told her I
was home and ready for dinner.

"I put my car in the garage, came in the house and must
have taken about five minutes to wash up and get ready for
dinner. So we sat down, I should judge, at ten minutes after
seven. I guess it took half an hour to eat dinner.

"It was quite a cold night and the gas wasn't working very
well. Mrs. MacLean complained of a chill, and I went upstairs
to get the little electric heater we usually have in the bathroom.
I went in the front room and lit the gas radiator and also the
radiator in the back room upstairs. As I went into the front
room to get my house coat and put it on, I heard a noice or an
explosion that sounded like a shot.

"I continued to work with the heater, unscrewed the
thing and came downstairs. I met Christina in the dining room.
She said, 'Mr. MacLean, did you hear a shot?'

"I said, 'Yes, Christina, if it was a shot.'

"I walked on into the living room and Mrs. MacLean said,
'I don't think it was a shot, do you?' I said no, I didn't think
so, I thought it was the backfire of an automobile.

"Mrs. MacLean suggested we play some dominoes, so I
got everything out and we played for quite a while, talked a
little, and then went to bed.

"In the morning I heard someone screaming in the court.
At first it was just a lot of jumbled noise. We sat bolt upright
in bed and listened. Finally we heard someone yell, 'Oh, Lord.
Oh, my God, Mr. Taylor is dead! Help! Come quick!'

"In our little court the houses began to bulge forth people
in all sorts of attire. I remember distinctly a man coming out

of the house across the street from us and going over to Mr. Taylor's. He said to a woman who was leaning out of a window above, 'Murder.'

"Mrs. MacLean said, 'Do you think it could have been the shot we heard last night?' Then she said:

" 'You know, a funny thing happened last night while you were upstairs. I went to the door and looked out and I saw a man leaving that house.'

"I asked what the man looked like.

" 'Well, he was—I don't know—sort of a roughly dressed man.'

" 'Did you see his face?'

" 'No, I didn't.'

" 'Do you think it was Sands?'

" 'No, I don't think so.'

"I asked her to describe his clothes, but all she could remember was that he wore a cap and had something around his neck. She wasn't sure whether it was a muffler or not. When she talked with the officers later, she wasn't sure whether the coat collar might have been turned up, or whether what she saw was a muffler.

"At any rate, I hurried into my clothes and went over to Mr. Taylor's house. It was full of people. I saw Mr. Taylor lying on the floor and Mr. Jesserun, the landlord, said to me, 'Mr. Taylor is dead.'

"Shortly after that the police arrived and then a doctor. The doctor said that Mr. Taylor had died of a hemorrhage. I told Mr. Jesserun about hearing what we thought might have been a shot. And he said, 'Oh, yes, I heard that too.'

"Taylor looked immaculate. He was lying flat on his back, his feet separated a little, his hands at his side, perfectly flat on his back.

"I said to Mrs. MacLean, later on, 'He looked just like a dummy in a department store, so perfect, so immaculate.' I was impressed with the fact that he looked like a wax figure dressed up. His face was to the ceiling. It seemed to me that he was looking straight up."

Mabel stayed at home in a state of shock, almost in a state of collapse. I thank God for Julia Benson, R.N., who had been out of town when the murder took place, but who hurried home to look after Mabel. Mabel was concerned about a number of letters she had written to Taylor which she knew he had kept. They were innocent letters, she told me, but she knew they would make sensational copy if they fell into the hands of reporters.

Mary Miles Minter talked until dawn with Marshall Neilan Friday night after the murder. She, too, was worried about letters she had written to Taylor. Neilan gave her sound advice. "Tell everything you know," he said. "Don't hold back anything."

District Attorney Woolwine and his deputies and detectives asked Mrs. MacLean about the man she had seen near the Taylor house the night she and her husband heard the shot.

"I saw a man had already opened the door and was looking toward Alvarado Street."

"Did he seem in a hurry?"

"No, he was the coolest thing I have ever seen. He went around—he was facing Alvarado Street—and as I opened the door I saw him. He turned around and looked at me and hesitated. Then it seems to me that Mr. Taylor must have spoken to him from inside the house. Seemed like he pulled the door shut. He turned around and looking at me all the time, went down the couple of steps that go to Taylor's house. I thought it was just nothing, none of my business. I closed the door as he started in between the two houses. He went toward Maryland Street and the alley."

Mrs. MacLean thought the man she saw had a smooth face, but she didn't see his face distinctly. Her main impression was that he wore a cap and something like a muffler around his throat. She guessed that the man was about five feet nine and believed he wore a dark suit.

"He was not a well-dressed man. He was dressed like my idea of a motion picture burglar."

The next person questioned was William Davis, Mabel's chauffeur, who had driven her to Taylor's house the night of the murder. William had worked for Mabel since December 1920.

He said that he drove the car to Taylor's house at seven o'clock and waited thirty or thirty-five minutes while Mabel was inside. When Mabel came out, Taylor was with her, helped her into the car, and talked with her for a minute or two before she drove off. The only other person he remembers seeing come out of the house was Henry Peavey. He was not positive what Taylor wore that night, but thought that he had on street clothes and was bareheaded. He didn't recall any man's going toward the Taylor apartment while he was parked on Alvarado Street.

When Peavey left for the evening, while Mabel was inside with Taylor, he came out to the street and had a few words with Davis.

"I remember he kept saying what a fine man Mr. Taylor was. But it didn't interest me. I didn't pay any attention. He said 'Good night' and went on. I was reading the Police Gazette, so I never paid any attention to anybody going around there or anything."

Davis told the District Attorney that he drove Miss Normand away from the Taylor house at "between twenty and a quarter to eight. It was within five minutes of that because I looked at the clock and it showed about twenty minutes of eight before she came out. I was getting hungry. I forgot to mention the Negro told me that dinner was over. Anyway, Miss Normand told me when she went in it would only be a couple of minutes. I thought if she was going to stay to dinner, she would tell me to go and get mine."

Davis remembered that he had taken Mabel to Taylor's home one evening two or three weeks previously at about 7:30. She was to have dinner with Taylor, so she dismissed her chauffeur and told him that Mr. Taylor was bringing her home. Davis thought this was the only time he had ever left Mabel at Taylor's house.

Mary Miles Minter and her attorney, John G. Mott, were questioned by W. C. Doran, Chief Deputy District Attorney.

Mary said that she saw William Desmond Taylor for the

last time on December 23, 1921, when she drove her "little runabout" to his house late at night.

"I had gone to bed. I hadn't seen Mr. Taylor in five months at the time—three months. I know. Three months, and I just got to thinking about it and I decided I couldn't stand it any longer. I was going to go up and tell him 'good-bye.' I got up and dressed, went down to my grandmother's room and said:

" 'Mama, I am going over to say "good-bye" to Mr. Taylor,' and she advised me not to do it.

"She said it was too late. 'Do you know it is nearly twelve o'clock?' she said.

"I said, 'Yes, sure, but I just must do so.' I said, 'I realize that this is not the usual thing and I have never been there so late, but I must do so, Mama. I am going to give him a letter in which I have told him "good-bye." '

"She said, 'All right, then if you must. I would get up and go with you, but I don't feel well enough.' Mama often accompanied me on my trips, which were not very many during the entire time that I knew him.

"So I went over there and arrived at five minutes to twelve. I am strange about that. I am rather queer about that, I think of the time. Every time I was with him I would say, 'Well, this time yesterday I didn't see him and today I am with him,' and things like that. So I arrived at five minutes to twelve and left at twenty minutes to one."

Mary told Mr. Doran that she and Taylor would have been married if Taylor had been younger. But Taylor, who was forty-five years old, saw this wouldn't work.

She quoted him: "You know, Mary, to me you are the morning sun, bright, beautiful, and with the world and a future before you, and I am the setting sun, and don't you see, my dear, it simply cannot be."

Mary said, "I never even called him 'Bill' in my life. The man was too wonderful for that. I don't care what anybody says or what they prove against him. I knew he was the finest thing in the world.

"I had always known that this was just an exquisite chapter in my life that must necessarily be a brief one. I couldn't bear to part with it. It was just a beautiful thing that seldom occurs in the world today as I see it, as it is forced upon me. It was simply a beautiful white flame. I had always been a reserved, very retiring young girl, and he was the first man and the only man who ever embodied all the glories of manhood in one private body. He represented that to me. He never, by look, by word, or by deed gave me any reason to doubt any of my ideals that were placed in him absolutely."

Mary Miles went on to tell about calling on William Desmond Taylor the night of December 23.

"It's rather late, Mary," Taylor said as he opened the door.

"Yes, but don't you realize that I had to come to see you? You know Mama—my grandmother—has been sick for three months and you have been ill, and I have been frightfully worried, and you haven't even had the kindness to call me to tell me that you were ill and that I must not expect to see you.

"I don't care if you don't want to see me. It hurts me, but it wouldn't have hurt one millionth as much if you had just explained."

"Mary, I couldn't help it. I couldn't help it, and I can't explain it to you."

It had been in the papers that Mary Miles Minter was engaged to marry Marshall Neilan, and then there were stories that the engagement had been broken.

Not so, Mary said. "Thomas Dickson is the only one to whom I have been even remotely engaged, and that was a freak of despondency."

On Friday night, February 3, following the murder, Mary Miles Minter, Gloria Swanson, Jack Pickford, and Frank Urson went to Marshall Neilan's house. Mary told how she and Neilan then went on to the studio on Santa Monica Boulevard and talked until dawn about William Desmond Taylor. They talked about the many letters Mary had written to Taylor and wondered how they could recover them before the newspapers got hold of them.

Mary and her grandmother had driven to Alvarado Street as soon as Mary heard of Taylor's death. They did not go inside. It was that afternoon that Mary went to Mabel's house at 3089 West Seventh Street and talked in the bathroom. Mary quoted Mabel:

"Come in here and we will run the water in the bath tub

because if there are any dictagraphs they won't work with the water running."

On February 1, the night William Desmond Taylor was killed, Mary Miles Minter said she spent the entire evening at home with her mother, her sister and her grandmother. She remembered the evening because she was reading *Cruise of the Kawa*, a take-off on Frederick O'Brien's stories of the south seas.

It was Mabel Normand's turn next. She had been at 404½ South Alvarado Street the night the shot was fired.

I hoped for the best. I didn't know what to expect. I was sure of one thing only: Mabel would tell the truth.

The Night of February 1

OF ALL THE ACTRESSES who knew William Desmond Taylor, or who might have shed any light on his strange death, Mabel Normand was the only one called to the stand at the coroner's inquest.

She was ill, hardly able to get out of bed, but she was a trouper and she went with all flags flying. She wore a brown-checked sports coat with fur at the collar and cuffs, a black skirt, and a creamy lace shirtwaist. She had white gloves and a flowing lavender silk handkerchief. On her head a wide-brimmed, green velour fedora. She looked small and brave.

"Mabel," I said, "do you need——"

She gave me the old grin.

"Don't need a thing, Nappy. I look all right? Think the photogs will like me?"

"Be serious for once, Mabel."

"I'm serious, Nap. Dead serious. All I do is tell them what happened. 'Sall there is to it.

"And, old boy, don't ever forget this—*nothing* happened."

The inquest was mercifully short. Only a few questions, none of them, I thought, very pertinent. The main thing the coroner wanted was for Mabel to go to Taylor's house on South Alvarado Street and re-enact everything that had happened on the night of February 1.

I saw her eyes widen, but she didn't hesitate. Only Peavey—front-row Peavey; Peavey sat in the front row everywhere—only Peavey grew emotional and broke down in tears.

Mabel was as forthright as a lawyer when they took her to

Taylor's living room, made her show where she and Taylor had sat, and drew a diagram to indicate where his body was found on the floor.

"I want my letters," she said. No attempt at concealment. "I know where Bill kept them. In the top drawer of his dresser."

The officials looked, but the letters were gone.

"I don't know why anyone should be interested," Mabel said. "There's nothing in them that would interest the police. There were six or seven and some telegrams. I'd like to have them back. Now, I know where they were because I saw them the night he showed me over the house after he'd been robbed."

Mabel's letters, Mary Miles Minter's handkerchief, an unidentified nightgown, and a mysterious note a policeman said he found in the toe of a riding boot—all these things were missing. If Taylor died at eight o'clock the night of February 1, and his body was not discovered until 7:30 the next morning, and if murder was not suspected for several hours later, there had been plenty of time for any number of persons to enter the Taylor house, make off with the evidence, cover up clues, and steal. It may not have been the fault of the Los Angeles Police Department—the cops arrived late—but this was a mismanaged investigation.

The ruckus about letters, handkerchiefs, and nightgowns was just more ammunition for the scandalmongers.

After Mabel's examination the coroner's verdict was released to the press. For tight understatement I thought it might have been written by my old friend Calvin Coolidge.

It said that "William Desmond Taylor came to his death at the hands of an assassin."

But Mabel had to account for every moment of the day and night of February 1. When she had recovered from another collapse, she went to the office of the District Attorney, without a lawyer.

Q. You are an actress, are you not?

A. I think so. Some of them don't think I am, Mr. Woolwine.

Q. You knew William Desmond Taylor in his lifetime?

A. How will I answer? Just say yes? Yes.

Q. How long have you known him?

A. I've known Bill about six years.

Q. How long have you known him sufficiently well to go out with him?

A. Last year and a half.

Q. Now, you were with Mr. Taylor on the evening of his death, were you not?

A. Well, Mr. Woolwine, I didn't hear of his death until the next day.

Mabel's movements the afternoon and evening of Taylor's murder were easy to establish. She went downtown in the late afternoon to the Hellman Bank at Sixth and Main. There she got out her canceled checks and left her checkbook to have it balanced—the only time it was in balance was when the bank had it—talked to several persons in the safety-deposit vaults, and asked permission to use the telephone.

"The maid said, 'Mr. Taylor has called you three or four times and he sent a book to you from Parker's, the bookstore. He said to tell you he had stopped at Robinson's and picked up the book you wanted.'

"It was *Rosa Mundi*, by Ethel M. Dell, and the price mark is on the back—$2.00.

"I said good night to the people in the bank and had Davis drive me down Main Street, but I stopped when I saw a peanut man at the Pacific Electric. I got out and ran across the street and bought fifty cents worth of peanuts. But the peanut man didn't have change for my ten dollars, so I went in the drugstore and the girl at the counter changed it and smiled very nicely as if she recognized me. She gave me a lot of silver. I asked her not to give me so much silver but she did."

Somewhere between the Hellman Bank and South Alvarado Street Mabel made another stop which she forgot to mention to the District Attorney. She arrived at William Desmond Taylor's house equipped, not only with fifty cents' worth of peanuts, but an armful of magazines, which she dropped on the floor of the car, and a new *Police Gazette*.

"I got there at 7:00 o'clock. I ran up the court and rang the doorbell and Peavey came to the door.

" 'Good evening, Henry, is Mr. Taylor here?'

" 'Yes, ma'am, he is on the telephone.'

"I could hear Mr. Taylor talking on the telephone in that little place underneath the stairsteps. He was talking quite loudly. His place is rather small, so I waited outside. I didn't want to step inside and have to listen.

"No, I don't know to whom he was talking."

It seems to me that Mabel thought this conversation was important. She mentioned it several times, not only to the District Attorney, but to detectives and reporters who were working on the case. It was the last telephone conversation that William Desmond Taylor ever had, and it was important enough for him to keep Mabel Normand standing outside while he finished it.

I thought that Mabel was trying to suggest to the investigators that this was a real clue. But so far as I know they never checked that last telephone call.

Mabel heard Taylor say, "Good-by, good-by, good-by."

"Then he rushed out to me, as Peavey went to the kitchen, and took both my hands in his, and there I was with that big bagful of peanuts in my hands and that black bag I keep things in, and all those cancelled checks, and Mr. Taylor laughed at me.

"I sat down on the piano stool. I said, 'Oh, Lord, I'm all out of breath.' He said, 'I know why you came to see me. You want your book. Now don't sit there in that hard seat, come over here and sit down,' and he pulled up the rocking chair. I got up and then I noticed the room. It had been changed all around.

"I said, 'Oh, you've changed everything.' And he said, 'No, I haven't.'

"I noticed one thing in particular, and that was his desk was open and things all scattered about, checks and things like that. There was a photograph of mine on the desk.

"The landlord says I am mistaken about this, but Mr. Taylor had a little table and he said it was pushed way out in the room. But it wasn't pushed out when I was there.

"I stayed until about a quarter of eight. Mr. Taylor asked me if I had had dinner. I told him I had not and he said, 'Oh, then please let me take you out to dinner.' But I realized that Peavey had already served Mr. Taylor his dinner in the living room so I said, 'No, thank you, I'm too tired to go out.'

"Then Mr. Taylor started showing me different books. We talked about the *Three Soldiers* by that Chicago newspaperman, and then about a red book, something Peavey had spoken of.

"Then Mr. Taylor said, 'Mabel, we have rice pudding, don't you want some?' When I said 'no' again, he insisted on taking me out to dinner. 'Let me take you out and I promise to go home right after dinner.' "

It's possible that William Desmond Taylor's life hung on that invitation. If Mabel had accepted, he might be alive today.

Peavey cleared up the dishes, moving around unusually fast for him, went upstairs once, came through the front room, said, "Good night, Miss Normand," and "Good night, Mr. Taylor" and left at 7:30.

Mabel recalled that because she almost doubled up with laughter when Peavey came downstairs. He was wearing golf clothes.

"You ought to see him from the back, Mr. Woolwine. In plus-fours. He was so funny. I don't know why he was wearing golf clothes at night, but I said to Mr. Taylor, 'That's a good idea, why don't you let him play golf more often so he won't get in any more of that trouble in the park.'

"I teased Mr. Taylor to tell me about Peavey, but I never found out. Peavey was in pretty dutch at the City Prosecutor's office and the case was going to come off at 3:00 in the afternoon. But that's all I know about Peavey's trouble.

"Finally, I said I was tired, I had to go, and Mr. Taylor said, 'Well, this is the first of the month and I'm going to make out a lot of checks. Can I come up to your house later?'

"I said, 'Well, yes, if I have my dinner downstairs. If I don't, I'm going upstairs and have a bath and go to bed and I will be asleep. Bill, please don't call me until 9:00 o'clock.'

"I picked up my book and stood on the little porch and Mr. Taylor came with me and pointed out who lived in the other apartments. Then he closed the screen door. I'm not positive whether he closed the glass door or not, but I think he didn't. We went out to my car together. Davis was in the front seat and Mr. Taylor helped me in. He looked down on the floor and saw the Police Gazette and started to laugh.

"He said, 'Good Lord, Mabel, you're going in for terrible literature this year.'

"Then I suggested that we drop in to see Edna Purviance for a moment. Bill said, 'No, you wouldn't go out with me, now you have to go home to bed.'"

Mabel blew Taylor a kiss with both hands through the rear window as she drove away. The last thing she heard him say was "I'll call you at 9:00 o'clock."

Mabel remembered Edward F. Sands, the former butler, and the time William Desmond Taylor received some pawn tickets from Sacramento with a letter signed "Alias Jimmy Valentine." She said Taylor knew the letter was from Sands, who was then a fugitive under indictment for forgery, because Sands mentioned Mrs. Dennis Deane-Tanner, and Sands was the only one who knew his sister-in-law's name. Taylor hated Sands and told Mabel he'd like to take a good punch at him.

She could think of no one who might want to do Taylor an injury on account of herself.

Q. Can you look back upon any man you ever went with or whoever entertained affection for you, who might become jealous of Mr. Taylor?

A. No, I have thought—that is one of the first questions you all asked me.

Q. Are you satisfied?

A. Yes, sir; I am very satisfied.

Q. As I just intimated to you, a girl of attractiveness, even in a less degree than you have it, naturally has many admirers. I will ask you if you can look back along the years of your life and recall any man who might have entertained such an affection for you as to become jealous of Mr. Taylor? Can you think of any one?

A. No, because I like to be by myself quite a lot, and the husbands of the girls I went around with all went to the fights on Tuesday nights. Mr. Taylor didn't care very much about the fights and always wanted me to dine with him alone, because, you see, we always used to go around in such a crowd, and I didn't do it, and they used to think I was not terribly nice at times toward Mr. Taylor.

Q. Oh yes, going with him perhaps, I mean to the ex-

clusion of others, might have engendered some sort of jealousy
on the part of some persons toward him?

A. No, because, Mr. Woolwine, I haven't gone with anyone, I mean in a couple of years out here.

Q. And you haven't heard any echo, anything of that sort,
even from the men you have gone with before, or any of your
friends?

A. I would certainly know it from some of the girls if a
fellow had a crush on me. The girls would say, "Mabel likes to
go out and play, but as far as getting serious with any one she
can't be annoyed, she is too anxious about work."

Mabel had several quarrels with Taylor and she told about
them freely.

"It was like this. Suppose we were at a party or something
and I would run away from him and pay attention to a lot of
other people. Bill would say, 'You're not treating me very well.
When are we going home?'

"I'd say, 'For God's sake why do you stand around with
that trick dignity of yours? You make me sick.'

"And he'd say, 'I'm not trying to be dignified. Good God,
don't you know I like you?'

"I'd say, 'Good God, don't be melodramatic.' And then I
wouldn't talk to him.

"One time we went to a New Year's party at the Alexandria along with Wesley Ruggles and Pat Murphy and Rene
and Tom Moore, and somebody got awfully drunk. Bill
wanted me to leave the party and I wouldn't. And I didn't
speak to him all the way home."

Q. You got the pouts?

A. Yes, and I got a little nasty.

Q. And that was all there was to it?

A. That was all.

The next morning, New Year's Day, Peavey found Taylor
weeping. He gave the butler a note to send to Mabel and when
Peavey handed it to the chauffeur he learned about the quarrel.

"He cried all the way home in the car," the chauffeur said.

Checking on the time of Mabel's departure from Taylor's
house and on the time that she arrived home—both facts inde-
pendently substantiated—Mabel Normand was having dinner

by herself at eight o'clock that Wednesday night when some-one shot William Desmond Taylor.

Neither she nor any other person was accused or brought to trial. In some respects it would have been better for Mabel if she'd been indicted.

"I wish they'd accused me and tried me," she said more than once. "That way, everything would have been clean. As it is, poor Bill Taylor's death is a scandal and I'm a liability.

"I'm through with pictures, Mack. I won't cause you any more trouble."

"You're not through," I said. "And *Molly O's* not through and I'm not through. We're going right on with *Suzanna*."

"I'm tired," Mabel said. "I want to go away. I want to rest."

Erle Stanley Gardner, head man of "The Court of Last Resort" and probably today's most distinguished detective-story writer, examined the Taylor case minutely.

"Let us suppose a man did slip through the door and had commanded William Desmond Taylor to raise his hands," Mr. Gardner wrote. "The movie director complied; then why shoot him? If a man is perpetrating a robbery and the victim raises his hands, the next move is for the robber to go through his clothes and take his personal possessions. The use of firearms is resorted to when the victim *refuses* to comply with the order to stick up his hands.

"Moreover, robbery was apparently not the motive be-cause money and jewelry were found on the body of the director.

"It occurs to me that the police either overlooked or de-liberately failed to emphasize a far more logical theory than this stickup hypothesis.

"There was a checkbook on the desk and a fountain pen. When a person is writing, if he is right-handed, he rests his left elbow on the desk and slightly turns his body. That would have the effect of raising the coat just about the amount that would be required to match up the bullet holes in the coat and vest of William Desmond Taylor.

"Let us assume, therefore, that Taylor was writing at the time he was shot.

"What was he writing?

"Obviously it was not a check. He may have offered to write a check, but the person who shot him didn't want a check. He wanted something else *in writing*.

"If William Desmond Taylor had refused to write a check, the checkbook wouldn't have been left there on the desk with the fountain pen near by. If he had written a check, then it was to the interest of the person receiving that check to see that Taylor lived long enough for the check to be cashed. A man's checking account is frozen by his bank immediately upon notification of his death.

"It seems to me, therefore, that some person wanted, and quite probably obtained, a written statement from William Desmond Taylor. Once that statement had been properly written out and signed, the person had no further use for William Desmond Taylor and probably through a desire for vengeance, or else with the idea of sealing his lips, pulled the trigger of a gun which had been surreptitiously placed against the side of the director's body.

"It is interesting to speculate whether some woman may not have been concealed in the upstairs portion of the house at the time the shot was fired. The presence of a pink silk nightie indicates that at some time previously women, or at any rate a woman, had been there.

"Notice the manner in which the body had been 'laid out.'

"If the woman in an upstairs bedroom had heard voices below, followed by the sound of a shot, and then the noise made by a body falling to the floor, then the opening and closing of a door . . . perhaps, after ten or fifteen minutes of agonized waiting, she tiptoed down the stairs and found the body of the director sprawled on the floor. It is only natural that this woman, before slipping out into the concealment of the night, would have bent over the lifeless body, wept a few tears, and arranged the clothing as neatly as possible.

"The most interesting lead of all was offered by Mabel Normand in her comments about the telephone conversation. Quite obviously she was trying to impress upon the police that in her opinion this telephone conversation had some probable bearing upon the death of the director. It is almost certain that this was no mere casual conversation and that William Des-

mond Taylor discussed it with her while they were talking
together."

Mabel had been quoted in the newspapers about this. She
said that someone had called Taylor on the telephone.

Mr. Gardner continues:

"How else could Mabel Normand have known that the
person had called Taylor, not that Taylor had called this person? How did she know that the person at the other end of the
wire was very much interested in what Taylor was saying?

"Is it possible the police failed to appreciate the signifi-
cance of Miss Normand's statement? Or did Miss Normand,
after thinking things over, decide that she had gone too far
and that it would be better to forget all she might have been
told about that conversation?

"It is to be borne in mind that the police were undoubtedly subjected to great pressure at the time. They were also
confused by confessions which were arriving at the rate of ten
a day. That's an average of better than one an hour for each
hour of the working day.

"One thing is certain, no dyed-in-the-wool mystery fan
would have let Miss Normand's significant statement about the
telephone conversation pass unnoticed. And I think that most
really intelligent mystery readers would have given an interpre-
tation other than the stickup hypothesis to the fact that the
course of the bullet indicated the left shoulder had been
raised at the time of death.

". . . There is an interesting field for speculation in the
fact that police have the fingerprints of Edward Sands. It is becoming more and more common nowadays for all classes of
people to be fingerprinted and the prints passed on to the FBI.
Imagine what a furor there will be if some day the FBI, making a routine check of some fingerprint, comes upon that of
the missing secretary of the murdered motion-picture director.
That is a distinct possibility. . . ."

Murder or no murder, mystery or no mystery, we had to
pick up the slapstick where we had dropped it and go on making funny pictures. Mabel was crushed. Many women's clubs
passed resolutions banning *Molly O*, condemning Mabel in

trial without jury, trial without evidence, and guilt by association. Mary Miles Minter left the screen for good.

Gradually decency and common sense and American fair play began to make themselves felt. The theaters showed *Molly* in spite of the witches on the back fence. *Molly O* was not the great financial success that *Mickey* was, but nothing that earns a million dollars is a loss. We made *Suzanna*, a historical costume comedy, starring Mabel, and that, too, was a hit.

Over Mabel Normand's life from then on hung the pall of the William Desmond Taylor murder.

The police continued to work on the case.

CHAPTER 23

On with the Show

THEY SAY the show must go on. For the life of me I don't know why. Tie me to an Apache stake or hale me before a senatorial committee investigating the nonsensicalities of motion-picture producers, and I'd still be tongue-tied. The show doesn't have to go on for doctors, lawyers, and merchant chiefs, who often enough call a halt to their proceedings to play golf, consult their astrologers, or dose themselves with the latest things in antibiotics.

But come hell and hot water, theater folks are supposed to get out there and act. So our show went on. That is to say, our various shows went on. While I tried to get *Molly* on the road, Billy Bevan and Mildred June cut their antics in *Gymnasium Gym*, Ben Turpin was in the throes of a new caper, and we began *Suzanna*.

At that, this was the one time when there was a reason for going on with the show. We needed to toss Mabel Normand right back into the teeth of the fools and harpies who had damned her—and at the same time back into the laps of the people who liked her. *Suzanna* was a big one. As always, our plot was so simple that you could have written it in detail on the back of a visiting card, but the project was ambitious.

I proposed to make a historical costume drama of Southern California, circa 1835, the era of the missions, the Jesuits, the Spanish dons, and the Indians. With Mabel Normand as star there obviously would be comedy, but we worked out a romance this time, instead of a slapstick, and shot the works in eight reels.

It had to be authentic historically. I worked with Dick

Jones, who directed under my supervision, and created on the lot the great houses of the Castilian gentry, the wonderful old missions, and even—on backdrops—California scenery breathtaking enough to please the Chamber of Commerce. In addition to a large cast headed by George Nichols and Leon Bary, I threw in black bears, timber wolves, coyotes, imported fighting cocks, a Mexican bull, and ten thousand head of steer.

Suzanna was completed late in May and was another triumph for Mabel.

Robert E. Sherwood, who later became a Pulitzer Prize-winning playwright, was the country's leading motion-picture critic. He made several interesting comments under the title of "Dere Mabel":

"Once a year, perhaps, she steps forth to remind us that she is still the first comedienne of the silent drama . . . Miss Normand is the person who taught Charlie Chaplin to be a movie actor. . . . It is the presence of Mabel Normand in the cast which saves it from being just another of those things. You can't imagine this irrepressive gamin doing anything stupid or dull or obvious on the screen. She has a remarkable flare for impudent comedy. . . ."

So we were back in business again at the old stand, or so it seemed for a spell.

But Mabel was weary. In June, with a good many millions of people smiling at *Molly* and at *Suzanna*, she begged off and said she had to take a long rest. She made reservations for a trip to Europe. On her way to New York reporters grabbed her in Chicago and she made a statement:

"I want to appeal to the public. I want to ask them to give me a square deal. The public was very kind to me once. . . . And then just when my biggest picture was released, this terrible thing came and the newspapers were full of horrible stories about us out there.

"I don't know anything about my future. I have left that in Mr. Sennett's hands."

Mabel sailed for Europe on the *Aquitania*, June 13, and did not return until September 13—and made the headlines all over again almost every day. I wish she had been content, as she said, to leave everything in my hands.

At the Prix de Longchamp, her gold cloth gown, embroidered with jade, with diamonds in the hem, was the talk of all the better-known continents.

I have a scrapbook jammed with pictures and articles devoted exclusively to Mabel's love affair with Paris dressmakers. She bought a gown of silver cloth, a blouse with metallic embroidery in antique and green gold on a foundation of chiffon, and a street costume of crepe-back satin in golden cocoa. She liked a coat in Canton crepe in dead white with rows of silk fringe a foot deep—so she bought two copies of the same garment. It also appears that she needed a pearl-gray afternoon coat with embroidered steel nailheads and sleeves looped up with steel buckles.

She spent $100,000 on clothes. She wore her new pretties once, then forgot them or gave them away.

She went to London and threw both Piccadilly and Mayfair into uproars by playing "Beaver" from Limehouse to Buck House. You play "Beaver" by screaming and pointing when you see a man with a beard, extra points for a man with a red beard. Mabel became London's champ screamer and pointer. She went to Deauville, where the biggest diamonds, pearls, and emeralds in the world were being worn that season, and outshone everybody. I wish she had confined her affections to dressmakers. Stories of Mabel Normand's secret wedding now made the front pages.

She married nobody, but the only publications which didn't carry pictures of her touring Europe with Prince Ibrahim, nephew of the Khedive of Egypt, must have been published in Braille.

Publicity about extravagances by motion-picture stars is bad medicine in Hollywood today, but after the bad taste of the Taylor tragedy I welcomed this splurge as possibly a good thing for Mabel professionally. And I thought, in spite of all the excesses which kept her away from me and away from the kind of pictures I now knew how to make for her, that it was a good thing for Mabel personally. I was wrong. Mabel returned with a shattering cough and needed a long rest to recover from exhaustion.

But I wasn't through, not by a country mile. In my up-and-down Odyssey, from boilermaking in the vicinity of Mr.

Coolidge to burlesque in the Bowery, to Hollywood, I had been down more often than up. This was a time when nothing was exactly right, but I thought I could peer around current difficulties to pretty good going ahead—that is, to much bigger and much better motion pictures starring Mabel Normand. We would make no more pie comedies with her, never again use her as the foil for rough guys in droopy pantaloons. We would contrive big stories, eight-reel stories, romantic and dramatic stories. We'd go the limit. Now there was money to do it with.

I thought of one of the times when I'd been at lowest ebb. That was when both Ford Sterling, my leading comedian, and Pathé Lehrman, my chief director, had walked out on me at the same time. I remembered the scene:

Lehrman and Ford were packing up their belongings and shouting back and forth through the dressing rooms about the marvels they were going to put on film when they got away from me. I was the head of the studio but I was slapping on make-up in a hurry to go on in a two-reel comedy as a rube—because I had to.

Ford and Lehrman sneered.

"All right, you guys, tell you something," I said. "I can act in the pictures, I can direct the pictures, I can produce the pictures, I can advertise the pictures—and damn it, I can finance the pictures.

"I'll be a success when you fellows have fallen on your cans and been forgotten!"

There'd been other bad times, as when Mary Pickford looked at the script of *Molly O*, turned it down flat, and left me holding the feed bag with no food in sight.

But then I'd invited her to the first screening of *Molly* and Mary had come through like the gentleman she is.

"How could I have been so dumb? I should have bought that one from you, Mack."

And so, in spite of Mabel's shenanigans and her ennui, I figured everything was going to be all right.

Then Dick Jones quit me. He went to Hal Roach, my chief competitor who produced the Laurel and Hardy and the "Our Gang" comedies. Hal named him a vice-president and doubled his salary, making him far and away the highest-paid director in town. I was scairt.

I could stand up to losing Jones, good as he was. But this boy was too smart, knew too much, had all my methods and trade secrets at the tips of his very talented fingers. He'd take all that knowledge to Roach, and Roach would beat me to death at the box office. I thought this over and had night-sweats about it.

After several weeks of fright I called up Jesse Lasky and made devious conversation about this and that and nothing much.

"Let's have lunch together someday," Jesse said, uttering a Hollywood cliché which no one ever takes seriously. I took it seriously. We met the next day and I listened to Mr. Lasky's troubles. Producers always have troubles and no listeners. I cupped an ear, thereby establishing myself with Jesse as a charming and intelligent fellow.

His trouble was his new *Bulldog Drummond* picture. Couldn't find the right director, he said.

I was aware of that. Why do you think I was having lunch with Mr. Lasky?

"Know just the man," I said. "That is, if you can get him. Greatest talent in the business. But I doubt if you can steal him. I doubt if you could pay his price."

Jesse rose to that last line like a carp to a fly.

"Don't be silly," he said. "This isn't one of your slap-sticks. This is an 'A' picture. I can pay anything for the best. Who you talking about?"

"Feller who used to work for me. Knows everything I know and then some. So good I couldn't keep him. You know, way too good for my little studio. Hal Roach stole him away from me. You might try, if you're willing to open up your pocketbook. Man's name is Dick Jones."

My strategy worked fine. Lasky approached Dick, contract and checkbook in hand, and lifted him out from under Hal Roach's nose.

The little dog laughed to see such fun and the cow jumped over the moon.

Hal Roach went right on making first-rate comedies, but he didn't learn a single Sennett trick from Richard F. Jones.

The sign at the front gate in Edendale informed Edendale that this was the Mack Sennett Studio. I set store by my name up there, valued it more, even, than the money now pouring into the cashbox by way of the parent company, Triangle. But our pictures were actually released as Keystone Comedies and that is how the world knew them. Suddenly we were offered a shining opportunity.

The grand sachems and high cockalorums of motion pictures were Adolph Zukor and Jesse Lasky. These two astute men had put their brains and their money together to form Famous Players-Lasky Corporation. In Hollywood, Famous Players-Lasky was as awesome as Tiffany's to a Main Street watch mender. Now Zukor and Lasky approached us and proposed that D. W. Griffith, Thomas H. Ince, and Mack Sennett—in short, Triangle—join forces with them.

This was impossible for reasons in which I presume only Price, Waterhouse, the accountants, would be interested. At any rate, I discontinued with my various partners and from then on went it alone under my own moniker. At long last all my pictures now went out under the label—as big as I could get it on the screen—"Mack Sennett Comedies." Part of the deal was an arrangement with Mr. Zukor and Mr. Lasky to release my pictures through a company they owned called Paramount.

Naturally you can't mention Paramount without mentioning Bing Crosby and Bob Hope. Unfortunately for me Mr. Hope was never one of my boys. I would have had him in a trice, whatever a trice is, if I could have laid hands on him. I have already laid claim to most of the great comedians who became rich and famous in Hollywood, and richer and more famous after I discovered them and was the first to put them in pictures. So I shall not omit Harry Lillis Crosby.

As everybody knows by now, Crosby made his real start with the Rhythm Boys and Paul Whiteman. Shortly after I began to produce everything under my own name, with a bow to Zukor and Lasky, Crosby turned up for an engagement at the famous Cocoanut Grove in the Ambassador Hotel. I heard him sing and thought he was great. I noticed that numbers of sophisticated and show-wise people were repeat customers.

I talked to my studio associates about giving this boy a contract.

Nobody to this day has been backward about telling me when they think I'm wrong. My talent scouts and directors had looked Crosby over too. Now they looked me over as a candidate for the loony bin.

"You out of your mind, Mack?" they said. "A crooner in slapstick comedies?"

"Boys, I admit I never heard of a crooner in slapstick comedy," I argued, "but until we flung 'em, nobody ever heard of a custard pie in slapstick comedy. All I know is, this boy entertains. And I don't care what people do, they can stand on their heads or count up to ten—if they're entertaining, I want 'em. I'm going to sign Crosby."

I did sign Crosby, at $400 a week. I believe he spends more than that today on his sons' shoeshines. But when I beckoned him over to me one night at the Grove, it was some years before the United States Treasury was compelled to build Fort Knox as a private sugar bowl for Bing.

Bing came to work. He braced me immediately on a matter that was bothering him.

"What about make-up, Mr. Sennett?"

"Make-up? What do you mean, Bing?"

"You know—on the face? What do you want me to do about eyes and chin and mouth and stuff like that there?"

I looked him over and laughed.

"Boy, I like you on the hoof, as is. Don't change anything."

"But I took a lot of tests, you know, at most of the big studios, and they all spent hours making me up before they put a camera on me."

"I know," I said. "I know all about that. They covered you with goo—and you didn't get a job. Now we'll just put you out there and let you look like yourself."

To be honest, I wasn't as confident as all that in Bing Crosby. I knew he could sing. But whether he could read a line convincingly and make with a funny were unknown quantities. I decided to take no chances with him as an actor. In his first picture I cast a well-known comedian along with him and gave the comedian all the important dialogue. Aside from singing

—and we threw in song cues for him on the slightest pretexts— I saw to it that Crosby barely uttered.

When the first rushes were run off in the screening room, we all discovered instanter something that has made hundreds of millions of people happy ever since: Mr. Crosby, with or without benefit of writer to give him the best lines, was as skill-ful a comedian as ever stole a scene. He underplayed and made off with every sequence from every comedian we put in his pictures—under the impression we were helping him out. He has been doing it ever since.

Because I always had from six to ten two-reel comedies going at the same time, I toured the lot every day to see how my people were getting along, and particularly to see if they were getting any laughs.

I came to the Crosby set. He was singing that "Blue of the Night" piece of his, the one with the boo-boo-boo-boo's in it. Being used to action and fun piled on top of action and fun, I thought this production number was a slow-paced lullaby which would induce audiences to take naps. I called Bing over.

"Don't you think you could speed that up a little bit, old boy?" I said.

Bing just stood there looking at me solemnly with those big blue eyes. His silence was considerably more eloquent than anything he might have said. I realized that the ex-boilermaker basso was telling the best crooner in the world how to perform his specialty.

"Skip it, Bing," I said. "Come to think of it, I like it better your way."

Crosby made eight or ten pictures for me, all crackerjacks. Then he went on to inspire riots with personal appearances at the Paramount Theater in New York. I went on a yachting trip to Alaska with Don Lee, leaving instructions to my executives to pick up Bing's option, raise his salary, and put him under a long-term contract.

When I returned from Alaska it was the same old story. Bing Crosby was under exclusive contract to Paramount.

Even so, my Mack Sennett company made something more than a million dollars' profit its first year. I soon left Edendale. A group of enterprising real-estate operators in the

San Fernando Valley thought it would be a fine thing if they could lure a motion-picture studio into their community. They offered me a gift of twenty acres of land near the trickle known as the Los Angeles River. I spent $500,000 in cash building a brand-new, equipped-with-everything motion-picture factory and was ready for sound and talk on film when they came along a few years later. That studio stands. It is known as Republic.

CHAPTER 24

Mr. Fields Meets a Whale

I BEGAN to think I was King Midas instead of the self-appointed "King of Comedy." I bought five hundred acres of Los Angeles real estate, 304 of these acres in Griffith Park, grabbed five thousand shares of Wall Street stock at a clip, borrowed money in lumps of $100,000 and more to finance new pictures, and acquired a gold mine.

One day in the middle 1920's, my chief business adviser, the only man who ever had an accurate notion of my financial position at any given time, came in and announced that it was his duty to tell me something.

"Mr. Sennett, I don't know what you want to do," he said, "but I have been running off totals and it's my job to tell you that you are worth fifteen million dollars."

"Well!" I said.

"That means, Mr. Sennett, that if you want to liquidate, you can be assured of an income of $150,000 a year at a gilt-edged, guaranteed 4 per cent."

It seems to me now that this statement should have struck me all of a heap. But it didn't. Even now, when we're all used to fancy figures, fifteen million dollars is too great a sum for one person actually to comprehend. I said:

"What the hell would I do with a pension? I can't loaf. I can't stand to be idle. I like this life. Let's get on with making pictures."

It was all mine. After I got my own corporation I never had a partner. I sold no stock in my company. I wanted to go it alone without having to be responsible to a bunch of pin-headed and penny-pinching share owners.

I engaged Charlie Bauman, the ex-New York bookie who had been my first backer, to represent me in the East at a salary of $500 a week. Charlie went to the track one afternoon and met a friend of mine from California. "Oh, I'm doing fine," Bauman told him. "Got a fellow working for me out on the coast. Name's Mack Sennett."

I burned a deep red and tried to fire Bauman, but he had a contract—and a long memory. He slipped an attachment on all the negatives I had sent to New York, and this stopped me as effectively as Tom Ince and I had stopped him when we hid the Keystone films in safety-deposit boxes all over Los Angeles. I had to put up a bond of $100,000 to get my film away from that wicked man.

That wasn't much trouble. In those days all I had to do was let a bank know I needed a little petty cash and they'd send it out by messenger boy.

I went into the gold-mining business. I bought a half interest in a mine adjacent to the North Star in Grass Valley, the biggest gold field in California.

My partners had sunk a shaft five hundred feet down. They told me they knew all about mining.

"Where is the gold?" I asked.

"We're blocking out tunnels," they told me.

"Why fiddle around in tunnels? Why not bring a little of that gold up?" I asked.

But they kept blocking out tunnels. I knew there was gold down there because I had put plenty in it—a quarter of a million dollars' worth.

I got out of that operation, leaving my $250,000 behind in the tunnels, convinced those Grass Valley chumps didn't understand a blooming thing about gold mining.

I bought a mountain. You can inspect the site today. It is the big mountain just off Griffith Park where the Don Lee TV tower and transmitter now dominate all of Hollywood. It used to be known as the old Brown Ranch. I paid $500 an acre for 304 acres, or $152,000, for my mountain—and then discovered that all I could do was look at it. There was no road, and the ascent to the top was impossible.

My idea was to build a big house up there. "It'll be good

exploitation," I explained when my friends wanted to know why in the name of this-and-that I needed a private mountain.

"I'll build an elevator," I said. "An elevator that goes zoop, right up the mountain! And a swimming pool. And everybody who goes by will point and say, 'That's where Mack Sennett lives.'"

Mother was always fascinated by anything like this, so she took charge. She put on an old straw hat and spent every day bossing the road gangs and steam rollers up and down that mountain. She got a road to the top, too, but we found the top wasn't flat. This meant slicing off sixty-nine feet of hard rock and shale to get a level site of about four acres. But Mother did it. As I have indicated several times before, she was a lady who could and did move mountains.

Only one thing upset her—snakes!

"They won't bite you, Mother," I said. "St. Anthony always looks after you."

"He does that," Mother said, "but this project isn't exactly under his jurisdiction. Now if we just had St. Patrick..."

Actually what was bothering Mrs. Sennett was the fear that a rattlesnake would kill one of the big Missouri mules pulling the scrapers and plows around the mountain. A Missouri mule cost $700. I made some inquiries on behalf of these aristocrats and was told by experts that the way to get rid of snakes was to sick some hogs onto them.

Mother and I started with half a dozen Berkshires, the best long bacon hogs purchasable, but they disappeared among the yucca plants. The snakes thrived and remained in command.

So I bought five hundred hogs and cut them loose to fight snakes. They did it, too. Hogs are immune to venom, and mine seemed to have a lot of fun playing tug of war with the reptiles on Mount Sennett. They not only ate up the snakes, but everything else.

My swine began to starve to death and we had to send studio trucks all over town buying up garbage to feed them. At one time I virtually cornered the Los Angeles garbage market.

Pork was high that year, but we didn't have any. My

snake-fed pigs turned wild and mean and refused to become bacon.

My new stars were Harry Langdon, Sally Eilers, Andy Clyde—and the man many intelligent critics argue was the greatest comic of them all—W. C. Fields.

None of the hundreds of thousands of words that have been printed about Bill Fields' prowess with the martini pitcher contains a syllable of exaggeration. Fields started before breakfast and drank steadily and copiously all day. His prescription for a perfect martini was a pitcherful of gin over which he had quickly cast the shadow of an empty vermouth bottle.

Bill used to go up to Svoboda Hot Springs, a spa.

"Why?" I asked. "Doesn't all that health appall you?"

"Nawp," Bill said. "I don't go for the baths. I just like to get drunk in a new atmosphere."

When Earl Carroll started his new restaurant on Sunset Boulevard, he asked numerous people in motion pictures to invest in it, and put Fields down for eight thousand dollars. He sent his brother out to Fields' home to fetch the money. Bill let him sit in the outer hall day after day.

A friend asked him why he treated the poor guy like that.

"Wants me to invest eight thousand dollars," Bill said.

"Whyn't you tell him you're not interested?"

"Oh, the hell with it," Bill replied. "Let him sit."

Fields was a superb golfer. One afternoon I played him a game at five dollars a hole. When I got home I began to worry about my score. "Did I count all my strokes in that sand trap?" I wondered. "I don't want Bill to think I'm a crook."

The next time I saw him I said, "I'm concerned about my score. I think I had five strokes instead of three in that trap."

"Don't worry any more," Bill said. "You had three. I counted 'em."

Bill would never admit that a proposed screen story was no good. A fine yarn, he'd say, but better for some other comedian, maybe Harry Langdon. And if you suggested a yarn you'd had written especially for him, he'd claim it wasn't funny. To get him to work in a picture I had to approach him like this:

"Bill you remember that story idea you had last week, the one you liked so much?"

"Yeah, yeah, yeah, now just how did it go?"

I'd tell him the new idea, being careful to insist it was his own, and he'd buy it every time.

I first met Bill Fields in New York when he was starring in the Ziegfeld Follies. Like everyone else, I thought all his routines were uproariously funny. Soon after that he headed for Hollywood, stopping off at various hamlets on the way to make secret bank deposits under fictitious names. (That's the way he kept his money. When he died there was hell to pay settling his estate.) The studios didn't appreciate his talent, so he spent his time playing golf. I ran across him at Lakeside. He said:

"Mack, I'm fed up with my frivolous existence. Why don't I come out to your studio and do something—anything. Gag, write, direct—any little chore. Money's no object. I just want to be busy."

Since money was no object, I arranged an appointment for the following morning.

"You've never been in pictures, Bill," I said. "Let's forget the gags and the writing and the directing and put you in a comedy."

"Well, Mack, that's fine. My regular salary for acting is $5000 a week."

Bill went to work on me while I was still anesthetized by his salary demand. He bullied me, cajoled me and charmed me, and walked out of the office with a $5000-a-week contract—$2500 payable at the beginning of each week, and $2500 payable in the middle of each week.

"Just in case of fire," he said with a casual wave.

Bill waltzed out and had a martini breakfast. He always talked business cold sober.

George Marshall, Arthur Ripley, Del Lord and I talked over a possible story for Mr. Fields. Our first discussion lasted three hours. As we broke up I yelled at the boys, "For God's sake, get a story fast. This actor has already earned $312."

Del Lord had an idea.

"Just the thing for Fields. He parachutes from an airplane into the ocean and lands on what he thinks is a small island. It's the back of a dead whale being devoured by ravenous sharks. Fields suddenly realizes where he is——"

We thought it was a brand-new suspense angle. Everyone cheered for it except Fields. He said, "I'm sure Mr. Sennett, that great comedy genius, and his brainy organization, can make comedies without going to all that expensive trouble. Or am I wrong about the King of Comedy?"

We went ahead anyway. We hired the *San Clemente*, a seventy-five-foot craft, and the crew finally sighted a whale off the Santa Barbara Islands. Bill was having lunch in the studio commissary when the news was announced. He was halfway through an abalone steak. His face turned pale and began to show splotches of green. He wobbled out of the room and talked to someone on the telephone. Then he came to me.

"Mack, I've just phoned my doctor, and he warns me I have a dreadful allergy. I'm allergic to water—particularly salt water."

But I was paying this man $5000 a week, and if the story called for him to act on the water, on the water he would act. For $5000 I might expect him to walk on it.

Fields had an extra special bout with his gin bottle that night and arrived late for work the next morning. His expensive automobile was out of whack, so he came by streetcar, trying to hold a newspaper in his twitching hands, while the rocking and swaying of the trolley made him weaker and sicker.

Now, there was a girl named Dora who worked for us. She boarded the streetcar and sat down by Fields, placing a small wicker basket between them. As always, the Sennett Studio was amply populated with critters—we had raccoons, wolves, eagles, chickens, varmints, and snakes. Dora was our snake charmer. The wicker contained a three-foot king snake.

As Mr. Fields tried to concentrate on his *Examiner*, the king snake slithered out of the basket, propped itself behind Fields, and peered over his shoulder.

"It cannot be," said Mr. Fields. "It does not happen. This, of course, is a damnable illusion, a mere figment of the gin-inspired cerebellum. I shall, I will, be brave."

He reached up and stroked the king snake's brow.

"Indubitably authentic," he proclaimed, "and purring like a Bengal tiger."

Fields stumbled out of the streetcar. "I'll never tetch another drop," he screeched, "at least until I get in that bar."

He broke fast with five straight shots of gin.

We finally propped Mr. Fields up and got him out to sea by promising constant refreshment aboard the *San Clemente*. Del Lord cautioned our skipper to get us a lively whale, to harpoon him rather gently, not to kill him. In no time at all we sank a shaft into a ninety-foot mammal and there followed a chase sequence never put on screen before or since. That inexhaustible whale gallumphed through the sea, spouting geysers, and towing our seventy-five-foot boat behind him like a chip. He towed us all day and all night, in and out, it seems to me, of all the harbors between San Francisco and Ensenada.

Our cameramen used small, battery-driven Brie cameras strapped to their chests and got some remarkable shots, but not of W. C. Fields.

Mr. Fields lay in his bunk consuming and emitting martinis.

He came topside only once and leaned weakly over the rail just as we finally had to cut the line and release our too vigorous whale.

It was there that he uttered for the first time his imperishable classic: " 'Tain't a fit night out for man nor beast."

The whale incident cost me more than $20,000 and we wound up, of course, with no picture. Meantime W. C. Fields' semi-weekly $2500 had to be paid. I rushed him into a two-reel comedy as soon as I could and this time I shot it on a golf course, where I knew Bill Fields was a marvel. He always held the whale fiasco against me.

"The studio let me down," he complained. "It would've been the greatest comedy the world has ever seen. I can imagine myself now, balancing with the athletic skill and grace of a toreador, riding the back of that gigantic, bucking denizen of the deep amid huge, awe-inspiring waves on that wonderful ocean."

The Fields' two-reelers were immensely successful. Indeed they were so good that Fields was soon under contract to Paramount.

Two Quick Curtains

BUT EVEN with Bill Fields in full cry, assassi-
nating every character in sight with his murderous vocabulary
—and making money for me in spite of that $5000 a week—
even then the thing I wanted most was to be serious about
comedy with Mabel Normand.

While she was away, kicking over champagne buckets in
France or in New England recuperating from kicking over
champagne buckets, I tried to start a picture along the lines of
Molly O, Mickey, and *Suzanna.* I wrote a script called *The
Extra Girl* and made a pass at shooting it as if I had never
heard of Mabel Normand.

Good actresses were available. We discussed Priscilla
Bonner. I thought she was great. But not just right. Next
Sigrid Holmquist. Then Evelyn Brent, Virginia Browne Fair,
Betty Francisco, and finally one of my all-time favorites, Phyllis
Haver.

Phyllis was purely wonderful, but——

"But the hell with it," I said to myself. "She'd do. This
might make her the biggest star in Hollywood, or it might
make any of these girls great stars. *But they ain't Mabel.*"

I gave up and started trying to reach Mabel on the telephone, long distance. Finally I got her in New York.

"You all right?" I asked.

"Never better, Nappy," Mabel told me. "Every day in
every way I'm getting sassier and sassier. What outrageous
enterprise is bedeviling your giant intellect now, Old Man?"

The to-hell-with-you was back in her voice again. She was

swinging the rope and I was doing the jumping, and it felt good. Like old times.

"Work," I said. "Aren't you through resting your lazy self by now? Do you want to work?"

Mabel giggled about eight dollars' worth of long-distance toll charges and then let me have it. She said:

"Mr. Sennett, I should indeed be most happy to be in your employ, now that you have tried out Phyllis, Betty, Virginia, Priscilla, Sigrid, and Evelyn. Seventh-choice Mabel, that's me.

"But all right, Mack, I'll make *The Extra Girl* for you. My price is $3000 a week."

"Good Lord, Mabel," I began. But she interrupted me.

"Three thousand dollars a week and 25 per cent of the net profits."

I knew of course that Mabel had no agent or financial adviser who'd inspired her to throw this terse demand in my teeth. She was as casual about money as an Indian with an oil well. But I knew exactly what she meant. She was putting me firmly in my place and serving notice that no ferryboat diamonds could bemuse her now. Knowing Mabel's arithmetic, I praised the Lord it hadn't occurred to her to ask for $75,000 a week and 125 per cent of the profits.

She returned to the coast as happy as Easter morning and we made *The Extra Girl*, with Dick Jones directing. This was the picture in which Mabel, who never used a double in any picture, led an enormous young lion named Duke around the lot, pretending she had a great Dane on the leash. This made a funny, suspenseful sequence, and, as I think I mentioned before, Mabel Normand was the only actress in the world who could look unconcerned while a lion breathed down her neck.

The Extra Girl was a good one. We set it for national release just before Christmas. Mabel was exhausted after the long shooting schedule and planned to enter a hospital for a checkup and a long rest immediately after the holidays.

A day or so before Christmas, Edna Purviance brought a man named Cortland S. Dines to see Mabel. Dines was at that time a playboy, the son of a Colorado petroleum millionaire. He was having fun in Hollywood.

Mabel mentioned meeting Cortland Dines when she came to my house for dinner New Year's Eve. She was rather formal with me that evening. After my party Edna and Mabel went to Dines' apartment on North Vermont Avenue to drink a toast. Mabel's new chauffeur, Joe Kelly, drove her there.

I wasn't invited. I don't know exactly what happened, but I've been told that when the hour grew late, Kelly returned to Mabel's home, talked to Mamie Owens, Mabel's housekeeper, and the two of them decided it was time for Miss Normand to leave the party.

Kelly appeared at Dines' apartment and asked Mabel to leave. Dines tried to throw Kelly out, and there was a scuffle. Suddenly there were three pistol shots.

Cortland S. Dines was wounded by bullets from a .25-caliber pearl-handled revolver which the police identified as the property of Mabel Normand.

And just as in the William Desmond Taylor murder case, still fresh in everyone's mind, it turned out that one of the leading characters in this drama was masquerading under an assumed name. Joe Kelly was Joe Greer. He was wanted for breaking prison in Oakland, California. He was a cocaine addict.

There were scarehead lines all over again. Dines recovered and Kelly pleaded self-defense and was released.

But *The Extra Girl* couldn't be released, not with its star again smirched by another Hollywood scandal. And what about Mabel's owning a pistol?

I knew about the pistol. It was a toy. Dick Jones and some of the boys had given it to Mabel as a joke, had amused themselves one afternoon urging her to shoot a mountain. She missed.

Kelly had picked up the gun during the Cortland Dines party when he went home to confer with the housekeeper, Mamie Owens.

Mabel's innocence was never in question, but this second shooting was too much.

"All I do is cause trouble, Mack," she told me. "I'm through. I'm washed up. This is the end. And I'm so awfully tired."

She wasn't through at all. She was ill and harassed and

she seemed to feel that every eye looked at her with suspicion. But she wasn't through.

I offered to start her in a new picture immediately, but she wouldn't consider the idea. She did a gallant and pitiful thing.

Mabel went to school to learn how to act on the stage. Her teacher was Alla Nazimova, who could tell Mabel Normand very little indeed about pace or gesture, but who tried to develop her small voice so the gallery could hear it.

Mabel then went to New York and rehearsed a play called *The Little Mouse* for Al Woods. It was a disaster. She was pretty and charming, but the stage was not her métier and she could barely be heard in the third row orchestra. The critics lambasted her without mercy.

She returned, but not to me. She returned to Lew Cody.

Lew Cody, who had played the city slicker in several of Mabel's best pictures, was born in Waterville, Maine, attended McGill University in Montreal, acted for the Shuberts, and was brought to Hollywood by Ince.

One evening Mabel gave a small dinner party. She invited Margaret McNamara, the singer, James Lord, and John Stahl. Just before dinner Stahl telephoned that he was unable to come. To fill out her table, Mabel appealed to Lew Cody, as an old friend, to accept a last-minute invitation.

As Mabel told the story afterwards—though never to me— Cody wanted to act after dinner. He wanted to act out an old-fashioned proposal in which he pleaded with Mabel to marry him. Mabel fell into her part like a trouper and this pair of first-rate mimes put on a show for the other guests. Then comes the incredible part. I have never understood it, I cannot explain it. I do not even believe it. But it happened.

Mabel and Lew Cody, accompanied by the dinner-party guests and Julia Benson, R.N., who was never left out of any-thing, drove up to Santa Barbara under police escort, and were married by County Recorder Thomas H. Meilandt.

Mabel returned to her home, Cody to his. Miss Benson declares that she spent that night in Mabel's bedroom as usual and that at no time did Mabel and Cody ever live together as man and wife.

Miss Benson overheard part of the telephone conversation next morning between Mabel and Lew. She did not know what Lew was saying, of course, but she believes he was arguing. One sentence of Mabel's stuck in her mind:

"No, Lew, you know I don't love you."

Mabel made a few two-reel pictures for Hal Roach after her marriage to Lew Cody, but she was failing and the knockabout slapsticks were difficult for her. She said many times that she had thought she was through with that type of picture and wanted more than anything in the world to make more films like *Molly O* or *Suzanna*.

I would have made them for her. I could have made them. I could have made them better than any man in the world.

But after Mabel Normand became Mrs. Lew Cody I never saw her or spoke to her again.

Miss Benson was with Mabel for more than ten years. She lived with her in Marilyn Miller's apartment, 100 West Fifty-ninth Street, New York; was with her when her play failed on Broadway, knew all of Mabel's New York friends during this unhappy time when she lived in one house and her husband in another. Mabel shuttled back and forth, coast to coast. In Manhattan she enjoyed knowing Heywood Broun, Edna St. Vincent Millay, Carl van Vechten, Margaret Illington, Covarrubias, and Major Bowes. In Hollywood she saw few people. She was lonely and ill and tired. In January 1927 she went to the hospital with double pneumonia.

She seemed to recover, but shortly after that Miss Benson had a private interview with a doctor and told him what she thought. Mabel had tuberculosis.

She entered Dr. Francis Pottenger's sanitarium in Monrovia in September 1929 and was desperately ill there for six months. No one told her that Lew Cody had only a short time to live. He was suffering from heart disease. Lew, good man, insisted on keeping that from her.

One early morning Mabel pulled herself out of a coma and motioned for Julia Benson to come near.

"Those flowers over there," she whispered, pointing, "they're from Mack, aren't they? He didn't forget me."

A little later she called Miss Benson again.

"I do so hate to go without knowing what happened to poor Bill Taylor," she said.

Her last words were, "Julie, please don't leave me."

Mabel died at 2:25 A.M., February 23, 1930.

Mother was on the farm in Canada. It was the old Curley place, the acreage she had purchased years ago when she drafted the studio for cash without a by-your-leave-son to me. It was a good, prosperous farm and Mother had a magic way with the soil. Things sprouted and grew and increased for her. She had handsome cattle and prize pigs—including a 350-pound sow which she had raised by hand from a shoat and which now frequently invaded the house and tried to sit on people under the impression it was a lap dog.

She had many farm hands, but her most efficient worker was a half-breed collie named Major, who fetched the cattle back and forth from the pastures and was under the impression that he was the overseer.

I tried once to hunt partridges with Major. He had an acute nose and he could come to a point—but he pointed only at cows.

I had always avoided anything to do with agricultural labor since I escaped from the farm many years ago. But there soon came a time when I sought it out as a happy and restful place. I went there in 1935 to lick my wounds and think things over when Paramount-Publix failed.

The big studio went into bankruptcy and I went with it. I lost the studio, the mountain, the acres of land in Los Angeles—I lost the whole shebang once upon a time valued at $15,000,000.

The story of Paramount's crash is long and involved. It was a repercussion of the Wall Street debacle of '29, it was partly the result of too many millions invested in too many fancy theaters with Byzantine lobbies and Renaissance orchestras. The collapse was not the fault of my old friend Adolph Zukor, who did all he could to save us. More than likely it was chiefly the doings of Wall Street speculators who deliberately sold Paramount short, regardless of the fortunes and the men they ruined.

I was wiped out.

How does it feel to lose everything you've worked for all your life? How does it feel to lose $15,000,000?

Well, how does it feel to lose a leg? It hurts.

I was glad that Mother was in Canada and was therefore unaware of the extent of my financial wounds. She suspected something was wrong, but, as wise and as ripe as she was, I think she never knew that I had been ruined.

I spent a gentle three months with her, and then she died, peacefully, in her sleep.

The dog Major ran into the forest that night and was never seen again.

When my mother's will was read I discovered things I never knew until then about her good sense with money. I had thought all the time that I was pampering an old lady when I let her buy things. Now it turned out that she had never made a foolish purchase. The farm lands were valuable. There was a large insurance policy. Johns-Manville engineers pointed out that a rich vein of asbestos ran through the old farm. And petroleum engineers bugged their eyes at the artesian wells she had dug on her property so blessed by rainfall that it never needed water.

"Oil there, Mr. Sennett," they said.

She left it all to me.

CHAPTER 26

Happy Ending

IT COMES over me, on long nights, that I have been writing a book covering fifty-two years of show business, from the hind legs of a horse to Hollywood.

This awes me. I never set out to do such a thing. Now, as I think it all over, I wonder if I have told the truth, and if any man ever does, or can, tell the truth when he pretends to write his life story.

I wanted to tell about the comedies and how we made them, and about the funny fellows and pretty girls who acted in them. They are a lost breed. Their like may never walk, tumble, or pratt-fall again.

Most of all I wanted you to meet Mabel Normand.

Becoming an author has been an experience for me. I am not sure that I recommend it to anybody, even with the aid of a collaborator. I might say, *especially* with the aid of Cameron Shipp as collaborator. Mr. Barrymore characterized this man once when he said, "He has the heart of a Borgia and the curiosity of a postmistress."

Whether that line is accurate or not is in question, at least by Mr. Shipp. But I can say that any person who exposes himself to a reporter for more than two years, even when the reporter is an old friend, begins to feel like a frog perpetually under a biologist's scalpel.

We did our best. There were times when I hollered for mercy. There were times when I screamed that the skeletons in my closet should be left there, laughing to themselves. I never won those arguments.

There are a few more things to say and one more story to tell.

Art never makes progress—it merely changes. Or it dies. The art of motion-picture comedy was grievously stricken as long ago as 1923 when an exhibitor in Providence, Rhode Island, noted that young factory hands and their girls were through work for the day, washed and polished and out of the house by 6:30 P.M. The young people then wanted someplace to go where they could spend the entire evening. The Providence theater manager solved this social problem by initiating the double-feature bill—three to four full hours of movies.

When this double dosage became a national fact, the two-reel comedy ailed and pined away.

This removed the greatest training ground ever provided for screen actors, most especially for screen comedians. Crosby, Fields, Lloyd, and Charlie Chaplin all started there.

The next change, obviously, will be the effect of television on motion-picture art. I predict that within ten years the movie industry will be devoted exclusively to making films for television. New York will have the Paramount, the Roxy, and the Music Hall as great showcases, after which big pictures will go straight into TV runs. The neighborhood movie house is a doomed piece of real estate.

But the picture business will be rejuvenated. When the right method—advertising, or drop-a-coin-in-the-slot—is worked out, a producer will get his negative cost back from one night's showing before a great television audience. And television may revive the two-reel comedy. Let us pray!

Who killed William Desmond Taylor?
I don't know.

It seems highly probable that the murderer of William Desmond Taylor is walking the streets today, a free man. Perhaps you have seen him. At any rate, the gun that shot Taylor was never found. Without it there is small likelihood that any person will ever be brought to trial.

I never married. There was only one girl.

Here is the last story:

In early March 1954, Shipp called me on the telephone and said something like this:

"Mack, they want us to do about five minutes on a new radio show. H. V. Kaltenborn is starting one called 'So You Want to Write a Book?' And we're invited to say our piece on it."

"Do we get paid?" I asked hopefully.

"No," Shipp said, "we don't. But this makes you an author on a coast-to-coast hookup. It'll be easy, sort of an interview thing. I'll sit beside you and ask a few questions."

"Not on your life," I complained. "The kind of questions you ask, my good man, will be asked only in private. I'll do it only if there's a script. Can't I ever teach you about showmanship? We're not going on a national network unprepared and unrehearsed. You write a script and I'll do it."

You never heard such objections. I was not astonished. I am used to that reaction. Writers hate to write. But I had him. He wrote us a script, but the way he carried on about it you'd have thought I'd asked him to carve it in marble with a butter knife.

I set the afternoon of the show, March 10, 1954, as rehearsal time. Mr. and Mrs. Shipp appeared at my apartment at the appointed hour and my collaborator handed me one page of copy.

I blew up like a father whose daughter has been left at the altar.

"We're sunk," I roared. "Sit down, Mrs. Shipp, do excuse me, but holy jumping catfish in a rain barrel, Cam, here I've been trying to beat it through your head for all these years that comedy is a serious business and you hand me about enough copy to cover a postage stamp and expect me to do a show with it. Now let's get us a script, and let's rehearse it."

I made the writer write. I gave him gags, lines, and toppers. He put them all down in disinterested prose, and then tried to brush off the rehearsal. I made him rehearse for two hours.

"Where'll we have dinner?" Mrs. Shipp asked.

Why did he have to bring that girl along? She sat there and yawned at the script, looking at a magazine while we rehearsed, and all she had on her mind was dinner.

Presently Don Malmberg arrived from the studio. Maybe he'll make sense, I thought, so I asked him to look over the script.

"Oh, that'll be all right," he said, sticking the script in his pocket and not looking at it. "We're on the air in a few minutes. Let's go."

It took us no more than five minutes to drive from my apartment to NBC. During this short drive I tried to discuss the show with Cameron Shipp and the studio man, but Mrs. Shipp took charge of the conversation. She mentioned wanting her dinner at least eighteen times.

Don't these writers ever feed their women? I wondered.

I was a sad showman when we arrived. I'd been euchred into committing a flop, no two ways about it. Moreover I was accorded the reception of a delivery boy with muddy feet, barely spoken to, shunted into a bare dressing room, and told to stay there until I was needed. Mr. Shipp disappeared. Mr. Malmberg had the script. I squatted on a divan and pouted up a storm. I tried to get out. They had locked the door.

Finally a messenger boy came.

"You're on, Mr. Sennett," he said in a tone of command.

He led me behind some scenery, aimed me at the stage, and gave me a shove.

I walked forward uncertainly, not knowing where I was going. I was hit in the face by enough glaring light to illuminate a battleship. Two people came forward. One of them was Shipp. I scowled at him and grunted. The other man I did not recognize.

Then as I blinked my eyes, getting used to the lights, and peered around, I saw that three monstrous television cameras were taking aim at me.

Shipp grabbed me by my right arm as if he was about to put a hammer lock on me.

"It's all right, Mack," he said. "Now take it easy. I know all about this, and it's all right."

This from a man who had just proved to me that he knew absolutely nothing about putting on any kind of a show!

I glowered at him.

The other man moved in and seized me. "I'm Ralph

Edwards," he said. "You didn't expect to find me here, did you?"

I didn't expect to find myself there, let alone Ralph Edwards, whoever he was. The name seemed familiar.

I gave Mr. Cameron Shipp a look of sheer hatred, which he was kind enough to tell me later was seen by a television audience of fifty million persons. But I'm a polite man.

"Oh, sure," I said to Ralph Edwards, digging deep for something bright to say and coming up with the most ancient bromide possible, "Oh, sure, you're my favorite comedian."

Then they let me have it.

"We've all conspired to get you here, Mr. Sennett," Edwards said, "so that we could tell you that tonight *This Is Your Life*."

You could have knocked me over with Ben Turpin.

Many of you have seen Mr. Edwards's famous and often exciting television production, "This Is Your Life," and I know what you have wondered. You have wondered whether the show is honest. You've suspected that the subjects, or victims, were tipped off in advance. I can assure you that Mr. Edwards's production is the most honest enterprise ever based on skulduggery and connivance.

As they do for all their productions, Ralph Edwards's staff had worked for a month exploring the highlights of my life, getting in touch with my old friends, and arranging to fetch some of them thousands of miles by air to confront me in Hollywood. I hadn't the smallest hint that anything like this was going on, and may I say that my vision is 20–20, my hearing good, and my nose for a show as sharp as it ever was.

Little wonder that collaborator of mine had been dejected and reluctant when I made him write a script, and rehearse it, for the nonexistent H. V. Kaltenborn radio program. I don't regret that. He played a jape on me, but I made him sweat—and it was I, not he, who got the gold watch on the Ralph Edwards program.

It is a disconcerting and frantic experience to walk out on a stage populated by three searching TV cameras with their crews, with at least a thousand spectators in the audience waiting to see if you are going to collapse, weep, try to run away, or hit Ralph Edwards in the nose.

I was enthroned in an enormous easy chair in which I sat during most of the show, making faces and muttering.

But then—but then, it turned out to be a pretty wonderful thing. Edwards started at the beginning and touched lightly on my life in Canada and the ironworks. Then he began to bring people on out of the past. First, Rose Guilfoil—Rose Guilfoil, the girl in Northampton I'd blushed over and tried to court when I was seventeen years old, whose name David Belasco had admired, now Mrs. Rose Guilfoil Clark. I hadn't seen her since 1906, forty-eight years ago, and there she was and just as attractive as ever.

Before I had begun to recover from that surprise, one of the most thrilling voices in the world picked up a melody back stage. It was "Kiss Me Again," and the singer was, of course, Fritzi Scheff singing the hit song from *Mademoiselle Modiste*. I was a chorus boy in that show and she had been the star. I hadn't seen Fritzi for fifty years. It was the last show for a magnificent artist. Miss Scheff died on April 8, in New York.

Then came all the rest, Dell Henderson, Del Lord, Vernon Dent, Andy Clyde, Hank Mann, Heinie Conklin, and Chester Conklin, all in cop uniforms, falling over each other.

Then Phyllis Haver, Franklin Pangborn, Minta Durfee Arbuckle, Alberta Vaughn—and Jack Mulhall!

When I saw him I started to duck.

Next Sally Eilers, Louise Fazenda, and Harold Lloyd.

You know, of course, what Mr. Lloyd said. He told that television audience of fifty million how I'd looked him over nearly forty years ago, decided he was no comedian, and fired him.

But he also said something else. I never appreciated a good word more sincerely:

"Mack wasn't wrong often. His judgment was sound and was respected by all in the industry. He was always kind and considerate, a true leader of men—he was an inspiration always to all of us who followed in his footsteps. And they were pretty big steps."

Ever since I started this book, I've wondered where to find a place to mention that I once won an Academy Award. Since Ralph Edwards brought that out on "This Is Your Life," I'll say it here. The Academy of Motion Picture Arts and Sciences gave me my gold statuette in 1938 and for my pride and pleasure it could not have been presented by a more appropriate person. It was handed to me by the man who started with me many years ago as a youngster in the gag room and scenario department. This was Frank Capra, who became world-renowned for his distinguished comedies.

Aside from the gratification that comes from being victim-in-chief on Ralph Edwards's good show—and you can be very sure that I stopped growling and began to laugh before it was over—seeing a parade of my old friends and my old stars, on stage and in action again, in a show that was timed and paced like the two-reel comedies we used to make, was a happy thing for me, and a summation.

There it was, in one swift, tumbling act, with clowns, surprises, and pretty women.

Where Credit Is Due

THIS BOOK is based on interviews with Mack Sennett in his Hollywood apartment, taken down in shorthand by Johny Aitchison. Mr. Aitchison's verbatim transcriptions far exceed the number of words in the book.

In addition, a number of interviews with Mr. Sennett were covered with a tape recorder. These were transcribed by Caroline Shipp and Maynard Smith.

Over a period of two years a number of persons associated with Mr. Sennett were interviewed for background material and anecdotes. These were also taken in shorthand and transcribed. A special indebtedness for their contributions of fact and hilarity is due in this respect to Chester Conklin, Hank Mann, Dell Henderson, Del Lord, Craig Hutchison, Franklin Pangborn, and Vernon Dent. In Chapter 12, Mr. Sennett's description of his Keystone scenario department at work is supplemented by extracts from correspondence with Vernon Smith, scenario editor during the custard-pie era, now a resident of New Orleans.

Credit is given to Miss Louella Parsons, Miss Hedda Hopper, Miss Florabel Muir, Miss Julia Benson, R.N., and Miss Phyllis Haver in the various chapters in which they are quoted. Harry Crocker, the Los Angeles columnist, formerly assistant director and writer for Charlie Chaplin, was consulted on the two chapters which concern Mr. Chaplin.

Romeo Carraro, chief librarian of the Los Angeles *Times*, and William Gammon, chief librarian of the Los Angeles *Examiner*, kindly made their files available for factual checking, with particular reference to the William Desmond Taylor murder.

A number of books were consulted. Chief among them were: *A Million and One Nights, The History of the Motion Picture*, by Terry Ramsaye, published by Simon & Schuster, an invaluable source book for confirming dates, casts, and the development of the motion-picture industry; *A Pictorial History of the American Theater*, and *A Pictorial History of the Silent Screen*, both by Daniel Blum, published by Greenberg; *Show Biz*, by Abel Green and Joe Laurie, Jr., Henry Holt and Company, a readable memory-refresher on theatrical chronology; and various editions of *The Best Plays*, edited by Burns Mantle, published by Dodd, Mead and Company.

Mr. Sennett's recollections of Charlie Chaplin were abetted by reference to *Charlie Chaplin*, by the late Theodore Huff, published by Schuman, a scholarly and brilliant record.

Erle Stanley Gardner's summation of the William Desmond Taylor murder case, in Chapter 22, is from *True* magazine, June 1946, and is quoted by permission from Mr. Gardner.

There is considerable conflict in published sources about Mabel Normand's birthplace and early years, but the most accurate source of information is undoubtedly "Mabel Normand— Comedienne and Madcap," a series of articles by Sidney Sutherland, published by *Liberty* magazine in 1930, based on interviews with Miss Normand in 1929. Several references to Mabel's family, her childhood, and her experience as an artist's model rely on Mr. Sutherland's findings.

Other factual material concerning Mabel Normand's European trips and motion pictures she made during her sabbatical from Mack Sennett derives from more than forty-eight thousand clippings in scrapbooks preserved by Mr. Sennett. Other matters of fact were obtained from Mr. Sennett's correspondence files and from original contracts with his various players.

The extract from Ruth Taylor's diary in Chapter 15 is from an article by Adela Rogers St. John, in the *American Weekly* of December 19, 1948.

All quotations by persons questioned during the William Desmond Taylor murder investigation are from transcripts prepared by shorthand reporters in the Los Angeles District Attorney's office.

Henry Peavey's statement was taken down by B. N. Smith, February 9, 1922 in the presence of Thomas Lee Woolwine, District Attorney; W. C. Doran, Chief Deputy District Attorney; Detective Sergeants J. A. Winn, H. H. Cline, Edward King, William Cahill, W. E. Murphy, and E. R. Cato.

Douglas MacLean's statement was taken down February 9, 1922 by B. N. Smith in the presence of Mr. Woolwine, Mr. Doran, and the detective sergeants.

Mrs. Faith MacLean's statement was taken down by Mr. Smith, February 9, 1922, in the presence of the same officials.

William Davis's statement was taken down by Mr. Smith, February 10, 1922 in the presence of Mr. Woolwine, Mr. Doran, and Sergeants Cato, Cahill, and Winn.

Miss Mary Miles Minter's statement was taken down by G. H. Boone, in the District Attorney's office, February 7, 1922, in the presence of Mr. Doran and her attorney, John G. Mott.

Miss Normand's statement is from a transcript by Mr. Smith, dated April 10, 1922, made in the presence of Mr. Woolwine, Mr. Doran, and Sergeants Murphy and Winn.

The majority of Mr. Sennett's innumerable two-reel prints have been either lost or destroyed. The Library of Congress has a good but incomplete collection of early Sennett films. A print of *Mickey* is available and is sharp and clear. The print of *Molly O* is in possession of Warner Brothers but is in deplorable condition.

However, Mr. Sennett's library contains more than one thousand original scripts of two-reel comedies he produced in the silent days and two hundred fifty scripts of films in sound. He has presented to the Academy of Motion Picture Arts and Sciences upwards of 150,000 photographs of scenes and personalities in pictures between 1912 and 1935.

This book was written at the University of Southern California, where the resources of the Department of Cinema were available. All of the manuscript was typed—and retyped—by Maynard Smith, M.A., research consultant, whose documentary techniques were invaluable.